CULTURAL APPROACHES TO PARENTING

CROSSCURRENTS IN CONTEMPORARY PSYCHOLOGY

A series of volumes edited by Marc H. Bornstein

PSYCHOLOGICAL DEVELOPMENT FROM INFANCY:
Image to Intention
BORNSTEIN AND KESSEN

COMPARATIVE METHODS IN PSYCHOLOGY
BORNSTEIN

PSYCHOLOGY AND ITS ALLIED DISCIPLINES
Volume 1: Psychology and the Humanities
Volume 2: Psychology and the Social Sciences
Volume 3: Psychology and the Natural Sciences
BORNSTEIN

SENSITIVE PERIODS IN DEVELOPMENT:
Interdisciplinary Perspectives
BORNSTEIN

INTERACTION IN HUMAN DEVELOPMENT
BORNSTEIN AND BRUNER

CULTURAL APPROACHES TO PARENTING
BORNSTEIN

THE SEGMENTATION OF BEHAVIOR (*In preparation*)
BORNSTEIN

SIGNIFICANCE OF THE ATYPICAL IN PSYCHOLOGY (*In preparation*)
BORNSTEIN

CULTURAL APPROACHES TO PARENTING

Edited by

Marc H. Bornstein

National Institute of Child Health and Human Development

 LAWRENCE ERLBAUM ASSOCIATES, PUBLISHERS

1991   Hillsdale, New Jersey   Hove and London

Lawrence Erlbaum Associates, Inc., Publishers
365 Broadway
Hillsdale, New Jersey 07642

Library of Congress Cataloging-in-Publication Data

Cultural approaches to parenting / edited by Marc H. Bornstein.
        p.   cm.
    Includes bibliographical references and indexes.
      ISBN 0-8058-1002-1
      1. Parenting--Cross-cultural studies--Congresses. 2. Child
development--Cross-cultural studies--Congresses. 3. Child rearing-
Cross-cultural studies--Congresses. I. Bornstein, Marc H.
    II. Series.
    HQ755.8.C85   1991
    649'.1--dc20   91-7183
                                                         CIP

Printed in the United States of America
10 9 8 7 6 5 4 3 2 1

For

MAISIE

Series Prologue

CROSSCURRENTS IN CONTEMPORARY PSYCHOLOGY

Contemporary psychology is increasingly diversified, pluralistic, and specialized, and most psychologists venture beyond the confines of their substantive specialty only rarely. Yet psychologists with different specialties encounter similar problems, ask similar questions, and share similar concerns. Unfortunately, there are today very few arenas available to the expression or exploration of what is common across psychological subdisciplines. The *Crosscurrents in Contemporary Psychology* series is intended to serve as such a forum.

The chief aim of this series is to provide integrated perspectives on supradisciplinary themes in psychology. The first volume in the series was devoted to a consideration of *Psychological Development from Infancy*; the second volume to *Comparative Methods in Psychology*; volumes three, four, and five examined relations between *Psychology and Its Allied Disciplines* in the humanities, the social sciences, and the natural sciences; volume six concerned itself with *Sensitive Periods in Development*; and volume seven focused on *Interaction in Human Development*. The present volume is *Cultural Approaches to Parenting*. Future volumes in this series will be devoted to the segmentation of behavior and the role of the nonnormal in understanding the normal.

Each volume in this series treats a different issue and is self–contained, yet the series as a whole endeavors to interrelate psychological subdisciplines by bringing shared perspectives to bear on a variety of concerns common to psychological theory and research. As a consequence of this structure and the flexibility and scope it affords, volumes in the *Crosscurrents in Contemporary Psychology* series will appeal, individually or as a group, to scientists with diverse interests. Reflecting the nature and intent of this series, contributing authors are drawn from a broad spectrum of humanities and sciences—anthropology to zoology—but representational emphasis is placed on active contributing authorities to the contemporary psychological literature.

Crosscurrents in Contemporary Psychology is a series whose explicit intent is to explore a broad range of crossdisciplinary concerns. In its focus on such issues, the series is devoted to promoting interest in the interconnectedness of research and theory in psychological study.

Cultural Approaches to Parenting derives from original presentations given at a workshop of the same name held in Montréal, Canada, on 18 April 1990. The workshop was sponsored by the National Institute of Child Health and Human Development. I am particularly grateful to Barbara Wright, for boundless energy, faithful assistance, and limitless good cheer during the organization of the workshop and the production of this volume, to Art Lizza for unwavering competence and high standards in book production, and to Dr. Arthur S. Levine and Dr. Duane F. Alexander of the National Institute of Child Health and Human Development, for sponsoring the workshop and for their continuing support of research into all facets of human growth.

Marc H. Bornstein

Contributors to this Volume

Dr. Marc H. Bornstein, Child and Family Research, National Institute of Child Health, and Human Development, Building 31—Room B2B15, 9000 Rockville Pike, Bethesda, MD 20892

Dr. T. Berry Brazelton, 23 Hawthorn Street, Cambridge, MA 02138

Dr. Jane Brown, 110 Henderson Building South, Department of Individual and Family Studies, The Pennsylvania State University, University Park, PA 16802

Dr. Judith F. Dunn, 110 Henderson Building South, Department of Individual and Family Studies, The Pennsylvania State University, University Park, PA 16802

Dr. Artin Göncü, College of Education, University of Illinois - Chicago, Box 4348, Chicago, IL 60680

Dr. William Kessen, Department of Psychology, Yale University, 2 Hillhouse Avenue, New Haven, CT 06520

Dr. Gérard Malcuit, Laboratoire d'Étude du Nourrisson, Département de Psychologie, Université du Québec à Montréal, C.P. 8888, Succ. A , Montréal, Québec H3C 3P8 , CANADA

Dr. Jayanthi Mistry, CDEE - Kekelaokalani, Kamehameha Schools, Kapalama Heights, Honolulu, HI 96817

Dr. Gilda A. Morelli, Department of Psychology, Boston College, Chestnut Hill, MA 02167

Dr. Christine Mosier, Department of Psychology, University of Utah, Salt Lake City, UT 84112

Dr. Hanuš Papoušek, Interfaculty of Human Movement Sciences, Department of Educational Sciences, Free University Amsterdam, P.O. Box 7161, 1007 MC Amsterdam, THE NETHERLANDS

Dr. Mechthild Papoušek, *Department of Social Pediatrics, Munich University, Heiglhofstrasse 63, 8000 Munich 70, WEST GERMANY*

Dr. Andrée Pomerleau, *Laboratoire d'Étude du Nourrisson, Département de Psychologie, Université du Québec à Montréal, C.P. 8888, Succ. A , Montréal, Québec H3C 3P8, CANADA*

Dr. Barbara Rogoff, *Department of Psychology, University of Utah, Salt Lake City, UT 84112*

Dr. Colette Sabatier, *Laboratoire d'Étude du Nourrisson, Département de Psychologie, Université du Québec à Montréal,, C.P. 8888, Succ. A, Montréal, Québec H3C 3P8, CANADA*

Dr. Marilyn Shatz, *Department of Psychology, University of Michigan, 330 Packard Road, Ann Arbor, MI 48104*

Dr. Marian Sigman, *68237 Department of Psychiatry, UCLA School of Medicine, University of California, Los Angeles, CA 90024*

Dr. Joseph Tal, *Child and Family Research, National Institute of Child Health and Human Development, Building 31—Room B2B15, 9000 Rockville Pike, Bethesda, MD 20892*

Dr. Catherine Tamis–LeMonda, *Infancy Studies Program, Department of Psychology, New York University, 6 Washington Place—Room 308, New York, NY 10003*

Dr. Edward Tronick, *Child Development Unit, The Children's Hospital, 300 Longwood Avenue, Boston, MA 02115*

Dr. Theodore D. Wachs, *Department of Psychological Sciences, Purdue University, West Lafayette, IN 47907*

Contents

INTRODUCTION

1 Approaches to Parenting in Culture

Marc H. Bornstein
National Institute of Child Health and Human Development

INTRODUCTION

Human beings, who are at once uniquely and commonly endowed, experience widely varying conditions in growing up. For example, children's immediate social networks vary from one culture to another, thereby dramatically influencing socialization and enculturation patterns. Presumably, cultural variations in the various domains of childrearing exert significant and differential influences over mental, emotional, and social development of children, just as variation clearly dictates the language children eventually speak. Whiting and Child (1953) developed this essential idea in their seminal study *Child Training and Personality*, arguing that modal developmental behaviors could be linked to different cultural treatments if it could be assumed that consistent individual relationships mediated society–wide effects. They found—and it is widely accepted—that parents in different cultures adopt some similar, as well as some different, approaches to childrearing, and that parenting is *a* principal reason why individuals in different cultures are who they are, and are often so different from one another.

Further, it is a truism of contemporary psychological study that the cultural contexts in which children are reared constitute central, yet often neglected, factors in developmental study. *Cultural Approaches to Parenting* is concerned with elucidating similarities and differences in enculturation processes that help to account for the ways in which individuals in different cultures develop.

MOTIVES FOR APPROACHING CULTURE IN PARENTING

The scope of developmental psychology embraces both description and explanation of the nature of human behavior over the life span. Among the many perspectives from which to pursue these twin charges, the cross–cultural developmental method of comparison occupies a significant position because it encompasses the full spectrum of human variation across a worldwide context and over a lifespan ontogeny.

3

The rationales for cross–cultural developmental study are many. Lay and professional people alike are perennially curious about human growth and behavior in other cultures. Social inquiry has as a matter of course almost always invited reports of alternative childrearing practices. One of the classic instances of one culture's over–the–shoulder interest in the parenting style of another is the legendary Athenian reverence for, and perhaps idealization of, traditional Spartan childrearing practices (French, 1977, 1990). Among the Greeks, Xenophone and Aristotle expressed special fascination with the Lycurgan system of training youth in Sparta, called the *agogé*. Their histories compared child management systems and documented how the Spartans intentionally set about developing a disciplined and obedient, self–denying and competitive, physically tough and mentally austere generation of young adults who confidently met and endured the harsh existence of the Peloponese. Xenophon, an Athenian who lived at the turn of the 4th century BC, specifically contrasted Spartan with other Greek childrearing practices in the *Constitution of the Lacedaemonians* of 380. Likewise, Aristotle's lost essay on *Education* is thought to have compared childrearing and child management in Sparta with family practices in other local cultures. Later, in his "Life of Lycurgus" and throughout the *Moralia*, Plutarch also focused on Spartan childrearing.

Comprehensive description of cultures is prerequisite to formal explanation of cultural phenomena:

> If children are studied within the confines of a single culture, many events are taken as natural, obvious, or a part of human nature and are therefore not reported and not considered as variables. It is only when it is discovered that other peoples do not follow these practices that have been attributed to human nature that they are adopted as legitimate variables (Whiting & Whiting, 1960, p. 933).

Further, epistemological inquiry has provoked many philosophers, following Bacon and Descartes, to ponder the origins and development of mind and morals under varying rearing conditions. Romantic fancy, like Rousseau's "noble savage," springs from considerations of development in the context of alternative cultures. Historical commentaries, such as those of De Toqueville and Spengler, have explored the psychological characteristics of a society that are, as Compte speculated, inculcated by one generation in the next *during childhood*. All of our more direct forbearers in psychology—Darwin, Freud, Piaget, Skinner—dwelt on the question of cultural approaches to parenting.

From the perspective of more formal inquiry, the disciplines of anthropology, sociology, and psychology have also attempted to approach the study of human development cross–culturally because of the unique and extraordinary power that this perspective is thought to furnish social scientific analysis (e.g., Bronfenbrenner, 1970; Erikson, 1950; Kessen, 1975; LeVine, 1977; Montagu, 1974; Munroe & Munroe, 1975; Werner, 1979; Whiting & Whiting, 1960). For example, many theories postulate that individual aptitude and performance capacity form in early life. Psychoanalytic theory, learning theory, and ethological theory all place a strong emphasis on early childhood experiences as determinants of adult patterns of behavior. In these views, childhood training also exerts a significant influence on the values, attitudes, and behaviors of whole communities.

> We are not saying here that their treatment in babyhood *causes* a group of adults to have certain traits—as if you turned a few knobs in your child–training system and you fabricated this or that kind of tribal or national character. ... We are speaking of goals and values and of the energy put at their disposal by child–training systems. Such values persist because the cultural ethos continues to consider them "natural" ... . They persist because they have become an essential part of an individual's sense of identity, which he must preserve as a core of sanity and efficiency. But values do not persist unless they work, economically, psychologically, and spiritually; and I argue that to this end *they must continue to be anchored, generation after generation, in early child training* (Erikson, 1950, pp. 137–138, emphasis added).

Cross–cultural developmental comparison also provides unique opportunities to test specific social–scientific hypotheses or predictions, to evaluate the generalizability or constraints on phenomena of interest, and to generate new hypotheses. Notable in this connection are the variety and value of unique information cross–cultural study is acknowledged to provide about cultural universals and specifics of human growth. Statistically, cross–cultural developmental psychology extends the range of variation being assessed. The study of development as culturally contextualized is also valuable for the check it provides against an ethnocentric world view ... as well as the implications of such a view.

Many critics today point to culture–bound assumptions and limitations of the prevailing, however restricted, Western psychologies. In actuality, "three different cultural limitations have constrained the scope of psychological theory: a narrow subject data base, a biased sampling of world cultures in its authorship, and a corresponding bias in the audience to which it is addressed" (Serpell, 1990, p. 99). Calls for cross–cultural investigation have in recent years echoed an increasingly strident critique of the monocultural perspective (see Berry, 1983; Kennedy, Scheirer, & Rogers, 1984; Moghaddam, 1987; Russell, 1984; Segall, 1986; Sexton & Misiak, 1984; Triandis, 1980; Valsiner, 1989). In response to such criticism, cultural context is achieving greater recognition in mainstream psychology, and most contemporary psychological investigators acknowledge that cross–cultural developmental inquiry is integral to understanding both substance and process in development. Description and explanation therefore constitute compelling reasons to undertake cross–cultural developmental comparisons. To discuss or reach conclusions about the growth of perception, cognition, communication, emotion, personality, or social interaction outside of a cross–cultural developmental framework is perilous.

A.R. Luria (1930/1978, p. 45) put the grander rationale for this catholic perspective most succinctly:

> ... no psychological function can be understood except in terms of its development (the genetic approach) and its particular social conditions (the sociological approach).

In brief, absent the cross–cultural developmental perspective, the true diversity and expanse of human behavior cannot be grasped, nor can it be known how diverse forces interact to shape our propensities to perceive, think, speak, feel, and act in the ways we do. *Cultural Approaches to Parenting* meets contemporary challenges to psychology to expand the subject data base, to contextualize thinking, and to promote internationalism.

MOTIVES FOR APPROACHING PARENTING IN CULTURE

This book is concerned with a full range of cultural approaches to phenomena associated with caretaking young children. A major issue of *Cultural Approaches to Parenting* is how children become members of the culture, given the behaviors, language, and physical surroundings they experience. In this construal, culture constitutes a kind of independent variable in individual development. (Like another taboo subject, we may not always or so easily be able to define culture, but still know it when we see it.) At the very heart of the concept of culture is the expectation that different peoples possess different values, beliefs, and motives and behave in different ways (Segall, 1986, p. 542). It is a particular and continuing task of parents and other caretakers to enculturate children, that is to prepare them for socially accepted physical, economic, and psychological situations that are characteristic of the culture in which they are to survive and thrive (Benedict, 1938; LeVine, 1977). In essence, culture (plus genetics) determines the structure and nature of the social and physical environments the individual is reared in and that influence the course and outcome of development. In that caretakers play the most critical role:

> I maintain that a good part of what we call ... development is dependent on the selection by caretakers among possible lines of development in children. In content we can, *as holders of the culture*, select physics or music, and in strategy we can emphasize social–interactional solutions to problems or we can emphasize analytic–"scientific" solutions (Kessen, 1984, p. 427, emphasis added).

Thus, young children everywhere have the potential to learn intricate culture complexities of, say, language, but at the same time they master the language to which they are exposed. *Cultural Approaches to Parenting* elaborates on the many assumptions, models, and data of parenting enculturation patterns and practices.

CULTURAL APPROACHES TO PARENTING

All of the contributors to this volume on *Cultural Approaches to Parenting* investigate and compare at least one substantive issue of parenting young children in at least two different cultures. Structurally, these chapters review the substantive parenting topics, describe the relevant cultures (albeit in psychological ethnography, rather than from an anthropological stance), report on the parenting–in–

culture results, and discuss the meaningfulness of cross–cultural investigation for understanding the parenting issue of interest. All of the presentations thus attempt to meet high standards for cross–cultural psychological investigation. These include, most importantly, the assessment of comparable behaviors observed in different cultural settings with obtained similarities and differences being related to particular features of the cultures involved in ways that articulate with theory and prediction (see Lamb & Wozniak, 1990). Super and Harkness (1986) defined three components of a "developmental niche": the physical and social setting in which the child lives, the customs of child care and childrearing, and the psychology of the child's caretakers. Chapters in *Cultural Approaches to Parenting* are addressed to each of these central aspects of development.

Two words of caution about *Cultural Approaches to Parenting* are appropriate at this introductory juncture. First, this volume houses contributions concerned with a diversity of substantive issues looked at in a diversity of ways across a diversity of cultural settings. Variety in all three of these domains faithfully reflects characteristics of contemporary cross–cultural developmental study. Across the ten chapters, specific issues of study include: speech form—interaction context relations, environment and interactive style, responsiveness, activity patterns, distributions of social involvement with children, structural patterns of interaction, language and the transmission of culture, development of the social self, and apprenticeship. Despite this range, language and interaction are consistent foci of interest and analysis throughout the book. Contributors to *Cultural Approaches to Parenting* have also employed a variety of methods, thereby enriching the range of data and the reader's understanding of how cross–cultural research is conducted. Methodologies include: questionnaires, interviews, experiments, and biochemical analyses of food intake. By far, however, the most popular method among cross–cultural developmental researchers is direct observation of behavior. The national settings for these reports number a baker's dozen. They include: Canada (Québécois, Vietnamese, and Haitian of Montréal), Egypt, England, France, Germany, Guatemala, India, Japan, Kenya, Korea, Turkey, the United States (Mandarin Chinese and Caucasian), and Zaïre (Efe and Lese). Not unexpectedly, the modal comparison is with U.S. samples. In virtually all cases, however, contributors have exercised care to discuss the target phenomena of parenting as specifically related to the cultures actually studied, choosing to under– rather than overgeneralize.

Second, virtually all of the principal contributors to this volume are of Western origin, and the categories and determinations of parenting represented here must be weighted by their Western orientation. Since it is difficult, if not impossible, to overcome one's own enculturation before taking up cross–cultural investigation, it is critical that contributors to *Cultural Approaches to Parenting* have acknowledged their own origins, as they have the essential foreignness of other cultures. Happily, most have undertaken collaborative studies with colleagues from the cultures being investigated. Both arrogance and danger attend projecting essentially Western ideas onto the behavior and experience of peoples living their lives in other cultural contexts. The degree to which applications of sets of descriptions "work" across culturally–diverse settings is an empirical question. Two factors are important to appreciate in this connection, however. One is that, for better or worse, researchers in many different cultures have today been schooled almost exclusively in the framework of Western psychologies. Therefore, many use (if not embrace) the same concepts and paradigms. The other is that there exists, despite different cultural perspectives, a "common core" of primary family experiences that underwrites the possibility of cross–cultural comparisons of parenting. This core recurs as central subject matter in *Cultural Approaches to Parenting*, and it is discussed more fully below.

The cultural approaches to parenting represented in this volume are divided into two broad categories: *conceptions of parenting* and *consequences of parenting*. In one way or another, each of the chapters in the first section considers characteristic relations between cultural attitudes and actions: For the Papoušeks, it is activity in discourse; for Pomerleau, Malcuit, and Sabatier, consistency across environment, interaction, and beliefs; for Bornstein, Tal, and Tamis–LeMonda, activity and responsiveness; and for Morelli and Tronick, distributions of different types of involvement among the child's main partners. In one way or another, each of the chapters in the second section of the book concerns itself with dynamics of enculturation: For Sigman and Wachs, it is the structure of interaction as conditioned by nutritional status; for Shatz, the role of language in cultural transmission; for Dunn and Brown, development and expression of the social self in language and play; and for Rogoff, Mistry, Göncü, and Mosier cultural apprenticeship.

These chapters examine topics in belief—behavior relations or enculturation dynamics, respectively, but all do so in comparative contexts. Hence, the accent on conceptions and consequences. Of course, there are many different conceivable ways to organize a collection of papers such as this one, just as there are important topics in cultural approaches to parenting that are not represented—like segmentation of the lifespan, rites of passage, culture from the child's eye view, and treatment of the aged to name a prominent few. This volume is not intended to be comprehensive by topic, method, or place; that would be impossible. Rather, its purposes are to illustrate, to examine, and to sensitize—to provide a forum in which writer and reader share the conduct of cross–cultural studies of parenting and the meanings that such cross–cultural study portends for advancing an understanding of substantive issues in parenting. A more detailed examination of individual chapters will serve to elucidate these objectives.

In the first chapter of "conceptions," on "Innate and Cultural Guidance of Infants' Integrative Competencies," Hanuš and Mechthild Papoušek examine culture–universal and culture–specific linkages as mothers use baby talk in some specific parenting contexts. Through a carefully constructed argument, the Papoušeks' work leads to the conclusion that certain intonation contours in mothers' speech to baby recur with greater–than–chance regularity in particular interactions, and that these regularities characterize "tone" as well as "stress" languages. The Papoušeks' work is laboratory–based and quantitative, contrasting U.S. American, German, and Chinese mothers speaking American English, German, and Mandarin, respectively. Their West—East selection of samples juxtaposes cultural traditions and childrearing philosophies, as well as language structures: tone (Mandarin Chinese) versus non–tonal stress (American English and German). The Papoušeks not only find that the same "caregiving frames" occupy similar amounts of interactive time in these different cultures, but also that contour–context relations are similar in different cultures and language groups. Their universalist results articulate with the more general notion they proffer of "intuitive parenting." In intuitive parenting, caretakers are thought to engage— naturally and unconsciously—in certain behavior patterns, the use of particular formats of maternal speech in particular kinds of interactional contexts being one example.

In "Child–Rearing Practices and Parental Beliefs in Three Cultural Groups of Montréal," Andrée Pomerleau, Gérard Malcuit, and Collette Sabatier compare and contrast the results of home–based observations and extensive questionnaire interviews with mothers of three subcultures in Montréal, including Québécois, Vietnamese, and Haitian. Pomerleau and her colleagues position their study in the important context of contemporary immigration and acculturation, wherein individuals strive to establish a critical balance between maintaining their unique cultural identity and adapting to the mazeways of the new cultural settings in which they find themselves. The study assesses beliefs on the one hand and behaviors on the other and, happily, in the conclusions ties attitudes and actions together. First, they identify important beliefs about babies among these three groups. From this mass of data, Pomerleau, Malcuit, and Sabatier analyze particular themes to illustrate similarities and differences among the cultural groups, controlling for SES differences. For example, they underscore variations in the social and physical environments that distinguish immigrants and natives. Finally, they explore the complexities of attitude–action relations, and point out how these can sometimes interact with culture.

Marc Bornstein, Joseph Tal, and Catherine Tamis–LeMonda describe naturally–occurring activities of "Parenting in Cross–Cultural Perspective" by comparing and contrasting U.S. American, French, and Japanese mothers. Based on observations of everyday patterns of interaction in the home, these investigators have unearthed similarities as well as culturally–specific differences among these three groups of mothers. Their work shows how comparisons of Western with Western as well as Western with Eastern cultures afford unique views on parenting identities and distinctions. For example, Bornstein and his colleagues find that, across all three cultures, mothers respond more to their infants' vocalizing than to infants' looking, and that a high degree of shared specificity and appropriateness characterizes maternal responsiveness: Mothers respond to their infants' exploration of the environment with encouragement to the environment, to infants' nondistress vocalizations with imitation, and to infants' distress vocalizations with nurturance. On the other hand, they observe that the most salient West—East differences involve Japanese and Americans with respect to dyadic versus extradyadic loci of interaction. In their chapter, Bornstein, Tal, and Tamis–LeMonda elaborate on sources of variation and implications of those differences for the child's development in different cultural contexts.

Gilda Morelli and Edward Tronick take a careful look at "Parenting and Child Development in the Efe Foragers and Lese Farmers of Zaïre." The two have meticulously catalogued daily caretaking routines in these two comparable but very different peoples. The Efe are foragers, hunters and gatherers who live in transient camps established in small, forested areas cleared of vegetation. The Lese are slash–and–burn horticulturalists. The contrasting orientations of these ecologies for childrearing beliefs and practices constitute the critical parenting patterns Morelli and Tronick examine. At base, these authors have compared children at extremes of contrasting ecologies, and in this sense their work exposes the relations and roles of economic factors in the caretaking experience of the young child and growth of the child's understanding of the caretaking community. In their view, social participation in a culture structures a child's reality and experience in ways that increase the likelihood that the child will acquire an accurate image of the society and develop into a culturally successful member of the society. Their chapter constitutes a rich descriptive comparison of linkages between divergent ecological demands in two communities on the one hand and individual growth on the other; in particular, Efe multiple caregiving patterns call into question the "continuous care and contact" model of parenting developed in Western societies.

In the first chapter of the second section of the book on "consequences," Marian Sigman and Theodore Wachs explore "Structure, Continuity, and Nutritional Correlates of Caregiver Behavior Patterns in Kenya and Egypt." Specifically, their presentation opposes the nature of caregiving provided to toddlers in a small village near Cairo with that in a rural village in the foothills of Mount Kenya. In the process, they arrive at a factor–analytic solution to making comparisons between data based on parallel but different observational strategies. Their results reveal similar structures of toddler caretaking relative to verbal interaction and responsiveness between the two groups—Saharan Egyptian and subSaharan Kenyan Embu. However, Sigman and Wachs show different relations between toddler nutritional intake and parenting activities in the two cultures. Egyptian caregivers react to vocalizations made by toddlers using both verbal and nonverbal responses; Kenyan caregivers are more likely to react to toddlers' vocalizations with verbal responses. Although caregiving behavior in both groups changes over the course of the second year, the changes are different in the two locales, with Egyptians becoming more responsive and Kenyans remaining consistent. Importantly, Egyptian toddlers are better fed than are their Kenyan counterparts who have a relatively low caloric, protein, and fat diet, and Sigman and Wachs use this feature of the results to explore important relations between responsiveness of parent and the diets of their children.

Marilyn Shatz illustrates the value of "Using Cross–Cultural Research to Inform Us about the Role of Language in Development." As she observes, talking is the most frequent parenting behavior, and language factors serve as powerful mediators of cognitive and social development in children. Shatz develops a straightforward model linking cultural values with language practices, language practices with child behaviors, and child behaviors with cultural values. In a pair of experimental studies designed to elucidate these associations, Shatz succeeds in showing how cultural values relate to language practices on the one hand, and how language practices may be reflected in certain child behaviors on the other. Her first study examines the role of specific characteristics of language form and use in Japanese, Korean, and English on children's sentence processing and reasoning. Her second study examines maternal speech in two cultures with different languages, contrasting German and American (and British) in order to assess whether and how variations in parental language style relate to widely–acknowledged differences in cultural values. These studies coordinate to show how variation in language practices associated with different cultures bear on children's development. Shatz compares cultures which are more "alike" than not, and the reasons she provides for using this comparative approach are compelling.

In an assessment of "Becoming American or English," Judy Dunn and Jane Brown analyze cultural variation in mothers' speech to young children about the social world and demonstrate how cultural messages are commonly embedded in daily interactions. The families involved are English and American. As Dunn and Brown vividly show, discourse about the social world varies dramatically between Center County, Pennsylvania and Cambridge, England, and does so in interaction with topic; assessments of transgressions of social rules and of prescriptions exemplify such interactions. Dunn and Brown further find that family discussions of feeling states, pretend play, and narratives of family life vary enormously within cultures, as they do between, thereby stressing the issue of within– versus between–culture variability and posing the question of when differences within groups conceptually outweigh differences between groups.

Barbara Rogoff, Jayanthi Mistry, Artin Göncü, and Christine Mosier describe "Cultural Variation in Role Relations of Toddlers and Their Families" in cultural communities in Turkey, Guatemala, India, and the United States, respectively. They defend the central point that in most places in the world young children are tended by multiple caretakers, and that, while important, the well–studied dyadic case of mother–and–child is not the rule. This cross–cultural perspective enriches the reader's understanding of the nature of parenting: In acknowledging the multiple–caregiver view, we admit to a global—and more comprehensive and accurate—perception of young children's social relations in growing up. In making their argument, Rogoff and her colleagues provide a textured description of the multiple settings and differential outcomes toddlers experience in growing up in such culturally diverse situations. Moving beyond the mother–infant dyad, they assess relations toddlers have with other caretakers (including siblings and nonfamily members). In their view, toddlers are "active learners" who participate in cultural-ly–organized activities with many others whose skills in those activities vary widely. Such cultural "apprenticeship" involves and evokes many factors—routine and novel, explicitly and implicitly communicative, and so forth. Apprentices must learn to think, argue, act, and interact with all of the central characters in a culture in order to make themselves truly cultural beings.

Along the way and at the end, T. Berry Brazelton and William Kessen provide critical reviews of the contents and directions of individual chapters, and, significantly, of the cross–cultural cum developmental methodology as applied to problems of parenting in culture. Their discussion and commentary go well beyond mere overview, providing independent, insightful, and penetrating analysis.

Readers of *Cultural Approaches to Parenting* will take away several lessons. They will be introduced to particular places as well as to particular parenting activities important in those (and other) places. They will learn the consequences that cross–cultural study possesses for advancing our understanding of a set of substantive parenting and developmental issues. They will be exposed to the range of diverse methods researchers have developed to meet the challenges of cross–cultural developmental study. Finally, they will gain a deeper appreciation of the problems, procedures, possibilities, and profits associated with a truly comparative approach to understanding human growth and development.

RECURRING THEMES OF PARENTING ACROSS CULTURE

The chapters in this collection are wonderfully eclectic with respect to substantive topic, geographic location, and experimental method. At the same time, all approach parenting from a contextualized and culture–sensitive perspective, and in doing so implicitly raise or explicitly address a similar variety of themes. The most prominent of these concerns culture–specific versus culture–universal parenting activities; two others of note are relations between cultural attitudes and actions in parenting, and specifying what might be meant by "parent" in a cultural context. This section highlights those subtexts. Other seemingly momentous topics—like the nature of culture itself—are discussed in the following section.

One significant theme in cultural approaches to parenting turns on the question of culture–specific versus culture–universal parenting activities. Some authors find that certain aspects of parenting recur across cultures, even very different ones. This raises the question, why? Some argue that recurring patterns of caretaking arise because of factors indigenous to children and their biology. For example, by virtue of their helplessness or "babyish" characteristics, which are universal, infants may naively elicit universal patterns of caregiving from their mothers. Others argue that universal characteristics of parenting may be instinctual to a parenting stage of the life cycle. It is in the nature of being a parent to optimize the development and probability of success of one's offspring, possibly to ensure the success of one's genes. A third possible explanation for the universalist position points to the environment as cause. Insofar as existing economic or ecological factors are shared, those common factors may press for parents to think and behave in similar ways.

Some authors have identified behaviors of parents that are culturally unique and specifically contextualized. Not too surprisingly, the arguments marshalled by culture–specifists to defend their view are of the same kind invoked by culture–universalists. Certain culturally–consistent biological characteristics of infants, such as constitutionally–based characteristics of temperament, could promote parental activities and/or attitudes that vary systematically across cultures. Adults in different cultures could parent differently because of their own biological characteristics, for example, differential threshold sensitivity or attention to infant signals. Finally, ecological or economic conditions specific to a given cultural setting might promote parental activities and belief systems indigenous to that culture, ones evolved differentially to optimize adjustment and adaptation of offspring to the circumstances of the local situation.

Papers in this volume report many instances of diversity as well as of uniformity in cultural approaches to parenting. Of course, the null hypothesis dictates a general expectation of uniformity...as biologically and statistically appropriate. The necessary assumption is that human beings as a species probably share much in terms of parenting. Moreover, all of the contributors to this volume have studied parenting of infants or young toddlers. There are very special and exacting constraints and demands associated with parenting very young children, and opportunistically these may be more universal than not. Finally, the late twentieth–century has witnessed a worldwide pattern of change toward urbanization, modernization, media homogeneity, and Westernization, that cumulatively contribute to breaking down traditional cultural patterns. These facts render the tremendous variation observed and reported in the following chapters even more significant. In this regard, finally, it is important to note that authors of these chapters specifically assess the significance of within–culture, beyond between–culture, variation.

A second recurring theme concerns relations between cultural beliefs and behaviors and how the two do (or do not) articulate. This issue appears in various chapters, but is undeveloped in the text of any one chapter per se. Perhaps with good reason. Although attitude–action relations are critical in social psychology and in cultural studies, as Davidson and Thompson (1980) note, the study of attitudes and beliefs cross–culturally has not yielded systematic findings, and the question of belief–behavior consonance is generally not well understood. In some ways, their relation itself invokes the important question of what "culture" is at all.

A third theme that arises in surveying cultural approaches to parenting concerns what is meant by parent. Different cultures distribute caretaking responsibility in different ways. In some, mother is the principal caretaker of children; for others, multiple caretaking models are more accurate. Indeed, in the minds of some observers, multiple caretaking arrangements are so common as to be more significant in the lives of children. In many places, babies and toddlers spend much or even most of their time with significant others, including siblings, nonparental relatives, or nonfamilial caretakers. In the minds of many other observers, mother is still unique, the role of mother universal, and motherhood unequivocally principal to the development of the individual. Various categories of parenting, like nurturance, social interaction, and didactics, may be distributed across various members of the culture; however, perhaps the ultimate responsibility for young infants and toddlers within the context of the nuclear or fragmented family universally falls to mother. Chapters in *Culturcl Approaches to Parenting* amply illustrate instances of different cultural patterns.

PROBLEMS TO APPROACHING CULTURE AND PARENTING

The explorers in *Cultural Approaches to Parenting* have much in common. Together they share in the profits of mining the cross–cultural developmental field. As reviewed earlier, there are many. The same explorers also confront many pitfalls in following the cross–cultural developmental approach.

As researchers who engage in cross–cultural developmental studies know, the sheer logistics of this kind of work can be formidable. Little is said in these chapters about the nuts–and–bolts difficulties associated with establishing collegial relations, building laboratories, recruiting subjects, and ensuring quality control in data collection in locales ranging far afield from one's office. (See, e.g., Lewis's, 1986, entertaining–serious ruminations on practical aspects of research in a global context.) The problems range from repeated failures of the mail and telephone to more fundamental ones like absence of social and health statistics for most places in the world.

Cross–cultural developmental study is also among the least practicable or feasible of comparative methods for reasons other than the sheer enormity of time, effort, and energy it consumes. To do this hybrid kind of work means tackling myriad unresolved questions of developmental study, myriad unresolved questions of cross–cultural study, as well as those issues uniquely generated by the interaction of these two comparative approaches. For this reason, and doubtless others, cross–cultural developmental investigators (among others) are often outspokenly critical of themselves. Some of their critiques are worth noting.

One concerns how successfully the designs of most cross–cultural research can practically or even theoretically address the challenging questions posed of it. Cross–cultural developmentalists are naturally interested in relations between culture on the one hand and psychological behavior on the other. Yet, unlike their colleagues in other psychological subdisciplines, cross–cultural developmental researchers are not in a position experimentally to manipulate relevant independent variables; such manipulations are impractical, impossible, or ethically unacceptable. However, all still understand that much might be learned about the nature and course of human development from just such manipulations. To meet the challenge of capturing cultural influences, cross–culture developmentalists often turn to "natural experiments." Natural experiments consist of the essentially fortuitous occurrence of particular customs human beings have adopted or of particular environments to which human beings have adapted. Classic investigations are of prenatal influences of teratogens like thalidomide on anatomical development in Europe, the effects of physical restraint on motor development in the Middle East, and the part played by social climate on gender role development in the South Pacific. But in such experiments of opportunity, the investigator does not actually exercise control over the treatment—whether it be culture, ecology, or economy. Nor are comparison groups sampled randomly. Consequently, unknown uncorrelated variables may differentially influence conditions, or comparison groups may not have been equivalent to begin with.

Many thorny methodological questions arise when doing research cross–culturally and developmentally. Some investigators opt to apply standardized assessments or protocols to different societies, in some degree sacrificing cultural sensitivity. Others work with individually–tailored formulations, only to forego the degree of comparability that is at the heart of cross–cultural comparison in the first place. Issues of sample representativeness, the quality of experimenter–subject communication, and population matching challenge all comparative research, but are particularly acute in cross–cultural inquiries involving children and/or family privacy.

In practice, studies in this tradition have also been only marginally cross–cultural or developmental in the sense of sampling across place and time. Most experiments compare only two cultures, the idea being simply to incorporate "culture" as a variable in the experimental design. Comparison cultures are typically selected because of circumstances that lead the experimenter to expect a difference; sometimes, generalizability is being evaluated. Yet cultures differ in many ways. As stated above, by adopting common experimental comparison strategies investigators run a risk of confounding variables over which they have no control or may even have no knowledge. In parallel, usually only one time period, age, or stage, or at most two, are assessed. This stricture severely limits understanding developmental processes.

Additional difficulties spring from near–unresolvable tensions that are inherent in diverging agenda of the academic disciplines that underlie cross–cultural developmental inquiry in the first place. These include philosophy, history, biology, sociology, and anthropology. Anthropologists, for example, have made two principal substantive contributions to the theory and practice of cross–cultural developmental study. They have systematically (and nearly single–handedly) broadened our descriptive knowledge of childrearing practices. Anthropological ethnographies first documented cultural information about childrearing the world over that might otherwise have gone unrecognized or simply been lost. Anthropologists also originated formal observations of important cultural dimensions of socialization.

However, anthropological and developmental comparisons are impelled by different motives: Culture studies tend to be concerned with assessment of social aggregate phenomena, whereas developmental ones focus on individual ontogeny. Super and Harkness (1986, p. 546) articulated this key contradiction: Anthropological approaches to human development have been oriented primarily to the socialized adult, at the expense of understanding developmental processes. Developmental psychology, in contrast, has traditionally been concerned with the decontextualized "universal child." The two fields typically address different psychological states, static culture versus the changing individual. "Unlike the vertical theories of developmental psychology, anthropological theories have presented a horizontal panorama of human variation." Thus, the constructs that usefully describe behavior at the group level do not apply very well to explaining behavior at the individual level and vice versa.

Cross–cultural and developmental psychology themselves also still stand outside the mainstream of general psychology. Whereas general psychology aims to study the "central inherent processing mechanism of mental life [that] is presumed to be a transcendent, abstract, fixed and universal property of the human psyche," cross–cultural and developmental psychologists have as their raisons d'etre, respectively, the varying appearance of and influences on mechanisms in different cultures and different age–gradings (Shweder, 1990, p. 4). For general psychology, cultural and developmental perspectives are so much noise masking the important signal. Hence, the impoverished position of both in its grander view. Of course, this position is itself limited: "Cultural psychology offers an alternative discipline of interpretation of the fundamentals of mind. The mind, according to cultural psychology is content-driven, domain specific and constructively stimulus-bound; and it can not be extricated from the historically variable and cross–culturally diverse intentional worlds in which it plays a co–constituting part" (Shweder, 1990, p. 13).

Further critique questions what kind of research beasts cross–cultural developmental investigators can be, in terms of their general approach to studying psychological phenomena cross–culturally. Lloyd (1972) once imaginatively characterized cross–cultural investigators as either "explorers" who conduct individual studies over short time periods or "settlers" who live and work intensively among the peoples they study. One borders on the superficial—the other constitutes life–long pursuit. There is nothing new under the sun. In Xenophon, Aristotle, and Plutarch, we have in microcosm one settler and two explorers of Sparta. Athenian Xenophon lived among the Spartans for over twenty years and had his two sons educated in the agogé. Aristotle is thought to have written the comparative–based *Education* during his Lyceum period, a time when many research assistants were collecting contemporary data in far–flung observation posts. Plutarch, who wrote in the first half of the 2nd century AD, was removed from classical Sparta by nearly half a millennium.

A common and related criticism of the psychologist–in–the–field is that this brand of "scientism" is incompatible with commonsensical issues of "guesthood." Some investigators, including those represented in this volume, go out of their way to cope sensitively with problems raised in studying a culture not their own. For example, virtually all of the contributors to *Cultural Approaches to Parenting* have undertaken research in close collaboration with colleagues who are native to the cultures studied. Of course, observations and experiments can and do change things; researchers must continue to bear in mind that to use them is to view the world through a particular (and distorting) lens.

Each of these profound issues presents cross–cultural developmental investigation with formidable challenges. Still others, no less compelling, lurk immediately behind them. Three appear to be especially noteworthy. What is culture? Culture is considered by some to reflect a complex of variables, a set of separable (if related) contextual factors (e.g., Campbell, 1961; Jahoda, 1980; Munroe & Munroe, 1980; Triandis, 1989), and by others to constitute a considerably more abstract entity of learned meanings and shared information transmitted from one generation to the next through interaction (e.g., Rohner, 1984; Schwartz, 1981; Segall, 1986). Actively or passively, to a greater or lesser degree, intentionally or unwittingly, then, parents pass culture on to their offspring. What are the chief processes of enculturation? As culture is organized information, parenting consists of mechanisms for transmitting that information, and childhood of processing that information. Both parent and child "select, edit, and refashion" cultural information. So, minimally, enculturation involves bidirectional processes in which adult and child play active roles. Finally, not well worked out are functional or theoretical connections between culture and parenting (Bronfenbrenner, 1979, 1986; Maccoby & Martin, 1983). How do components of culture relate to parenting attitudes and actions? The concept of culture is frequently used as a means of understanding relations between physical and social environments on the one hand and individual psychological structures on the other. At base, studies in *Cultural Approaches to Parenting* emphasize the joint negotiation of personal meanings that underpin a co–constructivist approach to development and to enculturation.

When all is said and done, then, cultural cum developmental study as practiced finds itself in a rather compromised position. And, frankly, it has become more and more difficult for cross–cultural developmentalists to meet rigorous criteria and standards already established ... and still evolving. All of these practical and theoretical shortcomings permit only the most cautious and tenuous conclusions about culturally–mediated "human" similarities or differences.

Despite this excess of logistical, methodological, conceptual, and theoretical hardship, it is quite clear that the lure of cross–cultural investigation is more than appealing—perhaps it is addicting—to many, including the contributors to this volume. Cultural field studies offer a richness, complexity, and power certainly complementary to that of the laboratory. The rationales and benefits of this work are apparent and sufficiently compelling to convince us that cross–cultural extensions to developmental psychology are mandatory, that developmental comparisons to cross–cultural psychology are invaluable, and that *the* cross–cultural developmental approach can provide uniquely comprehensive and theoretically significant data about human behavior. Its shortcomings notwithstanding, then, past practice and future potential forge a promise to this mode of comparison not otherwise realizable. This Humpty Dumpty must be put back together: "Anthropology has ignored children in culture while developmental psychologists ... ignored culture in children. The result is ignorance of the process and content of the child's emerging competence as a member of a culture" (Schwartz, 1981, p. 4).

CODA: CULTURAL APPROACHES TO PARENTING

How to care for children, how to rear them, how to apprentice them into the culture are, as Ruth Benedict (1938) observed, perennial concerns of parents in every society. Greek lawgivers and philosophers gave special attention to the education of children, beginning in infancy, just as we do today.

In this book, developmental psychologists again take up the question of *Cultural Approaches to Parenting*. Cross–cultural developmental research is used to describe and explain behavior, test hypotheses, and alert us to possibilities that otherwise might escape notice. Cross–cultural developmental comparisons cause us to rethink the origins and ontogeny of development. Without it, our understanding of the basics of human nature, whether in motor control, language acquisition, or emotional expression, is at best shortsighted, ethnocentric, and suspect. In the absence of cross–cultural developmental research, our psychology would simply be incorrect. Thus, the knowledge gained from this approach alters our beliefs as ethnocentric parents about the nature of children, and our beliefs as ethnocentric psychologists about the nature of human development. Among its lessons can be counted a deeper understanding of the variability that characterizes individual and cultural behavior and, by reflection, a deeper understanding of ourselves. With lessons like these in mind, the pages of *Cultural Approaches to Parenting* inject a richer texture of diverse realities into what is otherwise and oftentimes a tragically narrow schoolroom pursuit.

ACKNOWLEDGMENTS

I wish to thank H. Bornstein, J. Suwalsky, J. Tal, and B. Wright for comments and assistance.

REFERENCES

Benedict, R. Continuities and discontinuities in cultural conditioning. *Psychiatry*, 1938, *1*, 161–167.

Berry, J. W. The sociogenesis of social sciences: An analysis of the cultural relativity of social psychology. In B. Bain (Ed.), *The sociogenesis of language and human conduct* (pp. 449–454). New York: Plenum, 1983.

Bronfenbrenner, U. *Two worlds of childhood: U.S. and U.S.S.R.*. New York: Simon & Schuster, 1970.

Bronfenbrenner, U. *The ecology of human development*. Cambridge, MA: Harvard University Press, 1979.

Bronfenbrenner, U. Ecology of the family as a context for human development: Research perspectives. *Developmental Psychology*, 1986, *22*, 723–742.

Campbell, D. T. The mutual methodological relevance of anthropology and psychology. In F. L. K. Hsu (Ed.), *Psychological anthropology* (pp. 333–352). Homewood, IL: Dorsey, 1961.

Davidson, A. R., & Thompson, E. Cross–cultural studies of attitudes and beliefs. In H. C. Triandis & R. W. Brislin (Eds.), *Handbook of cross–cultural psychology: Social psychology* (Vol. 5, pp. 25–71). Boston: Allyn & Bacon, 1980.

Erikson, E. H. *Childhood and society*. New York: Norton, 1950.

French, V. History of the child's influence: Ancient Mediterranean civilizations. In R. Q. Bell & L. V. Harper (Eds.), *Child effects on adults* (pp. 3–29). Hillsdale, NJ: Lawrence Erlbaum Associates, 1979.

French, V. *The Spartan family and the Spartan decline: Changes in child–rearing practices and failure to reform*. Unpublished manuscript, Department of History, The American University, 1990.

Jahoda, G. Cross–cultural comparisons. In M. H. Bornstein (Ed.), *Comparative methods in psychology* (pp. 105–148). Hillsdale, NJ: Lawrence Erlbaum Associates, 1980.

Kennedy, S., Scheirer, J., & Rogers, A. The price of success: Our monocultural science. *American Psychologist*, 1984, *39*, 996–997.

Kessen, W. *Childhood in China*. New Haven, CT: Yale University Press, 1975.

Kessen, W. Construction, deconstruction, and reconstruction of the child's mind. In C. Sophian (Ed.), *Origins of cognitive skills* (pp. 419–429). Hillsdale, NJ: Lawrence Erlbaum Associates, 1984.

Lamb, S., & Wozniak, R. H. Developmental co–construction: Metatheory in search of method. *Contemporary Psychology*, 1990, *35*, 853–854.

LeVine, R. A. Child rearing as cultural adaptation. In P. H. Leiderman, S. R. Tulkin, & A. Rosenfeld (Eds.), *Culture and infancy: Variations in the human experience* (pp. 15–27). New York: Academic, 1977.

Lewis, C. Children's social development in Japan: Research directions. In H. Stevenson, H. Azuma, & K. Hakuta (Eds.), *Child development and education in Japan* (pp. 186–200). New York: W. H. Freeman, 1986.

Lloyd, B. B. *Perception and cognition: A cross–cultural perspective*. Harmondsworth: Penguin Books, 1972.

Luria, A. R. A child's speech responses and the social environment (M. Vale, Trans.). In M. Cole (Ed.), *The selected writings of A. R. Luria* (pp. 45–77). New York: M. E. Sharpe, 1930/1978.

Maccoby, E. E., & Martin, J. A. Socialization in the context of the family: Parent–child interaction. In E. M. Hetherington (Ed.), P. H. Mussen (Series Ed.), *Handbook of child psychology. Socialization, personality, and social development* (Vol. 4, pp. 1–101). New York: Wiley, 1983.

Moghaddam, F. M. Psychology in three worlds. *American Psychologist*, 1987, *42*, 912–920.

Montagu, A. (Ed.). *Culture and human development: Insights into growing humans*. Englewood Cliffs, NJ: Prentice–Hall, 1974.

Munroe, R. L., & Munroe, R. H. *Cross–cultural human development*. Monterey, CA: Brooks/Cole, 1975.

Munroe, R. L., & Munroe, R. H. Perspectives suggested by anthropological data. In H. C. Triandis & W. W. Lambert (Eds.), *Handbook of cross–cultural psychology: Perspectives* (Vol. 1, pp. 253–317). Boston: Allyn & Bacon, 1980.

Rohner, R. Toward a conception of culture for cross–cultural psychology. *Journal of Cross–Cultural Psychology*, 1984, *15*, 111–138.

Russell, R. Psychology in its world context. *American Psychologist*, 1984, *39*, 1017–1025.

Schwartz, T. The acquisition of culture. *Ethos*, 1981, *9*, 4–17.

Segall, M. H. Culture and behavior: Psychology in global perspective. *Annual Review of Psychology*, 1986, *37*, 523–564.

Serpell, R. Audience, culture and psychological explanation: A reformulation of the emic–etic problem in cross–cultural psychology. *Quarterly Newsletter of the Laboratory of Comparative Human Cognition*, 1990, *12*, 99–132.

Sexton, V. S., & Misiak, H. American psychologists and psychology abroad. *American Psychologist*, 1984, *39*, 1026–1031.

Shweder, R. A. Cultural psychology: What is it? In J. W. Stigler, R. A. Shweder, & G. Herdt (Eds.), *Cultural psychology: The Chicago symposia on culture and human development*. New York: Cambridge University Press, 1990.

Super, C. M., & Harkness, S. (1986). The developmental niche: A conceptualization of the interface of child and culture. *International Journal of Behavioral Development*, *9*, 546–569.

Triandis, H. C. The self and social behavior in differing cultural contexts. *Psychological Review*, 1989, *96*, 506–520.

Valsiner, J. *Human development and culture*. Cambridge, MA: Lexington Books, 1989.

Werner, E. E. *Cross–cultural human development*. Monterey, CA: Brooks/Cole, 1979.

Whiting, J. W. M., & Child, I. L. *Child training and personality: A cross–cultural study*. New Haven: Yale University Press, 1953.

Whiting, J. W. M., & Whiting, B. B. Contributions of anthropology to the methods of studying child rearing. In P. H. Mussen (Ed.), *Handbook of research methods in child development* (pp. 918–944). New York: Wiley, 1960.

I CONCEPTIONS

Innate and Cultural Guidance of Infants' Integrative Competencies: China, The United States, and Germany

2

Hanuš Papoušek

Free University of Amsterdam, Faculty of Movement Sciences

Mechthild Papoušek

Institute of Social Pediatrics, University of Munich

INTRODUCTION

Intuitive Parenting: A Challenge for Cross–Cultural Research

In a recent review on cross–cultural developmental comparisons between Japanese and American cultures, Bornstein (1989a) discussed the main rationales for cross–cultural research in general and drew attention to specific problems in comparing mother–infant interactions. To give an example, Bornstein pointed out that attempts to analyze simple phenomena such as the quantity of infant activity can lead to considerable methodological and conceptual problems, if activity is to be measured within interactional situations where contexts constantly vary and provoke varying activity levels.

The move from simple S–R designs investigating effects of stimuli on isolated infants to complex interactional designs constituted an ecologically sound and necessary step. However, only a thoroughgoing appreciation of functional aspects of the dyadic mother–infant system can guarantee that such steps will prove fruitful in cross–cultural research. In contemporary approaches, parent–infant interactions are viewed in a dyadic system of interacting partners each of whom develops and matures as a dynamic process of reciprocal adaptation (Fogel & Thelen, 1987;Kaye, 1982). Similarly, vocalization and language develop in dynamic interactions with progress in neuromotor, perceptual, integrative, imitative, and communicative skills (Bruner & Bornstein, 1989; Papoušek & Papoušek, 1982; in press a).

The dyadic parent–infant system specifically differs from general systems of interaction between two conspecifics on account of the acute biological relevance of parent–infant interdependence and some antipodal differences between the two interacting partners (Papoušek & Papoušek, 1984, 1987). Although infancy researchers have discovered an astonishing adaptive competence for infant learning and cognition, human infants still fully depend on the assistance of more mature and more experienced conspecific caretakers. For good reasons, therefore, infants are motivated to seek and maintain the presence of the caretaker, to identify, attend to, and communicate with the caretaker, and while interacting to process behavioral coherences and contingencies, to learn, to co–act, to imitate, and to conceptualize social experience.

Human caretakers—parents or others—are both biologically and culturally motivated not only to provide vital bodily care but also to share experiences, to communicate, and to guide the infant in mental advance. From this view, the amount of activity appears to be a too narrow aspect of interaction, as Bornstein (1989a) found. Researchers have increasingly become interested in the qualitative structures of activities, mutual contingencies, and communicative significance in particular.

Analyses of qualitative structures have been approached by the use of audiovisual documentation; multiple, repetitive, and interdisciplinary evaluations of audiovisual records; and microanalytic assessment of sequential regularities. This approach has evidenced unexpected forms of caretaking as well as an abundant presence of teaching episodes in "spontaneous" parent-infant interactions. Surprisingly, further analysis has shown that caretakers are unaware of their finely–tuned teaching interventions. Yet, no other environmental events can compete in frequency, richness, and didactic qualities with caretakers' nonconscious lessons (Papoušek & Papoušek, 1987). From this perspective, parent–infant communication is viewed by some authors as a primary, biologically–determined didactic system, and not a mere product of human culture.

The evidence of nonconscious behavioral tendencies actually raises the question of interdependence between genetic and cultural determinants. From biological perspectives, the proportion of genetic factors and evolutionary selection is expected to be particularly high in cases where behavioral tendencies relate to species–specific means of adaptation. In humans, the use of speech allowing accumulation of knowledge across generations, as well as cultures, is the most potent candidate for the position of a pivotal means of adaptation. For this reason, it seems legitimate to pay particular attention to whether human caretakers are preadapted for guiding infants toward speech acquisition in specific ways. Gaps in research on preverbal communication lend this task additional significance.

The inability to apply straightforward techniques for discriminating innate and sociocultural determinants in humans has forced researchers to look for indirect parameters. For instance, Papoušek and Papoušek (1987, in press b) suggest the following criteria of innate behavioral patterns:

(1) Functional involvement of the behavioral pattern in species–specific means of evolutionary adaptation.
(2) High probability in occurrence in response to cue elicitors or within given interactional contexts.
(3) Universality of the pattern across sex, age, culture, or species.
(4) Early emergence during ontogeny.
(5) Minimal awareness and rational control in subjects carrying out the given behavioral pattern.
(6) Co–evolution of counterparts to the pattern in conspecifics.
(7) Presence of the pattern in cases where environmental influence was for some reason seriously restricted or eliminated.
(8) Conceptual congruity in interpreting determinants in the given pattern and other functionally interrelated behavioral patterns.

In this context, cross–cultural comparisons serve to test the borders of universality in biological origins of behavioral tendencies: Cross–cultural universality supports the evidence of innateness. The degree of universality helps to elucidate the relative contributions of biological and cultural determinants. Conversely, various features of complex universals vary among cultures and among individuals and thus allow the identification of cultures or individuals as do other categories of universals, such as fingerprints or voiceprints.

Cross–cultural comparative analyses of intuitive parental communication with infants represent the observer's keyhole into biological programs related to species–specific forms of human adaptation. The fact that innateness may be interrelated with a lack of conscious awareness in subjects obviates the use of questionnaires or interviews in inquiries about cross–cultural universals in behaviors involved in parent–infant interactions.

Representative Parental Behaviors: Melodic Contours in Maternal Speech

In line with the assumption that speech is central in biological as well as cultural human adaptation, we have focused in a series of studies on forms of communication between preverbal infants and parents or caretakers. One research avenue includes analyses of vocal communication; another investigates potential support to infant learning and cognitive capacities which are expected to develop early and accelerate sufficiently before speech can appear.

Prior studies have confirmed that the rate of infant learning dramatically increases during the first postpartum months, not only on account of age but also on account of learning how to learn and in dependence on the arrangement of learning tasks (Papoušek, 1967, 1977). Assumptions for successful teaching were derived from those studies and later found to be enacted by parents in unintentional teaching interventions during interactions with infants (Papoušek & Papoušek, 1984).

Unknowingly, caretakers assess and, if necessary, modify infant alertness and attention, stimulate with contingent, simple, slowly displayed, and repetitive patterns, encourage and reward coping or matching responses in infants, and vary the quality and dosage of stimulation according to feedback cues in infant behaviors (Papoušek & Papoušek, 1984, 1987). Since rational control is not necessary, such behavioral adjustments can be carried out quickly, with short latencies, and without wearing the parent. Thus, human caregiving for preverbal infants includes species–specific behavioral patterns with an obvious didactic character in as much as it offers guidance and models for adaptative advance and/or compensates for infant constraints in perceptual, integrative, and communicative capacities (Papoušek & Papoušek, 1978, 1987).

In interactions with older preverbal and language–learning infants, similar didactic phenomena have been reported in mothers as "scaffolding" (Bruner, 1975), "tutoring" (Wood, 1989); "master–apprentice relation" (Fogel & Thelen, 1987), "parental framing" (Kaye, 1982), "instructive mode of parenting" (Bornstein, 1989b), or "guidance in development" (Rogoff, 1990). Scaffolding describes teaching interventions that support and augment the child's limited cognitive capacities. Vygotsky (1978) proposed the concept of the "zone of proximal development" to explain interactional advantages to the child's development. In the zone of proximal development, children perform beyond the limits of their existing individual skill when they are supported by a more experienced adult. Thus, children become capable of coping with more advanced problems than their unassisted skills would otherwise allow (Rogoff, 1990).

We have accumulated evidence that didactic parenting functions on a preadapted nonconscious basis from the earliest stages of preverbal communication as a universal dialectic counterpart to the infant's integrative capacities and constraints (for survey see Papoušek & Papoušek, 1987). This didactic potential of parental behaviors is exemplified especially well in the peculiar melodic structure of parental speech.

(1) Melodic contours are perceptually the most salient features of parental speech to infants in the first months of life (Fernald & Kuhl, 1987; Papoušek, Papoušek & Haekel, 1987; Stern, Spieker, Barnett, & MacKain, 1983). The acoustic properties of melodic contours in parental speech seem to be optimally adjusted to the infant's auditory sensitivities and preferences (Fernald, 1984). Infants in the first months of life prefer the melodic structure of infant-directed speech to adult–directed forms of speech (Fernald & Kuhl, 1987; Werker & McLeod, 1989).

(2) Elevated pitch and exaggerated melodic contours do more than simply draw the infant's attention to the mother's voice. Figure 2.1 illustrates the prototypical structure of infant–directed melodies with an example from a 3–minute dialogue of a German mother with her 2–month–old infant. The slow tempo, frequent repetitions, and distinctive prototypical character of melodic contours fulfill basic prerequisites to successful learning and integration in young infants (Papoušek, 1969; Papoušek & Papoušek, 1984). They enable the infant to detect, perceive, and categorize basic units in parental speech (Fernald, 1984; Papoušek et al., 1985; Stern et al., 1982; Trehub, 1990). At the same time, melodic contours offer models

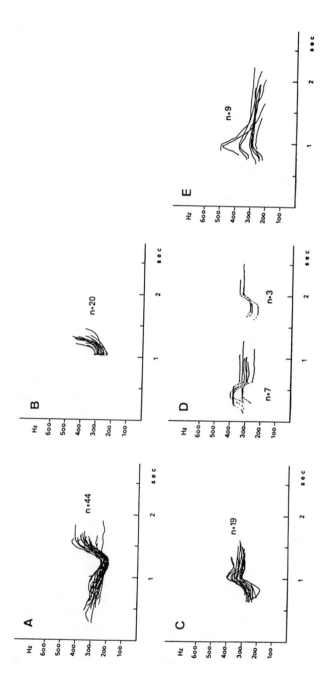

Figure 2.1. Prototypical adjustments of repetitive melodic contour types during a 3-minute dialogue of a German mother with her 2-month-old infant. Superimposed computer-generated F_0 contours of five repetitive melodies used for encouraging a vocal turn (A and B), for encouraging visual attention (C and D), and for contingent rewarding (E).

of those features that infants practice first in vowel–like sounds, namely, phonation, melodic modulation, and vowel–like resonances (Papoušek & Papoušek, 1989).

(3) Melodic contours in parental prosody have been shown to function as the earliest prototypical messages, presented to infants in close relation to the most relevant forms of intuitive parental guidance (Papoušek, Papoušek, & Koester, 1986).

Thus, melodic contours in parental speech represent a unique model for cross–cultural comparisons of preverbal communication. They play a key role in the broad behavioral repertoire of nonconscious parental didactics (Papoušek & Papoušek, 1987). In methodological terms, they lend themselves, better than other communicative behaviors, to quantitative structural analyses and comparisons across individuals, languages, or cultures.

Representative Cultural Traits: Tone versus Stress Languages

For a cross–cultural comparison of the forms and functions of melodic contours in maternal speech, it is crucial to select ethnic groups which widely differ not only in cultural tradition and child–rearing philosophy, but also in the structure of language, particularly in linguistic and paralinguistic uses of melodic patterns. We selected an Asian population with a tone language, Mandarin Chinese, for comparison with Caucasian populations using non–tonal stress languages, American English and German.

Although Chinese infant care has not yet attracted enough attention in developmental research, it seems to deviate from American and German in ways similar to infant care in other Asian countries. According to Ho (1986), most authors agree that Chinese parents emphasize emotional harmony and control as central to social relationships, whereas Caucasian American parents emphasize individuality, spontaneity, variety, and self–assertion (Wu, 1985). Kuchner (1989) observed that Chinese infants are less attentive to people in their environment and smile less, and that Chinese mothers are less affectionate with their 3–month–olds, introduce less change and novelty, and manipulate infant attention less often than Caucasian American mothers. Ho (1986) reviewed anthropological and psychological research in relation to early child rearing, and concluded that Chinese parents tend to be highly lenient and indulgent toward children under 4 years, but demand strict discipline later on. They discourage independent, active, exploratory activities in infants, and underemphasize self–mastery, creativity, autonomy, and assertiveness.

Equally significant may be the phonological differences between tone and stress languages used in these different cultures. In a stress language, melodic patterns are used on the word, phrase, or sentence level to manifest linguistic stress and intonation; they carry semantic, syntactic, and/or affective/attitudinal meaning (Crystal, 1975). In the phonological system of tone languages, melodic contours "carry an additional functional load" (Wang, 1972). Specific F_0 contours or "tones" are used contrastively on the syllable or segmental level and carry lexical meaning (Gandour, 1978). Mandarin Chinese has four tones (level, rising, dip–rising, and

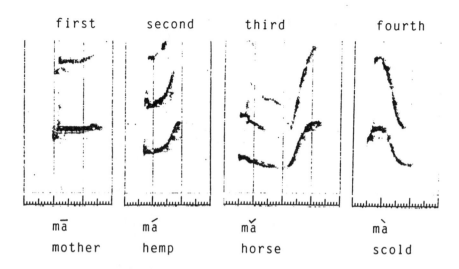

first   second   third   fourth

mā   má   mǎ   mà

mother   hemp   horse   scold

Figure 2.2. Models of the Mandarin Chinese syllable "ma" spoken by a native teacher of Mandarin with each of the four lexical tones. Narrow–band spectrograms (Kay Elemetrics Digital Sonagraph TM 7800), 11.3 Hz bandwidth, 0–2000 Hz F_0 range, 400 msec/time unit.

falling) and a neutral tone (Chao, 1968; Eady, 1982). Depending on the tone, the syllable "ma" can carry four different word meanings (Figure 2.2), or may be used in the function of a neutral–tone final particle, for instance, as a marker of yes–no questions (Gandour, 1978).

There is sufficient evidence that Mandarin speakers use more complex and more variable F_0 patterns in adult conversations than English American speakers. Eady (1982) found a higher average F_0 and a greater rate of F_0 change in Mandarin speech (i.e., more F_0 fluctuations per second and syllable in spite of equal overall F_0 ranges). Chen (1974) reported higher F_0 ranges and F_0 variability in conversational Mandarin utterances—particularly if spoken by native Mandarin Chinese speakers—than in American English utterances. Such fundamental differences in the phonological systems of English and Mandarin suggest that forms and functions of melodic contours in infant–directed speech may be similarly affected.

The aim of our research was to elucidate innate and cultural determinants in mothers' use of melodic contours during interactions with their presyllabic infants. By presyllabic we mean the period of age between birth and appearance of canonic, reduplicated syllables around 7 months. The crucial question was whether the tonal rules of Mandarin Chinese constrain mothers in the use of simplified prototypical caregiving melodies. Several hypothetical alternatives come into question. On the one hand, reduced talking to infants, reduced use of lexical utterances, reduced difference between infant–addressed and adult–addressed speech, or on the contrary didactic enhancement of tones from the beginning of infant life, would strongly indicate the prevalence of cultural determinants. On the other hand, neglect or violation of tone rules in favor of nonlinguistic prototypical melodic units would indicate primary biological determination. Of course, constraints on the display of melodic caregiving messages may also be caused by sociocultural rules of emotional expressivity.

COMPARATIVE DATA

Ten Chinese and 10 Caucasian American middle–class mothers and their 2–month–old infants from the Washington DC area participated in our study. Chinese parents were first–generation immigrants, mostly from Taiwan, and spoke exclusively Mandarin to their infants. Subjects were recruited through local Chinese newspapers or members of the local Chinese community, and were contacted by a native Mandarin–speaking Chinese student. Infants (5 girls and 5 boys in each sample) were born without complications, had developed normally, and were healthy at the time of observation. Data on 21 German middle–class mother–infant pairs who had previously been investigated under comparable conditions during spontaneous interactions in the laboratory (Papoušek et al., 1986) were used for additional comparisons.

Mothers were asked to speak and play with their infant as at home. Sessions were observed and videotaped through one–way mirrors with three synchronized cameras, and they were simultaneously audiotaped on a Revox 77 tape–recorder. Adult–directed speech samples were taken from the middle section of a subsequent interview, when mothers talked about their infant in an animated way in their native language.

Seven minutes of infant–directed speech and one minute of adult–directed speech from each mother were transcribed and translated into English in collaboration with a native Mandarin–speaking Chinese linguist. Maternal utterances were defined as units of vocal behavior embedded in a global intonational envelope, separated from adjoining utterances by natural pauses. All utterances were evaluated for lexical content, melodic contour type, and interactional caregiving context by experienced observers. Coding schemes were based on definitions, categories, and reliabilities that had been developed in previous investigations of vocal communication in German samples of mother–infant and father–infant interactions (Papoušek & Sandner, 1981; Papoušek et al., 1987).

Digital acoustic analyses of melodic contours focused on the prevalent melodic prototypes (i.e., on rising, falling, bell–shaped, and U–shaped contours). Programs for digital analyses were kindly provided and adjusted by D. Symmes (for details see Papoušek, Papoušek, & Symmes, in press).

Lexical Content of Maternal Utterances

Chinese and American mothers exhibited as strong tendencies to talk to infants as German mothers (32.4, 25.4, and 31.7 utterances per minute, differences nonsignificant). All three groups of mothers used predominantly nonverbal utterances (65.9%, 60.4%, and 60.8%, respectively) for promoting conversation–like turn–taking (with interjections, particles, emotional exclamations, calls), playful inter–changes (with melodic and rhythmic components of interactional games), or imitation (with matching and modelling sounds). Verbal utterances referred to the immediate interactional context, in particular to the infant's vocal, facial, and other motor behaviors.

A few differences were consistently observed: (1) Chinese mothers used a higher proportion of imitation–promoting utterances than American mothers (19.5% versus 9.7% of utterances; $p < .05$, U–test). (2) American mothers more often commented on or encouraged motor activity in their infants than Chinese mothers (23.1% versus 10.6% of utterances, $p < .01$, U–test). (3) Chinese mothers referred more often to smiling than American mothers (4.5% versus 0.3% of utterances; $p < .05$, U–test).

Melodic Contours

The three groups of mothers showed equal preference for the most simple unidirectional (level, rising, and falling: in 59.4%, 52.9%, and 54.2% of utterances, respectively) and bi–directional contours (U–shaped, and bell–shaped: in 24.3%, 28.0%, and 34.6% of utterances, respectively) (Figure 2.3). Both Chinese and American mothers doubled their overall speech frequency ranges from 14 and 13 semitones, respectively, in adult–directed speech to 28 and 29 semitones, respectively, in infant–directed speech. German mothers had an average range of 23 semitones. American mothers significantly expanded pitch excursions per utterance from 6 to 10 semitones. Chinese mothers used significantly wider pitch excursions in adult–directed utterances than American mothers (7 semitones), but

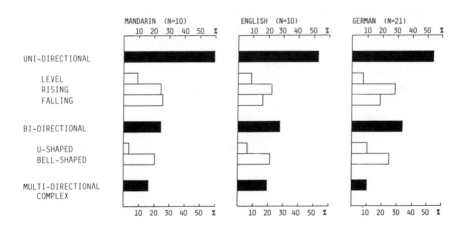

Figure 2.3. Average distributions of melodic contour types in infant–directed speech of Mandarin–, English–, and German–speaking mothers.

they did not expand F_o excursions in infant–directed utterances. German mothers averaged 6 semitones in infant–directed speech.

The average acoustic shapes and prototypical features of infant–directed rising, falling, bell–shaped, and U–shaped contours were strikingly similar in Chinese and American samples (Figure 2.4). Infant–directed contours were significantly shorter in duration, and higher in all measures of absolute fundamental frequency (F_o) than adult–directed contours. However, Mandarin–speaking mothers raised their pitch and expanded pitch excursions significantly less than American mothers. Interestingly, when compared to corresponding data from the German sample, the average pitch excursions (see above) and measures of absolute pitch in Chinese motherese (e.g., peak $F_o = 288$ Hz) were closer to those of German (peak $F_o = 298$ Hz) than to those of American (peak $F_o = 351$ Hz).

Interactional Caregiving Contexts

Previous analyses of interactions between German mothers and their 2–month–olds had revealed significant relations between the forms of melodic contours in maternal speech and their functions in eight interactional frames characterizing intuitive didactic guidance: Encouraging Infant Attention; Encouraging an Infant Turn; Encouraging Imitation; Encouraging Play; Contingent Rewarding for an Infant Turn; Discouraging Unfavorable Behavior; Evaluating Infant Behavioral–Emotional State; and Soothing a Hyperaroused or Distressed Infant (Papoušek, Papoušek, & Koester, 1986). The same caregiving frames constituted major proportions of the interaction time and occurred with similar frequencies in both the Chinese and American samples (Papoušek, Papoušek, & Symmes, in press). The overall correspondence in prevalent caregiving contexts implies that Chinese and American mothers used strikingly similar forms of interactional didactic care in guiding the infant to regulate arousal, attention, and readiness to interact; to develop control over vocal, facial, and gaze behaviors; and to practice elementary communicative skills, such as turn–taking, vocal imitation, and vocal playfulness. Only minor differences were observed: For instance, Chinese mothers more frequently engaged in Encouraging Imitation, whereas American mothers tended more to Reward Infant Behaviors.

The laboratory set–up of the study in which mothers and infants interacted in a standardized face–to–face position certainly emphasized cross–cultural similarities in interactional contexts. However, mothers and infants seemed to feel at ease, to interact spontaneously, and to follow their intuitive propensities to come to the fore. Future research will have to establish whether face–to–face communication plays similar roles and occurs with similar frequencies in normal everyday child–rearing practices in the two cultures.

Contour–Context Relations

Loglinear modelling techniques were used to analyze the effects of both caregiving context and language group (Chinese versus American) on the mothers' choice of

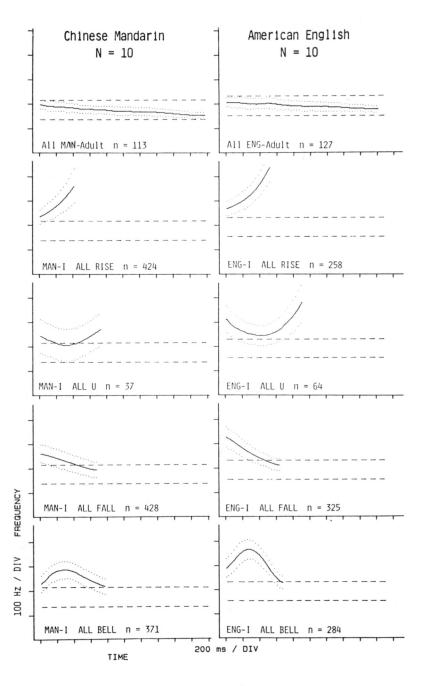

Figure 2.4. Average acoustic shapes of melodic contours (solid lines) in adult–directed utterances (top) and infant–directed utterances with rising, U–shaped, falling, and bell–shaped melodies. Dotted lines represent 2 standard errors of the mean, dashed lines represent overall speech frequency ranges of adult–directed speech.

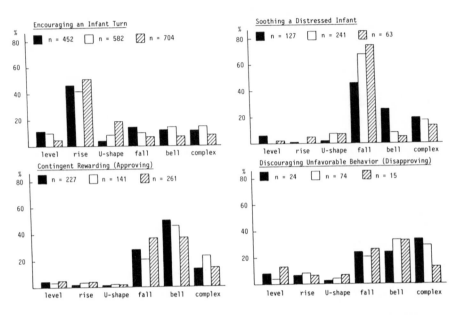

Figure 2.5. Average distributions of melodic contour types in four interactional caregiving contexts. Black bars: Chinese mothers; White bars: American mothers; Hatched bars: German mothers.

melodic contour types. We found a large context effect, Likelihood ratio $X^2(35) = 896.5, p < .001$, next to very small language, $X^2(5) = 19.1, p < .001$, and interaction effects, $X^2(35) = 90.6, p < .001$. According to the data, Chinese and American mothers exhibited highly corresponding profiles of contour preferences in relation to the majority of interactional caregiving contexts (Papoušek & Papoušek, 1987). These profiles were also congruent with the distributions of melodic contour types in German motherese (Figure 2.5).

All mothers preferentially used rising contours for encouraging infant attention and participation in a dialogue. They used low–pitch, slowly falling melodies for soothing a hyperaroused or distressed infant. They contingently rewarded infant smiling, pleasant vocalizations, or other desirable infant turns with falling or bell–shaped contours, and they discouraged infant fussiness or other undesired behaviors with brief, steeply falling or bell–shaped contours at a high pitch (Papoušek & Papoušek, 1987; Papoušek et al., 1986; in press).

The above results accord with previous reports on maternal and paternal uses of falling melodies for soothing a crying infant (Fernald et al., 1989); on maternal use of bell–shaped contours for maintaining positive affect (Stern et al., 1982); and on use of rising melodies for encouraging a visual or vocal turn (Ryan, 1978; Stern et al., 1982). Recently, Fernald (1990) found evidence of similar attention–directing, rewarding, prohibiting, and soothing melodies in maternal speech to 1–year–olds.

In American and Chinese samples, we also analyzed the effects of context and language group on acoustic measures of rising, falling, and bell–shaped contours with the help of multivariate analyses of variance (Papoušek et al., in press). In most cases, results suggested significant main effects for context, and small but significant language and interaction effects. Context effects on the acoustic configuration of melodic contours were of the same kind in both language groups.

MELODIC CONTOURS AS UNIVERSALS

Cross–Cultural Similarities in Forms and Functions of Melodic Contours

The present data show that mothers who speak a tone language, Mandarin Chinese, use a distinct prosodic register when talking to their presyllabic infants in much the same way as mothers who speak non–tonal stress languages, American English or German. As compared to adult–directed speech, maternal speech to 2–month–olds is characterized by a high proportion of non–lexical utterances, widely expanded speech frequency range, and a predominance of simple, distinctive and repetitive uni– and bidirectional melodic prototypes with significantly raised start, maximum, minimum, and terminal frequencies.

The data are well in accord with the findings of earlier monocultural studies (Fernald & Simon, 1984; Garnica, 1977; Grieser & Kuhl, 1988; Papoušek et al., 1987; Stern et al., 1983) and with a recent truly comparative study of maternal speech prosody across languages with different prosodic organizations (Fernald et al., 1989). The data lend further support to the assumption that an infant–directed high–pitch prosodic register with exaggerated intonation is universal across cultures (Ferguson, 1964).

Yet, the present data go beyond the general characteristics of maternal prosody to arrive at a more detailed comparative account of the structure and functions of prevalent prosodic contours. Digital acoustic analyses of the prevalent melodic contours evidenced the same kind of didactic prototypical adjustments in Chinese and American motherese which had been found in the German study (cf. Figure 2.1). They closely correspond to infants' earliest perceptual/integrative constraints (Fernald & Kuhl, 1987; Papoušek et al., 1987; Sachs, 1977; Trehub, 1990). The adjustments allow the presyllabic infant to detect and process potentially meaningful units in caretaker speech. Interestingly, Chinese and American mothers did not differ in the distribution and overall acoustic configuration of prevalent melodic prototypes. Thus, mothers with both tonal and nontonal languages seem to provide requisites for successful presyllabic communication in the very same way.

As reported for German motherese (Papoušek, Papoušek & Koester, 1986), Chinese and American mothers used melodic prototypes in speech to 2–month–olds as linguistically independent units in close relation to immediate interactional caregiving frames. The present analyses of form–function relations revealed striking similarities among the three samples in terms of both context–related contour types and acoustic shapes of prevalent contours (Papoušek et al., in press).

Interestingly, Attention– or Turn–Encouraging rises and Soothing falls represent opposite tendencies along a dimension of arousing/soothing interventions (Cruttenden, 1981) with short, high–pitch, wide–range, and steep melodies on one end and long, low–pitch, low–range, and flat melodies on the other. In the contexts of Evaluating Infant State and Soothing, mothers respond to infant cues of tension, exhaustion, or hyperarousal. They reduce the rate and intensity of stimulation and calm the infant. Accordingly, maternal melodies are significantly prolonged, flattened, and reduced in the level and range of fundamental frequencies. In contexts of Encouraging a Turn or Encouraging Attention, mothers respond to infant cues of passivity and inattentiveness. They use various strategies to increase the infant's alertness and responsivity. Melodic contours in motherese become significantly shorter and steeper, fundamental frequency rises, and pitch range increases. Thus, mothers adjust the acoustic properties of melodies to infant behavioral states in counteractive ways, as if to bring the infant from inconvenient transitory states either into the state of optimal waking alertness or into quiet sleep.

Another contrast in mothers' melodic contours relates to the approving/disapproving dimension of maternal interventions in Rewarding and Discouraging contexts. In both contexts, falling and bell–shaped contours prevail. Interactions with 2–month–olds seldom require discouraging; in most cases, mothers disapprove of infant fussiness and display corresponding contours distinctly while attempting to stop infant fussiness and recapture infant attention. Impressive discouraging responses remind us of warning signals in threatening contexts among humans or non–human primates (Jürgens, 1979). The attention–getting, disruptive and/or warning properties of discouraging falls or bells are expressed in brief staccato–like, steep, high–pitch F_0 contours in vocal sounds and in their somewhat negative hedonic quality. In contrast, Rewarding falls and bells are longer than those in the other contexts, and are displayed in vocal sounds with intermediate frequency ranges and a positive hedonic quality.

The consistent association of distinctive melodic prototypes with relevant forms of intuitive parental care suggests that these prototypes may facilitate infant processing of contextual information and function as didactic guiding messages in early mother–infant communication (Papoušek & Papoušek, 1987). This assumption has recently been verified experimentally (Papoušek, Bornstein, Nuzzo, Papoušek, & Symmes, 1990). In an infant–controlled design of auditory preference, 4–month–olds were found to respond appropriately to a contrastive pair of approving and disapproving bell–shaped contours. Infants looked significantly more at one of two identical faces which was contingently associated with a rewarding contour, and looked less at the face which was presented with a discouraging contour. Thus, the melodic prototypes of parental speech may represent the first meaningful units in parental speech which the infant is able to process and answer.

No evidence was found in the present study that melodic prototypes in Chinese motherese represent exaggerated lexical tones. Neither were they used for other linguistic purposes such as highlighting contrastive speech sounds or new words; nor did they encompass meaningful linguistic units in most utterances. The majority of melodic prototypes in maternal speech were found in non-lexical utterances, and—according to Mandarin Chinese listeners—did not resemble exaggerated didactic models of the four tones. They were much more variable in pitch level and shape, particularly in imitation–promoting utterances. In contrast, lexical utterances were generally spoken fast with flattened tones (Papoušek & Hwang, in press). Although there was no indication that Chinese mothers were teaching tones to their 2–month–olds, they encouraged the infant to practice and control pitch and pitch modulation. Chinese mothers matched and modelled various melodic patterns on widely varying pitch levels twice as often as American mothers. Reciprocal vocal matching and modelling has been shown to be a regular part of presyllabic communication in German mother–infant dyads, and may support infants' procedural learning and practicing sound features, as well as their imitative development (Papoušek & Papoušek, 1989).

Infants growing up in linguistic environments of tone languages do not evidence acquisition of tones prior to the acquisition of first words (Li & Thompson, 1978; Tuaycharoen, 1978). However, according to a recent cross–cultural study of infant babbling, listeners were able to correctly identify the target language from the babbling of 10–month–old infants, and specific tonal configurations on the syllable level were identified in sonagraphic analyses of canonical babbling of 10–month–olds (Ichijima, 1987). The present data suggest that melodic practice may be emphasized in presyllabic dialogues of Chinese mother–infant pairs as early as in the first postpartum months.

Cross–Cultural Differences

Cross–cultural differences between Mandarin and English melodies did not concern the didactic structural features of melodic prototypes, nor their function as primary didactic caregiving messages. Differences only concerned the extent of melodic expansions and raised speech frequencies. American mothers raised their overall pitch and expanded pitch excursions in utterances significantly more than Chinese and German mothers, particularly in falling and bell–shaped contours (Papoušek & Papoušek, 1987).

These findings are supported by recent reports on relatively low F_0 excursions in Mandarin Chinese motherese (Grieser & Kuhl, 1988), and on similar differences in the extent of prosodic modifications in American English, Japanese, and four European languages in maternal speech to one–year–olds (Fernald et al., 1989). In the latter study, American English parents raised their pitch and expanded pitch excursions more than parents from all other language groups. In the present study, American mothers similarly surpassed both Chinese and German mothers in the extent at which they raised pitch and expanded pitch excursions.

Both linguistic and cultural interpretations of these differences need to be considered. First, the lexical tone system of Mandarin Chinese may constrain speakers in non–lexical modulations of pitch. This explanation applies only in part, in as much as Chinese mothers—as American mothers—used significantly higher pitch, varied pitch levels more frequently, and expanded pitch excursions more extensively in imitation–promoting utterances in which tonal constraints were minimal because of a low proportion of lexical items and a preponderance of imitative and modelling melodies (Papoušek et al., in press). In general, however, Chinese mothers seemed effectively to outwit potential tonal constraints by simply avoiding lexical utterances as American and German mothers do.

Second, Chinese, English, and German languages differ in the degree to which they use intonational cues for emotional, attitudinal, or syntactic information. Whereas English depends almost exclusively on intonation, German and Chinese can also utilize supplementary means, such as modal particles in German (Schubiger, 1980) or word– and sentence–final particles with neutral tone in Chinese (Alleton, 1981; Chao, 1968). In friendly, polite conversations of Mandarin Chinese speakers, the use of modal particles is obligatory for expressing attitude and interest, and is conditioned by the context of their intersubjective relations (Alleton, 1981). For marking linguistic emphasis and sentence types, Chinese speakers typically use particles rather than intonational cues (Chao, 1968), as Japanese speakers do (Kuno, 1973). In speaking to 2–month–old infants, Chinese mothers used particles abundantly in their lexical utterances. Interestingly, however, they utilized particles as a means to modulate and expand melodic contours rather than as substitutes for intonation (see below).

A third explanation may be found in different cultural conventions for the display of attitudes or emotions. For instance, cultural display rules in the Japanese society prescribe masking of emotions in many social situations, whereas in American middle class society amplification of emotional expressions, particularly in relation to young children, is regarded as socially acceptable or even desirable (Fernald et al., 1989; Kuno, 1973). Similar differences in social display rules seem to apply to Chinese–American comparisons of mother–infant interactions (Kuchner, 1989) and to account for the present finding that American mothers modified infant–directed prosody more extensively than Chinese and German mothers.

Interesting as they are, these cross–cultural differences appear negligible in comparison with the reported cross–linguistic similarities in maternal speech to 2–month–olds.

Determinants of Maternal Speech Adjustments

The crucial question remains how Chinese mothers, who were expected to produce more complex F_0–patterns with a higher rate of F_0–change per time unit (Eady, 1982), managed to provide infants with the same prototypes as American or German mothers. The most straightforward "strategy" used by all Chinese mothers in the sample was to avoid lexical utterances and use more exclamations and interjections which allow for continuous, smooth modulations in pitch. Chinese mothers evidently share this intuitive tendency with American and German mothers and fathers (Papoušek et al., 1985).

In order to cope with conflicts between tones and prototypical melodies in lexical utterances, some Chinese mothers seemed to adopt other interesting strategies. A common pattern was a disproportional lengthening of the last tone–

bearing syllable in an utterance, or, even more frequently, of a neutral–tone final particle. In adult–directed conversational utterances, short final particles with neutral tone ("ma", "ne", "le") are used to mark the speaker's attitude or intention, or to mark syntactic functions (Alleton, 1981; Chao, 1968). In maternal speech to 2–month–olds (Papoušek & Hwang, in press), the final particles were lengthened and carried a major part of the sentence intonation, while lexical tones were shortened and flattened in favor of a simplified global contour (Figure 2.6). In the same vein, initial or final exclamations were incorporated into the overall intonation pattern. In other cases, mothers used special kin or address forms of lexical items in which the lexical tones were neglected or even violated. For instance, three mothers repeatedly asked their 2–month–olds to imitate the word "mama", a duplicated noun with two level tones, in which the tone of the second syllable is typically changed into a neutral tone (Chao, 1968). The Chinese mothers obviously did not care about correct pronunciation of lexical tones, but instead used a variety of melodies, and rising contours in particular (i.e., the contour type which all mothers regularly use for Encouraging an Infant Turn) (Figure 2.7; see Papoušek & Hwang, in press, for detailed analyses of this finding).

Although such forms of tonal neglect were found only in a small sample of utterances, they strongly support the assumption that Chinese mothers may have been driven less by the rules of their language than by biologically preadapted adjustments to the needs of communication with presyllabic infants.

The intuitive nature of prosodic and other structural adjustments in infant–directed speech has found little attention among students of babytalk. These adjustments would hardly be possible on the basis of conscious rational decision making (Papoušek & Papoušek, 1987). As evident from subsequent interviews in the present study, most Chinese and American mothers did not realize in which ways they were modifying their speech. Yet, a "biological preadaptedness" seems to be evidenced in the intuitive nature of maternal recourse to basic nonlinguistic

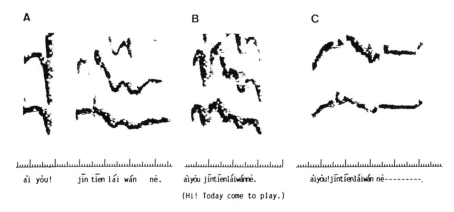

A   B   C

aì yòu!   jīn tīen lái wán   nè.   aìyòu jīntīenláiwánnè.   aìyòu!jīntīenláiwán nè--------.
                                         (Hi! Today come to play.)

Figure 2.6. Mandarin Chinese utterance spoken in three different registers. A: foreign language instruction, B: adult conversation, C: maternal speech to her 2–month–old. (Spectrogram specifications are in Figure 2.2.)

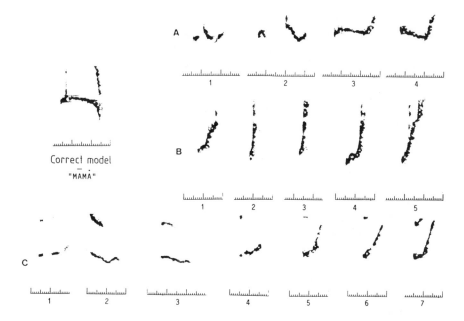

Figure 2.7. Melodic contours in utterances of 3 mothers (A, B, C) encouraging imitation of the word "mama" in their 2–month–olds: Correct lexical model or caregiving message? (Sonagraphic specifications are in Figure 2.2.)

units of vocal communication, in adequate adjustments of speech units to the infant's level of perceptual and integrative processing, and in the structural and functional universals of melodic prototypes across age, gender, and some highly diverse languages/cultures. As a matter of fact, all criteria of innateness mentioned above relate to the caretaker's intuitive adjustments in infant–directed speech and their didactic significance.

The present comparison of tonal and nontonal language groups crucially supports the assumption that the use of melodic units in parental speech to presyllabic infants coevolved in the social environment independent of cultural differences, and that it did so as species–specific environmental support for infant communicative development.

CONCLUSIONS

Analyses of the parent–infant system can elucidate specific forms of preadaptedness in the two partners which may contribute to human precocity in communicative development. Infant ability to perceive and process communicative messages in the social environment meets corresponding counterparts in caretaker ability to adjust interventions to infant behavioral/emotional state and to the actual stage of integrative development. Resulting parent–infant interchanges bear the character of a primary didactic system which is partly based on co–evolution of corresponding biological premises. Because biological origins can hardly be examined in direct experiments, the nonconscious (or preconscious) regulation of interchanges and their universality rise to the status of particularly significant indices.

Cross–cultural comparisons gain a new relevant dimension from this view. Behavioral and cultural traits were selected in this study to represent crucial aspects of early preverbal communication: the structure and functions of prosodic melodies in vocal mother–infant dialogues in tonal (Mandarin Chinese) versus stress languages (American English and German). Cross–cultural universality does not contradict the presence of cultural and individual variation. Both forms and functions of melodic contours, related to the presyllabic period of development in the present report, change with infant age and progress towards syllabic and verbal communication. Increasing influence of specific traits distinguishing tonal and non–tonal stress languages is predictable beyond the presyllabic age.

Together with the intuitive nature of infant–directed speech, evidenced from systematic interviews with observed caretakers, the presence of cross–cultural universals strengthen the assumption that the highly adaptive process of speech acquisition in humans depends on the co–evolution of species–specific supportive constituents.

ACKNOWLEDGMENTS

Analyses of vocal sounds in this chapter profited substantially from conceptual and methodological help provided by David Symmes, an outstanding primatologist from the Laboratory of Comparative Ethology at the National Institutes of Health, Bethesda, MD. David Symmes died on April 8, 1990. Acknowledging his friendly cooperation and skilled contribution, the authors dedicate this presentation to David Symmes.

The study is part of a collaborative research project on "Intuitive parenting of infants in comparative perspectives", organized by the authors at the Laboratory of Comparative Ethology, NICHD, Bethesda, MD during a Sabbatic Year in 1985/86. This research has been generously supported by the NICHD and by the German grant foundation Deutsche Forschungsgemeinschaft. The authors owe special thanks to Shu–fen Hwang, G. Kneitinger, M. Radmacher, C. Rahn, S. Suomi, J. Sykes, W. Thompson, and A. Yassourides.

REFERENCES

Alleton, V. Final particles and expression of modality in modern Chinese. *Journal of Chinese Linguistics*, 1981, *9*, 91–115.

Bornstein, M. H. Cross–cultural developmental comparisons: The case of Japanese–American infant and mother activities and interactions. What we know, what we need to know, and why we need to know. *Developmental Review*, 1989, *9*, 171–204 (a).

Bornstein, M. H. Between caretakers and their young: Two modes of interaction and their consequences for cognitive growth. In M. H. Bornstein & J. S. Bruner (Eds.), *Interaction in human development* (pp. 197–214). Hillsdale, NJ: Lawrence Erlbaum Associates, 1989 (b).

Bruner, J. S. The ontogenesis of speech acts. *Journal of Child Language*, 1975, 2, 1–19.

Bruner, J. S., & Bornstein, M. H. On interaction. In M. H. Bornstein & J. S. Bruner (Eds.), *Interaction in human development* (pp. 1–14). Hillsdale, NJ: Lawrence Erlbaum Associates, 1989.

Chao, Y. R. *A grammar of spoken Chinese*. Berkeley and Los Angeles: University of California Press, 1968.

Chen, G. The pitch range of English and Chinese speakers. *Journal of Chinese Linguistics*, 1974, 2, 159–171.

Cruttenden, A. Falls and rises: Meanings and universals. *Journal of Linguistics*, 1981, 17, 77–91.

Crystal, D. *The English tone of voice*. London: Edward Arnold, 1975.

Eady, S. J. Differences in the F_0 patterns of speech: Tone language versus stress language. *Language and Speech*, 1982, 25, 29–42.

Ferguson, C. A. Baby talk in six languages. *American Anthropologist*, 1964, 66, 103–114.

Fernald, A. The perceptual and affective salience of mothers' speech to infants. In L. Feagans, C. Garvey, & R. Golinkoff (Eds.), *The origins and growth of communication* (pp. 5–29). Norwood, NJ: Ablex, 1984.

Fernald, A. Intonation and communicative intent in mothers' speech to infants: Is the melody the message? *Child Development*, 1990, 60, 1497–1510.

Fernald, A., & Kuhl, P. K. Acoustic determinants of infant preference for motherese speech. *Infant Behavior and Development*, 1987, 10, 279–293.

Fernald, A., & Simon, T. Expanded intonation contours in mothers' speech to newborns. *Developmental Psychology*, 1984, 20, 104–113.

Fernald, A., Taeschner, T., Dunn, J., Papoušek, M., Boysson–Bardies, B., & Fukui, I. A cross–language study of prosodic modifications in mothers' and fathers' speech to preverbal infants. *Journal of Child Language*, 1989, 16, 977–1001.

Fogel, A., & Thelen, E. Development of early expressive and communicative action: Reinterpreting the evidence from a dynamic systems perspective. *Developmental Psychology*, 1987, 23, 747–761.

Gandour, J. T. The perception of tone. In V. A. Fromkin (Ed.), *Tone: A linguistic survey* (pp. 41–76). New York: Academic, 1978.

Garnica, O. K. Some prosodic and paralinguistic features of speech to young children. In C. E. Snow, & C. A. Ferguson (Eds.), *Talking to children: Language input and acquisition* (pp. 63–88). Cambridge: Cambridge University Press, 1977.

Grieser, D. L., & Kuhl, P. K. Maternal speech to infants in a tonal language: Support for universal prosodic features in motherese. *Developmental Psychology*, 1988, 24, 14–20.

Ho, D. Y. F. Chinese patterns of socialization: a critical review. In M. H. Bond (Ed.), *The psychology of the Chinese people* (pp. 1–37). New York: Oxford University Press, 1986.

Ichijima, T. *A study of infants' utterances during the babbling period: Cross–linguistic analysis through perceptual and acoustic experiments*. Paper presented at the Meetings of the International Society for the Study of Behavioral Development, Tokyo, July, 1987.

Jürgens, U. Vocalization as an emotional indicator. A neuroethological study in the squirrel monkey. *Behaviour*, 1979, 69, 88–117.

Kaye, K. *The mental and social life of babies*. Cambridge: Cambridge University Press, 1982.

Kuchner, J. F. *Chinese-American and European–American mothers and infants: Cultural influences in the first three months of life*. Presentation at the 7th Biennial Meetings of the Society for Research in Child Development, Kansas City, April 1989.

Kuno, S. *The structure of the Japanese language*. Cambridge: MIT Press, 1973.

Li, C. N., & Thompson, S. A. The acquisition of tone. In V. A. Fromkin (Ed.), *Tone: A linguistic survey* (pp. 271–284). New York: Academic, 1978.

Papoušek, H. Experimental studies of appetitional behavior in human newborns and infants. In H. W. Stevenson, E. H. Hess & H. L. Rheingold (Eds.), *Early behavior: Comparative and developmental approaches* (pp. 249–277). New York: Wiley, 1967.

Papoušek, H. Individual variability in learned responses in human infants. In R. J. Robinson (Ed.), *Brain and early behavior* (pp. 229–252). London: Academic, 1969.

Papoušek, H. Entwicklung der Lernfähigkeit im Säuglingsalter. In G. Nissen (Ed.), *Intelligenz, Lernen und Lernstörungen* (pp. 89–107). Berlin: Springer, 1977.

Papoušek, H., & Papoušek, M. Interdisciplinary parallels in studies of early human behavior: from physical to cognitive needs, from attachment to dyadic education. *International Journal of Behavioral Development*, 1978, *1*, 37–49.

Papoušek, H., & Papoušek, M. Infant–adult social interactions: Their origins, dimensions, and failures. In T. M. Field, A. Huston, H. C. Quay, L. Troll, & G. A. Finley (Eds.), *Review of developmental psychology* (pp. 148–163). New York: Wiley, 1982.

Papoušek, H., & Papoušek, M. Learning and cognition in the everyday life of human infants. In J. Rosenblatt (Ed.), *Advances in the study of behavior* (Vol. 14, pp. 127–163). New York: Academic, 1984.

Papoušek, H., & Papoušek, M. Intuitive parenting: A dialectic counterpart to the infant's integrative competence. In J. D. Osofsky (Ed.), *Handbook of infant development* (2nd. Ed., pp. 669–720). New York: Wiley, 1987.

Papoušek, H. & Papoušek, M. Early interactional signalling: The role of facial movements. In A. F. Kalverboer, B. Hopkins, & R. H. Geuze (Eds.), *A longitudinal approach to the study of motor development in early and later childhood.* New York: Cambridge University Press, in press.

Papoušek, H., Papoušek, M., & Koester, L. S. Sharing emotionality and sharing knowledge: A microanalytic approach to parent–infant communication. In C. E. Izard & P. Read (Eds.), *Measuring emotions in infants and children* (Vol. 2, pp. 93–123). Cambridge: Cambridge University Press, 1986.

Papoušek, M., Bornstein, M. H., Nuzzo, C., Papoušek, H., & Symmes, D. Infant responses to prototypical melodic contours in parental speech. *Infant Behavior and Development*, 1990, *13*, 539–545.

Papoušek, M., & Hwang, S. C. Tone and intonation in Mandarin babytalk to presyllabic infants: Comparisons with registers of adult conversation and foreign language instruction. *Journal of Applied Psycholinguistics*, in press.

Papoušek, M., & Papoušek, H. *Models and messages in maternal speech to presyllabic infants in tone and stress languages.* Presentation at the Sixth Biennial Meetings of the Society for Research in Child Development, Baltimore, April 1987.

Papoušek, M., & Papoušek, H. Forms and functions of vocal matching in precanonical mother–infant interactions. *First Language*, 1989, *9*, 137–158.

Papoušek, M., & Papoušek, H. Preverbal vocal communication from zero to one: preparing the ground for language acquisition. In M. E. Lamb & H. Keller (Eds.), *Perspectives on infant development: Contributions from German speaking countries.* Hillsdale, NJ: Lawrence Erlbaum Associates, in press.

Papoušek, M., Papoušek, H., & Bornstein, M. H. The naturalistic vocal environment of young infants: On the significance of homogeneity and variability in parental speech. In T. Field & N. Fox (Eds.), *Social perception in infants* (pp. 269–297). Norwood, NJ: Ablex, 1985.

Papoušek, M., Papoušek, H., & Haekel, M. Didactic adjustments in fathers' and mothers' speech to their three–month–old infants. *Journal of Psycholinguistic Research*, 1987, *16*, 491–516.

Papoušek, M., Papoušek, H., & Symmes, D. The meanings of melodies in motherese in tonal and nontonal languages. *Infant Behavior and Development*, in press.

Papoušek, M., & Sandner, G. W. Mikroanalyse musikalischer Ausdruckselemente in Sprache und praeverbaler Lautentwicklung. *Sozialpädiatrie in Praxis und Klinik*, 1981, *3*, 326–331.

Rogoff, B. *Apprenticeship in thinking: Cognitive development in social context.* New York: Oxford University Press, 1990.

Ryan, M. L. Contour in context. In R. N. Cambell & P. T. Smith (Eds.), *Recent advances in the psychology of language* (pp. 237–251). New York: Plenum, 1978.

Sachs, J. The adaptive significance of linguistic input to prelinguistic infants. In C. E. Snow & C. A. Ferguson (Eds.), *Talking to children: Language input and acquisition* (pp. 51–61). Cambridge: Cambridge University Press, 1977.

Schubiger, M. English intonation and German modal particles II: A comparative study. In L. R. Waugh & C. H. Schooneveld (Eds.), *The melody of language* (pp. 279–298). Baltimore: University Park Press, 1980.

Stern, D. N., Spieker, S., & MacKain, K. Intonation contours as signals in maternal speech to prelinguistic infants. *Developmental Psychology*, 1982, *18*, 727–735.

Stern, D. N., Spieker, S., Barnett, R. K., & MacKain, K. The prosody of maternal speech: Infant age and context related changes. *Journal of Child Language*, 1983, *10*, 1–15.

Trehub, S. E. The perception of musical patterns by human infants: The provision of similar patterns by their parents. In W. C. Stebbins & M. Berkley (Eds.), *Comparative perception* (Vol. 1). New York: Wiley Interscience, 1990.

Tuaycharoen, P. The babbling of a Thai baby: Echoes and responses to the sounds made by adults. In N. Waterson & C. E. Snow (Eds.), *The development of communication* (pp. 111–125). Chichester, New York: Wiley, 1978.

Vygotsky, L. S. *Mind in society: The development of higher psychological processes*. Cambridge, MA: Cambridge University Press, 1978.

Wang, W. S. The many uses of F_0. In A. Valdman (Ed.), *Papers in linguistics and phonetics to the memory of Pierre Delattre* (pp. 487–496). The Hague: Mouton, 1972.

Werker, J. F., & McLeod, P. J. Infant preference for both male and female infant–directed talk: A developmental study of attentional and affective responsiveness. *Canadian Journal of Psychology*, 1989, *43*, 230–246.

Wood, D. Social interaction as tutoring. In M. H. Bornstein & J. S. Bruner (Eds.), *Interaction in human development* (pp. 59–80). Hillsdale, NJ: Lawrence Erlbaum Associates, 1989.

Wu, D. Y. H. Child training in Chinese culture. In W.–S. Tseng & D. Y. H. Wu (Eds.), *Chinese culture and mental health* (pp. 113–134). Orlando: Academic Press, 1985.

Child–Rearing Practices and Parental Beliefs in Three Cultural Groups of Montréal: Québécois, Vietnamese, Haitian

3

Andrée Pomerleau, Gérard Malcuit, and Colette Sabatier

Université du Québec à Montréal, Laboratoire d'Etude du Nourrisson, Canada

INTRODUCTION

This research reports a multi–dimensional study of mother–infant interaction and child–rearing practices in three cultural groups living in Montréal, a multi–ethnic mostly French–speaking metropolis. Its goals are two–fold: first, to examine parental practices, belief systems, and frames of reference in different cultures and, second, to understand the norms and child–rearing practices of minority groups in order to elaborate social and health programs which would be more adapted to these populations. Three clusters of variables are examined: (1) the *physical and social environment* provided for the child as defined by the toys and the space made available (room, play area), infant accessories and furniture, as well as the social density of the household; (2) the *mothers' perceptions and beliefs concerning infant development* expressed in response to a questionnaire; and (3) *mother–infant interaction* patterns observed in a semi–structured context when the baby was 3½, 6, and 9 months of age.

INFANT SOCIALIZATION IN THE FAMILY CONTEXT

Traditionally, studies in developmental psychology have described the processes of infant socialization in accordance with the norms and stages appropriate to middle–class industrialized societies. Early intervention programs were planned and infants' needs were assessed according to these norms. Nowadays, parental behavior, as any behavior, tends to be considered in its socio–cultural context (LeVine, 1988). It is understood that a competent mother will be competent only within her own culture. The study of educational and socialization practices among immigrant families demands that both cultural variations and the adaptation process inherent in the immigration context be given serious consideration.

Cultural Variation

The different child–rearing practices noted across various cultures are multi-faceted: caretaking, stimulation patterns, hygiene, choice of toys and other stimulating objects, and so forth. In addition, adult perceptions of the neonate and of the developmental process vary across cultures. Three main categories of variables can be identified.

Parental belief systems and perception of the child. Each cultural group has its own concepts and perceptions of the newborn infant, as well as of the mechanisms underlying infant socialization. For instance, Munro (1975) stressed the influence of Confucianism on the Chinese educational system (human perfectibility, an innate need to choose the good path, and the role of models in social learning). This influence seems to have an impact on the parental practices of the Vietnamese (Phan Thi Dac, 1966). Adults' beliefs about children's capacities and needs, which are more or less explicitly verbalized, have an impact on the way they interact with infants (Sigel, 1985). Data on Japanese and American mothers support this point of view (Bornstein, 1989; Caudill & Schooler, 1973; Shand, 1985). The Japanese are described as being convinced of the independent character of their newborn child. They interact with the goal of shaping a social human being who is attached to his or her family and centered on the needs of others. In contrast, American mothers appear to be equally convinced of the extreme dependence of their infants. Consequently, they behave in a manner which would reinforce their infants' independent behaviors.

Zeskind (1983) and Smith and Freedman (1983) observed that, irrespective of the child's characteristics, mothers of diverse cultures refer to implicit cultural norms when they are questioned about the needs and temperament of their child. Such norms have an impact on their dyadic interactions. In the same vein, Bril, Zack, and Nkounkou–Hombessa (1989), Keller, Miranda, and Gauda (1984) and Ninio (1979) noted the existence of specific cultural norms which underlie mothers' conceptions of child development (the age of onset of infant walking, talking, and so forth), and the role of the environment on the acquisition of social behaviors and psychomotor abilities. This more or less explicit system of convictions, images, and rules concerning the education and socialization of the child relates to the concept of naïve theories or parental belief systems (Holden & Edwards, 1989; Sigel, 1985).

Educational practices. Different cultural groups also vary in the ways they stimulate their infants and in their caretaking habits. Many factors seem to underlie these differences across cultures. Konner (1981) stressed the importance of the level of the society. Among hunter–gatherers, the infant is continuously carried by an adult or by an older child during the day. At night, the infant sleeps with the mother. Children are weaned when they are approximately 4 years of age. In

North–America, on the other hand, infants are more frequently placed in a seat or playpen rather than carried, and they sleep in their own bed. They will likely be weaned at 4 months. In general, parental child–rearing practices appear to be related to cultural conceptions (LeVine, Miller, & West, 1988).

The impact of socioeconomic status among various minority groups has also been considered (Field & Widmayer, 1981; Johnson, Breckenridge, & McGowan, 1984). Family income, number of children in the family, and number of individuals in the household appeared to be related to the quality of the environment as measured by the HOME (Caldwell & Bradley, 1979). However, the correlations found between socioeconomic levels and parental practices or dyadic interactions were not as strong as the correlations with culture (Johnson et al., 1984).

Mother–infant interaction. Cross–cultural studies of mother–infant interaction have revealed both universal and culture–specific patterns of behavior. The universals are most likely linked to the perceptual abilities of the infants. Cross–cultural diversity in the elements of interactive patterns is observed in the rate, intensity, and rhythm of specific behaviors. In general, white American mothers, as compared with the minority groups or mothers in the Third–World countries, appear frequently to overstimulate and to express less sensitivity to their baby's reactions and activity cycles (Callaghan, 1981; Chisholm, 1989; Dixon, Tronick, Keffer, & Brazelton, 1981; Fajardo & Freedman, 1981; Muret–Wagstaff & More, 1989). Studies comparing Japanese and American mothers highlight the impact of cultural values on their interactive behaviors (Bornstein, 1989; Caudill & Weinstein, 1969; Fogel, Toda, & Kawai, 1988). Moreover, within cultural groups, economic and environmental conditions also play a role. They may reinforce or diminish the effects of the cultural values.

Immigration and Early Development

The cross–cultural differences in belief systems, educational practices, and mother–infant interaction patterns are compounded by the immigration experience. When people set up residence in a new country, they are faced with the task of adapting their customs to new codes of social conduct. Their parenting behaviors must change in order to integrate with their new living conditions. The shaping of new cultural practices is not the simple mixing of the old and new; similarly, the result is not a mid–way equilibrium between the two cultures. Even though values concerning the family seem more resistant to change, the confrontation with occidental values, for example, especially in the area of women's rights, may affect the stability of the family. Because immigrant women find access to the work place, they extend their social network and are exposed to models in which autonomy and independence are prized characteristics. Pressures from state institutions and laws make it necessary to modify relationships within the family. Mothers might have to change their styles of educating and socializing their infants. Their concepts and practices related to child–rearing as well as their modes of interaction will be affected.

These changes are not always achieved harmoniously. In societies where there is strong pressure to assimilate, and when there is little or no social cohesion in the immigrant group, the rupture with traditions may be so sudden that a loss of identity and of any reference point may result (Bastide, 1969). Parents, understandably, feel overwhelmed in this situation.

POPULATIONS OBSERVED IN THIS STUDY

Haitians and Vietnamese were chosen as target groups because they are both important new visible minority groups in Montréal. There are approximately 40,000 Haitians and 25,000 Vietnamese in Montréal, and their number is growing. A Québécois sample from the dominant, French–speaking, Caucasian community of Montréal was also selected. This last group, while culturally distinct from the main Anglosaxon North–American population, is nevertheless an affluent Western society and, as such, shares many common practices and beliefs with its North–American neighbors.

The Haitian and Vietnamese groups have in common poor economic conditions, the high rate of illiteracy and of infant mortality of their countries of origin, and a somewhat similar history of immigration to Québec. These two groups differ in other aspects: racial origin, language, cultural values, for example. A comparison of child–rearing conceptions and practices in these two groups of different racial and cultural backgrounds, and in a group of mothers from the culture of the majority may indicate different processes of adaptation to an environmental context during a given historical moment.

Cultural Backgrounds

Québécois. Québec is the largest province of Canada in area and the second largest in terms of population and economic strength. As such, Québec society ranks among the world's wealthy and highly–developed nations. Its population is over 6.5 million (1986 census), the majority of which are French–speaking (80%) and of Catholic background. It is essentially an urban society (78%) with almost half of the population living in the greater Montréal area. Along with most Western societies, Québec is faced with a drastic decrease in birth rate which is, at this point, one of the lowest in the world. Consequently, immigration is very important for the demography and economy of the province.

Québec society, despite its cultural and linguistic distinctiveness, shares the social values inherent in other North–American societies of European origin. Much emphasis is placed on the individual and his or her autonomy. The education of the child, both at home and at school, places more stress on creativity and personal expression than on the acquisition of formal content and social responsibility. In spite of the high value placed on the individual, Québec has developed egalitarian educational, social, and medical organisms. Accordingly, health and social services are public, universal, and free of charge, based on freedom of choice. They were developed with the concept of interdependence of clinical, social, community, and prevention services. These interrelations make it possible to effect changes rather quickly in life styles related to health; they permit easy universal access to socio–health services, and thus can reach out to minority and immigrant populations.

Haitians. Officially, Haitians are Francophone and Catholic, however the majority speaks Creole and practices voodoo. The family structure is patriarchal and matrifocal. The household consists of an extended family made up of many adults and children. During infancy, children are considered vulnerable (Durand, 1980). Many beliefs and practices can be related to this perceived infant vulnerability. They are never left alone, they sleep in their parents' room at night, and are always carried by an adult or an older child. Their cries are responded to quickly. Infants are groomed, positively encouraged in their developing skills, enjoyed, and played with. At the same time, adults believe that they must mold the children to display desirable characteristics in order to integrate them into the social group. At a later age, education becomes more severe. It bears mostly on discipline, good manners, and belief in God.

Vietnamese. Hierarchy and social cohesion characterize the traditional Vietnamese society. Social values take precedence over individual needs. Three cohabitating religions (Confucianism, Buddhism, and Taoism) permeate the life structures and reinforce family cohesion. The family organization is patriarchal. Infancy is considered to be a period requiring attention and care. Since the character and future of the infant are thought to be predetermined, parental education is not conceived of as having a powerful impact. Infants sleep in their mother's bed, and adults respond quickly to their cries. Parents believe in progressive learning through imitation and social conformity. The principal objective of child–rearing seems to be the immediate well–being of the child and his or her social participation. Continuously carried by an adult or an older child, the infant experiences frequent social contacts, and dyadic interactions have a reserved and gentle quality. The objectives of education for the older children are to teach hygiene, emotional reserve and discretion, respect for the hierarchy, piety, good manners, sharing, and solidarity.

THE CONTEXT OF LIVING IN IMMIGRANT GROUPS

Most cross–cultural research which deals with the aspects of the developmental context discussed here has considered only single factors. Leiderman, Tulkin, and Rosenfeld (1977) discussed the methodological and ethical problems encountered in cross–cultural research with infants. They suggest a multivariate approach in order to obtain a better understanding of the complexity of infant development and of the interplay of all the relevant factors. For example, by looking at only one dimension at a time, one loses sight of the relations between the educational practices observed and the maternal belief systems which are assumed to underlie these behaviors. Too often, relations are postulated a posteriori. The cultural values adopted by the mothers who participate in a given study, and the norms according to which they judge the needs and characteristics of their children are not examined. We are not aware of their concept of infant learning abilities, the norms that guide their actions, or their methods of stimulating their babies. Therefore, it is invaluable first to explore these parental attitudes and then to determine the eventual links between explicit and implicit norms of development, education, and dyadic interaction. The present research was conceived within this perspective. Our comparison of two immigrant groups and one group of Québécois cannot address the question of behavioral changes before and after immigration, but it permits an examination of cross–cultural differences in three clusters of variables, early physical and social environment, mother's beliefs, and dyadic interaction, during the infants' first year of life.

Within this context, a total of 109 primiparous mothers and their full–term healthy infants (38 Haitians, 45 Québécois, 26 Vietnamese) participated in the study. They were recruited mainly through the birth registry of the Government of Québec and contacted via telephone. Fifty percent of the Haitian, 35% of the Québécois and 57% of the Vietnamese mothers who were contacted agreed to participate in the study. Data were collected when the infants were 3½, 6, and 9–month–old. Two home visits were made at each age. The study was a combined longitudinal and cross–sectional design. Some dyads were seen at all three ages, some at two, and others at only one age.

Both parents were of the same ethnic origin and born in their home country. Haitian and Vietnamese mothers were first generation immigrants; the majority immigrated as adults. Their mean time of residence in Québec is 5.6 years. The main demographic characteristics of the sample appear in Table 3.1. The Vietnamese mothers are slightly older than the mothers of the other two groups and more educated than the Haitians. In spite of efforts to match the socioeconomic levels of the three groups, the family income data reveal that there are more lower income families in the immigrant groups. The housing conditions reflect the differential income levels. The annual income of 65% of the Québécois group is in the $20–40,000 category, and the majority of these families are tenants in duplexes or triplexes with 4 or 5 rooms. The Haitian group has the lowest income: 76% of families earn less than $20,000 annually. Most are tenants in small apartments. The average family income of the Vietnamese is comparable to that of the Québécois, but a larger proportion of families earn above $40,000 and below $20,000 and, understandably, their housing conditions vary as well.

Female assistants of the same ethnic origin as the mothers participated in the collection of the data. All questionnaires were translated, via back translation, into Creole and Vietnamese. Inter–observer agreement was evaluated on 20% of the data in each cluster of variables.

Maternal conceptions were recorded once at the first visit during a semi–structured interview which lasted approximately one–half hour. The questionnaire contains 66 items (some open, others closed) and was based on the work of Ninio (1979). It assesses the mothers' conceptions of infant competence (the development process and intent accorded to infants' signals), their expectations of infant be-

TABLE 3.1
Socio-Demographic Characteristics and Type of Housing of the Sample

	Haitian		Québécois		Vietnamese		
Mothers							
	M	Range	M	Range	M	Range	F
Age	26.4	20-33	25.9	21-33	29.5	21-38	9.41***
Education (years)	11.1	6-15	11.6	9-13	12.3	9-20	3.51*
Years in Canada	6.3	1-15			5.0	1-11	1.77
Age at arrival	20.1	7-30			24.7	14-35	9.38**
Family income (%)							X^2
> $40,000	3		13		19		
$20-$40,000	21		65		31		***
< $20,000	76		22		50		
Housing conditions							
Type of housing (%)							
Individual house	6		5		20		
Duplex/triplex	36		60		12		**
Apartment bldg	58		35		68		
Owner/tenant (%)							
Owner	3		20		36		
Tenant	97		80		64		**
Size of the house (%)							
Large (> 5 rooms)	6		5		16		
Medium (4-5 rooms)	42		93		48		**
Small (2-3 rooms)	52		2		36		
	M	SD	M	SD	M	SD	F
Density (no pers/no room)	.70	.24	.44	.07	.62	.25	16.74***

*$p < .05$ ** $p < .01$ *** $p < .001$

haviors, their beliefs concerning the role parents play in the child–rearing process, and their daily socialization practices.

The *organization of the infants' environment* was assessed at the 3½– and 9–month visits via questions directed to the mother as well as by direct observation. The number of toys, their type, and potential for stimulation were noted on a checklist. Accessories available to the child (playpen, walker, bed) were noted as well. Information was also obtained concerning the space made available for the infant and the organization of his/her social life (presence of adults, other children, outings).

The *interactive styles* of the dyad were recorded on video at each age, within a structured context (a teaching task similar to the task used by Dixon, LeVine, Richman, & Brazelton, 1984). The mother was asked to teach her infant four tasks which were difficult for his or her age level. At 3½ months, the mother attempted to elicit toy holding, visual following of a moving puppet, visual attention to his/her mirror image, and vocal imitation. At the 6–month visit, she was asked to teach her infant to play peek–a–boo, to pull a string in order to obtain a ring, to obtain a cube behind a plexiglass barrier, and to bang a toy on table. At 9 months, she was asked to teach her child how to open a box, to turn a tray in order to obtain a cube, to stir a spoon in a cup, and to play ball. Each task lasted 1 minute. Eight maternal behaviors were coded from the video tapes: demonstration, facilitation, guidance, active prohibition, static restraint, observation, stimulation, and vocalization. In addition, ten infant behaviors were coded: observation, trial, success, prehension attempt, off–task exploration, mouthing, retaining object, deviation from the task, opposition, and negative vocalization. The frequency and duration of each infant and maternal behavior were analyzed.

INDIGENOUS AND IMMIGRANT EXPERIENCES AND CHILD–REARING PRACTICES

Social and Physical Environment

Immigrant infants live in somewhat different social environments than the Québécois. The social density of the household (number of people/number of rooms) is higher among the immigrant families of both groups (see Table 3.1). In the Québécois sample, the household usually consists of the two parents and the child. In the immigrant groups, a quarter of the families includes from one to five members of the extended family in addition to the nuclear family. Twenty–six percent of the Haitian babies and 8% of the Vietnamese (none of the Québécois) live with other children in their homes (cousins, half–siblings). However, according to the mothers' reports, the number of adults who take care of the infant does not differ among the three groups.

Babies of immigrant families live in close proximity to their parents: 87% of Haitian babies and 64% of Vietnamese sleep in their parents' room, compared with only 7% of the Québécois infants. By comparison with the Québécois, very few immigrant infants have the opportunity to visit other homes even at 9 months of age: 27% of the Haitians and 60% of the Vietnamese, as compared with 77% of the Québécois infants, are taken on visits more than twice a week.

These differences in the physical environments of the immigrant and Québécois babies are reflected in Tables 3.2 and 3.3. On the whole, with the exception of walkers and infant seats, Québécois infants have accessories more than the other two groups. They have many more toys than the babies of the immigrant groups, and this discrepancy increases with age. In the same vein, we found that infants who have the largest number of toys also have access to more miscellaneous objects to play with. In order to control for differences in income across our three groups, and to isolate a cultural effect from a financial one, an analysis of covariance with income as the covariate was carried out. As shown in Table 3.3, the differences between groups in quantity of toys remain. Thus we seem to be dealing with a cultural rather than an economic phenomenon.

TABLE 3.2
Percentage of Households with Infant Furniture and Accessories at
3 and 9 Months of Age

| | Haitian | | Québécois | | Vietnamese | | X^2 | |
	3	9	3	9	3	9	3	9
Infant carrier	13	9	50	61	0	15	**	***
Infant seat	93	100	96	100	80	75		
High chair	20	27	67	86	40	40	*	***
Playpen	13	45	67	71	60	45	*	
Swing	13	27	62	62	0	25	*	*
"Jolly-Jumper"	0	0	8	24	10	10		*
Walker	20	91	29	67	60	90		
Other	7	9	42	43	20	20	*	*

*p < .05   ** p < .01   *** p < .001

TABLE 3.3
Mean Number of Toys in the Three Groups at 3 and 9 Months
for the Total Sample and for the Higher Income Families

| | Haitian | | Québécois | | Vietnamese | |
	M	Range	M	Range	M	Range
Total						
3 mo	8.5	0-47	26.9	12-73	6.7	2-10
9 mo	10.8	2-33	58.3	25-119	15.8	4-54
Income > $20,000						
3 mo	5.0(n=1)		25.7(n=19)	12-38	6.0(n=6)	2-10
9 mo	11.6(n=7)	2-25	62.0(n=13)	25-119	19.7(n=10)	8-54

ANOVA: Groups: $F = 73.17$ − Age: $F = 27.91$ − Age × Group: $F = 12.94$
ANCOVA: Groups: $F = 63.66$ − Age: $F = 28.25$ − Age × Group: $F = 13.27$

Maternal Beliefs

Learning models and sources of information. The sources of information of which mothers avail themselves in order to learn about the maternal role do not differ greatly across these three cultural groups. Most mothers direct questions to their physicians, to members of their family, or read books or articles. However, when asked how they have learned to bring up their child, more Québécois mothers credit their instinct, natural abilities, trial and error, judgment or experience, whereas the majority of Vietnamese mothers report relying on formal social learning, including books (see Table 3.4). The most reliable source of information, according to the mothers of all three groups, seems to come more from the medical world, rather than from family.

Conceptions about infant abilities. We asked mothers to report the age at which they consider that infants acquire various abilities in the perceptual, cognitive, social, and motor domains. They were required to locate these developmental milestones as precisely as possible. Of the 19 questions related to the age of acquisition of these abilities, 16 show significant differences among the groups (see Table 3.5). No significant differences were found for crawling, identifying objects from pictures, and giving up of the pacifier. All differences, with the exception of three (onset of language, ability to sit and to walk) are in the same direction: The Québécois mothers expect infant perceptual and cognitive abilities to develop at the earliest age. On the other hand, the Haitian mothers expect earlier development of motor abilities (with the exception of crawling). They also expect earlier development of language. The Vietnamese placed most of these milestones at the latest age.

We asked the mothers two questions related to their interpretation of two common infant behaviors: "Why does a baby mouth objects?" and "Why does a baby cry?" The mothers of the three groups gave a variety of answers. Most of them indicated physical needs as the main reason for crying. In addition, the Québécois mothers stressed affective needs (Q: 64% versus H: 24% and V: 27%) and the Vietnamese, a need to communicate (V: 42% versus H: 13% and Q: 27%). In contrast with the others, the Québécois mothers mentioned mouthing of objects as a means of exploration (Q: 56% versus H: 10% and V: 11%). A third of the Vietnamese mothers consider hunger and the need to suck as motivating factors for infant mouthing, but these factors were rarely recognized by the Haitians and Québécois.

In order to gain information concerning possible cultural variations in maternal expectations of an ideal infant, we asked mothers of our three groups to describe "a good baby". Mothers differ somewhat in their concept of "a good baby" (see

TABLE 3.4
Percentage of Maternal Responses to Questions Concerning Sources of Learning and Information

	Haitian	Québécois	Vietnamese	X^2
Which is the most trustworthy source of information for parents?				
Medical world	70	42	48	
Family	15	11	24	
Books	8	27	16	
How did you learn to bring up your child?				
The family	50	40	46	
Informal learning	68	87	61	
• peers	26	40	42	
• trial and error	10	40	8	*
• judgment/experience	26	51	8	*
Formal social learning	53	58	85	*
• books	32	40	73	*
• lectures	21	24	23	
• physicians	16	7	11	
• media	3	0	4	
Instinct	8	31	0	*

*$p < .05$

TABLE 3.5
Mean Age (in days) of Acquisition of Infant Abilities According to the Mothers of the Three Groups:
Analysis of Variance and Scheffé Tests

	Haitian		Québécois		Vietnamese		F	Scheffé Comparisons H Q V vs Q V H
	M	(SD)	M	(SD)	M	(SD)		
Hear	27.6	(32.8)	4.9	(12.2)	52.8	(39.2)	23.66***	· ·
See	30.4	(33.2)	18.9	(22.2)	48.2	(33.2)	8.36***	· ·
Recognize mother	62.4	(53.2)	37.6	(43.0)	78.3	(65.5)	5.29**	·
Recognize father	73.9	(56.7)	44.9	(41.5)	98.3	(63.1)	8.74***	· ·
Recognize others	135.3	(75.9)	97.7	(51.2)	153.2	(81.1)	6.25**	·
Think	405.1	(527.4)	91.8	(118.3)	609.0	(918.5)	7.91***	· ·
Understand words	292.4	(138.1)	215.6	(95.5)	267.3	(116.9)	4.57*	·
Identify objects	387.4	(173.1)	368.0	(173.0)	385.2	(144.5)	0.16	
Babble	92.3	(75.9)	69.9	(44.8)	140.4	(87.4)	11.05***	· ·
Talk	276.5	(70.0)	320.6	(164.6)	376.1	(111.3)	4.84**	·
Interact with peers	578.3	(452.7)	291.8	(199.2)	457.7	(320.0)	7.64***	· ·
Sit	137.4	(36.8)	174.1	(40.2)	193.6	(52.8)	14.88***	· ·
Crawl	180.3	(46.7)	180.8	(37.6)	197.1	(42.6)	1.52	
Walk	279.3	(52.2)	311.7	(41.8)	335.7	(41.5)	12.40***	· ·
Drink: training cup	237.6	(95.4)	242.5	(66.8)	308.8	(125.8)	5.34**	·
Drink: cup	387.2	(215.6)	322.3	(115.0)	444.0	(213.1)	3.92*	·
Give up bottle	569.0	(240.8)	410.9	(159.1)	613.8	(251.9)	9.17***	· ·
Give up pacifier	406.2	(337.3)	475.5	(308.5)	528.1	(498.1)	0.87	
Sleep in his/her own room	463.9	(436.1)	44.7	(112.3)	540.3	(805.6)	12.12***	·

*p < .05   **p < .01   ***p < .001

Table 3.6). Although most mothers consider the infant's basic physiology (regularity of feeding and sleep, good health, infrequent unmotivated crying) as important, the Haitians and Vietnamese stress the importance of facility of feeding. The Québécois mothers also mention social behaviors, such as smiling and playful activity, as defining criteria of a good baby.

All mothers had difficulty answering the question about what abilities they consider important for their infants to develop for the future. Nevertheless, as shown in Table 3.6, there were differences among the groups. The immigrant mothers, particularly the Haitians, value the acquisition of social norms: kindness, good manners, social awareness, respect for parents and the rules of life, sharing, and so forth. More immigrant than Québécois mothers, particularly the Vietnamese mothers, stress the importance of providing their children with a good formal education. The Québécois mothers more frequently mentioned the importance of psycho–affective development.

The mothers' answers to the general questions concerning their conceptions of the role and impact of parents on their infants' development indicate a similarity among the three groups. The more specific questions, on the other hand, reveal

TABLE 3.6
Percentage of Maternal Responses to Questions on Parental Expectations and Beliefs Related to: The Definition of a Good Baby, Ability to Foster, and the Role of Parents

	Haitian	Québécois	Vietnamese	X^2
What is a good baby?				
Basic physiology	84	96	92	
• Regularity of sleep	55	60	50	
• Regularity of feeding	3	11	11	
• Facility of feeding	45	11	35	**
• Good health	26	31	42	
• Infrequent unmotivated crying	58	67	61	
Social behavior	16	67	15	***
What developmental aspect is important to foster?				
Physical/motor	21	33	35	
Cognitive	50	42	50	
• Education	21	7	38	**
Psycho-affective	37	60	27	*
Moral and social	76	29	54	***
• Social awareness	42	4	19	***
What can parents do to foster the development of the child?				
Physical/motor	55	42	69	
• Basic care	45	24	58	*
Cognitive	47	44	42	
• Stimulation	34	38	19	
Psycho-affective	84	91	35	***
• Giving attention to the child	58	76	31	***
Moral and social	13	9	15	
• Social awareness	5	2	0	

$*p < .05$ $** p < .01$ $*** p < .001$

some cultural differences in maternal beliefs. When responses concerning the parental role are coded under four categories (physical/motor, cognitive, psycho–affective, moral/social), mothers of the three group differ, particularly in the psycho–affective category. While only a third of the Vietnamese mothers consider that parents can have an effect at this level, most of the Haitians and Québécois consider that they play an important role in this area. In general, the mothers do not differ in their view of the impact of the parental role in the physical/motor area. However, a large proportion of the immigrant mothers stress the importance of basic care (versus one Québécois out of four). In contrast with the stress placed by Haitian and Vietnamese mothers on the acquisition of social and moral abilities, few specify that they can do something at this level.

The responses to questions concerning the age at which mothers should initiate specific activities revealed group differences for 12 out of 15 identified activities (see Table 3.7). It comes as no surprise that the Québécois mothers, who expect the appearance of infant's cognitive abilities at an earlier age, report an earlier age of initiation of activities than the immigrant mothers. To our surprise, Québécois mothers, who do not consider moral development as a priority, report introducing punishment earlier than the Haitians. The two immigrant groups differ from each other on two issues: learning to clean up and the purchase of the first book. Vietnamese mothers, like the Québécois, consider initiating these activities earlier than Haitians.

Questions relating to infant stimulation may be classified into three groups: beliefs about the likelihood of accelerating three aspects of development (sitting, walking, and language), the type of learning of which infants are capable, and the need for exercise. Maternal responses related to the likelihood of accelerating sitting, walking, and language development do not yield clear–cut differences. Forty to sixty percent of the mothers in the three groups think that they can do something to influence the development of sitting and walking. The Québécois mothers appear to be more ambivalent on this subject; they more frequently express nuances in their responses. On the other hand, their point of view on the acquisition of language is more affirmative. While a majority of the mothers of all three groups think that it is possible to do something to accelerate language acquisition, almost all the Québécois mothers report that they can, indeed, have an effect.

All mothers think that it is possible to teach something to 9–month–old infants, but the groups differ as to what they consider possible to teach. Psychomotor abilities are more often stressed by the Québécois mothers than by the others. Surprisingly, whereas the Québécois mothers consider the verbal, cognitive, and affective aspects of development to be important, they do not stress the fact that they can teach verbal skills to 9–month–olds as much as the immigrant mothers.

The three groups of mothers do not differ in their attitudes toward infant exercise. They all consider this to be an important activity. However, the three groups do not appear to favor the same type of exercise. Most of the Québécois mothers stress psychomotor rather than learning exercises.

Mothers of all three groups think that play is important for the child. They report playing with their infant in various contexts (bathing, dressing, face to face

TABLE 3.7
Mean Age (in days) of Introduction of Specific Activities According to the Mothers of the Three Groups:
Analysis of Variance and Scheffé Tests

	Haitian		Québécois		Vietnamese		F	Scheffé Comparisons H Q V vs Q V H	
	M	(SD)	M	(SD)	M	(SD)		H Q V	Q V H
Talk to the child	38.0	(52.6)	4.2	(16.1)	71.6	(89.2)	13.04***	·	·
Tell stories	836.6	(1462.7)	332.3	(332.1)	742.0	(397.6)	3.54*	·	·
Talk about absent objects	577.6	(459.7)	347.2	(320.9)	421.5	(320.2)	3.85*	·	
Talk about absent persons	593.3	(451.6)	296.2	(297.3)	395.8	(295.3)	7.10**	·	
Look at television	290.1	(255.8)	405.5	(338.9)	385.0	(452.9)	1.22		
First book	781.6	(538.6)	363.9	(357.2)	476.3	(249.8)	11.00***	·	·
Wean	202.0	(136.8)	148.8	(98.3)	200.0	(100.2)	2.78		·
Take bottle unaided	217.2	(75.3)	154.3	(53.0)	217.0	(99.9)	9.24***	·	·
Eat by himself/herself	454.6	(210.5)	317.5	(105.7)	461.4	(193.4)	8.89***	·	·
Toilet train	487.1	(177.8)	511.2	(186.1)	507.8	(220.9)	0.18		
Sleep in a regular bed	912.4	(493.7)	716.6	(191.8)	906.6	(620.0)	2.74		
Dress by himself/herself	1010.6	(400.7)	776.5	(288.8)	843.5	(352.5)	4.84**	·	
Clean up	1158.4	(587.6)	736.9	(435.9)	773.5	(393.1)	8.68***	·	
Refrain from touching	543.2	(444.5)	368.1	(177.5)	557.6	(263.4)	4.26*	·	
Punish	859.0	(619.1)	489.7	(305.7)	657.5	(350.7)	6.94**	·	

*p < .05   **p < .01   ***p < .001

interactions). But here, too, there are some group differences. The Québécois and Vietnamese mothers, to a much larger extent than the Haitians, consider it important for the baby to play alone (H: 13%, Q: 76%, V: 61%), but the Haitians and Québécois consider it still more important that infants play with their parents (H: 95% and Q: 89% versus V: 46%). The Haitians, more than the others, consider that the baby should be played with at his/her request (H: 71%, Q: 53%, V: 31%).

Vietnamese mothers report more rigid attitudes concerning the regularity of feeding and sleeping (feeding H: 45%, Q: 42%, V: 69%; sleeping H: 45%, Q: 36%, V: 61%). A fair number (42%) also consider it important that the child eat all the food offered to her or him (versus H: 3% and Q: 2%). On the other hand, more Québécois mothers (51%) than Haitians (22%) and Vietnamese (31%) think that an infant should eat everything the parents eat. Most of the mothers do not let their baby cry at night.

Québécois mothers initiate punishment earlier than the other two groups (Table 3.7). However, when asked how one should punish an infant, there were no significant differences among the three groups in the number of mothers who consider using physical punishment. On the other hand, more Québécois report using verbal punishment as well (Q: 67% versus V: 42% and H: 37%). Their motivation for punishment is to help the child to understand (Q: 76% versus V: 50% and H: 39%), whereas more of the immigrants punish in order to correct the child (H: 50% and V: 65% versus Q: 27%). Following a punishment, most immigrant mothers explain or talk with their child (H: 82% and V: 72% versus Q: 51%); more Québécois mothers than immigrants prefer to wait until things settle down (Q: 42% versus H: 10% and V: 15%).

Dyadic Interactions: Learning Tasks

We employed two strategies of analysis in approaching the interaction data. First, MANOVAs were performed on all categories of mother and infant behaviors at each age for each task. This enabled us to determine whether the babies and mothers of the three groups behave differently in a given task. Second, repeated–measures ANOVAs were conducted on each category of behavior across the four tasks of each age. This allowed us to see whether the babies and mothers in the three groups differ in their use of specific behavioral categories across all tasks.

As indicated by the MANOVAs, mothers show different cultural patterns of behavior with their 3–month–old infants in two of the learning tasks. In both cases, the differences were mainly explained by the Vietnamese who resorted more to static restraint and to stimulation, and, in one case, by the Haitians who spent more time facilitating. In the same vein, during the 3–month sessions the groups of babies differed on two of the tasks. First, the Vietnamese produced more deviations from the task and more negative vocalizations and, second, they looked at their stimulating mothers more often than the other infants did.

During the 6–month sessions, the mothers showed cultural differences in all four tasks. In three of these tasks, the Vietnamese used the least active prohibition, and the Haitians used more stimulation and observation behaviors. The Haitians were also the mothers who vocalized the least. The Québécois vocalized the most and used more demonstrations. Six–month–old babies of the three groups displayed different categories of behaviors across the tasks. Québécois babies made more observations; reciprocally, their mothers made more demonstrations. Haitian babies produced the least deviations and off–task exploration across the tasks.

It is with their 9–month–old infants that the groups of mothers differed the most. They exhibited different patterns of behaviors in all four tasks *and* across tasks. The Vietnamese performed the fewest demonstrations and resorted more to guidance and static restraint. The Haitians used the least guidance and static restraint, and, along with the Québécois, performed the most demonstrations. The Québécois displayed mostly facilitation, stimulation, and demonstration behaviors. Like their mothers, 9–month–old infants exhibited different patterns of behaviors in the four tasks *and* across tasks. The Québécois babies spent more time than the others mouthing objects; they also showed the least opposition behaviors. The Haitian infants made the most prehension attempts, especially in those tasks where their mothers were the most demonstrative and used the least static restraint. Haitian babies also emitted more and longer negative vocalizations than the others; Vietnamese babies produced more opposition and deviation behaviors than the Québécois and Haitians.

HOW IMMIGRATION AND CHILD–REARING MATCH: ENVIRONMENT, BELIEFS, AND INTERACTIONS

This multidimensional study was designed to examine the conditions of development of infants of two immigrant groups from Third–World countries and of infants of their host culture. The results illustrate some differences between the immigrant and the Québécois populations. At the same time, they provide us with a fresh look at the cultural ideology of the host. Differences among the three groups could be discussed globally, considering the various aspects of the study together. However, it seems appropriate to distinguish three areas: (1) the mothers' verbal reports of their values and belief system concerning infant development, (2) the actual social and physical environment they provide for their infants, and (3) their behaviors while teaching their infants difficult perceptuo–motor tasks. Since knowledge of the nature of cultural specificities within cultural groups is crucial for the effective planning of social and health programs directed towards these populations, it is important to identify the differences in these three areas. Questions must also be raised concerning the links postulated between maternal belief systems and the actual environment provided for infants, as assessed through the physical and social milieu which they set up for their children, as well as through dyadic interaction patterns.

Before discussing our results, we must make some precautionary remarks on our samples. Because we did not match the groups on all factors (for example, the socioeconomic level), and since we are unable to evaluate the eventual modifications of parental practices and beliefs consequent to immigration, the effects of adaptation to a Western country, the stress of immigration, and poverty are not easy to disentangle. One can argue that economic factors explain most differences across groups. Certainly, low income leads to high density housing conditions and, consequently, there is less space for the child. However, research with minority group parents indicates that the educational level of the mother and of the father is a more potent contributing variable to beliefs and teaching strategies than is the family income (Laosa, 1981; Ninio, 1988). In the present research no differences in maternal education are observed between the immigrant and Québécois groups. Most (83%) of the mothers have between nine and thirteen years of education. The only difference appeared between the two immigrant groups. Several Haitians and Vietnamese parents living in Montréal had not found jobs related to their level of education. This explains in part the disparity between the income and the educational levels of both parents. This situation does not exist in the Québécois group. Moreover, a careful examination of the present data gives some indication that, in our three groups, actual child–rearing practices and beliefs derive more from cultural than from economic factors. As an illustration, the mean and the range of the number of toys provided to infants were different between groups even when differences in income levels were taken into account.

Social and Physical Environment

On the whole, the social and physical context of the infants' life is different in the immigrant and Québécois groups. These differences can be primarily linked to the situational context of immigration where lower affluence and social isolation are common. They also reflect cultural norms and customs. Compared to their Québécois counterparts, immigrant infants live in small apartments, and, in addition, their households often include a relative other than the immediate family. Even when immigrant infants have their own room, they tend to sleep in their parents' room. As a result, the opportunities to interact with familiar adults are enhanced, and social stimulation in a familiar context is frequently encountered. On the other hand, immigrant infants, particularly Haitians, do not seem to go on outings and visits to other homes as frequently as do Québécois babies. Consequently, infants of immigrant families tend to have more familiar social stimulation and less exposure to novelty than Québécois infants. The Québécois are surrounded by a multitude of toys and accessories, and their mothers consider it important that they play by themselves. This abundance of play objects does not appear to be a reflection of the level of affluence, but rather of a cultural view of the benefits of stimulation and the provision of practical learning experiences. These properties of the physical and social environment likely have an effect on the future cognitive development of the infant. In fact, as shown in recent work (Bradley et al., 1989), some aspects of the home environment (availability of stimulating play materials, parental responsivity) are strongly related to measures of cognitive development at the toddler stage. In our research, developmental testing (motor and mental scales of the Bayley) was carried out when the infants were 9 months of age. Although we did not find inter–group differences, we cannot make any predictions as to the effects of these different environments on the future cognitive development of the infants.

Parental Beliefs and Values

This research also revealed different values and beliefs among the three cultural groups. The most coherent patterns of differences were found in the area of developmental time–tables. Mothers born in Québec expect the earliest emergence of most infant competencies, especially at the perceptuo–cognitive level. Accordingly, they report introducing activities in these areas earlier than the other two groups. Mothers from Vietnam tend to underestimate the age of appearance of infant abilities. In most instances, they report the latest age of emergence of these abilities. However, with the exception of four items (talk to the child, tell stories, let the baby take the bottle alone, and eat unaided), the age at which they would introduce activities did not differ greatly from the Québécois. On the other hand, Haitians, who situated two motor milestones and language at the earliest age, and other milestones at an age between Québécois and Vietnamese mothers, report introducing most activities at the latest age.

Affective needs and psycho–affective factors in development were stressed mainly by the Québécois mothers. For instance, they put emphasis on the affective needs underlying infant crying, and on the importance of developing the psycho–affective characteristics of their infants. They also agreed, almost unanimously, on the importance of their role in the development of these aspects. In this last instance, they were on a par with the Haitians.

On the whole, the thoughts and beliefs expressed by the Québécois mothers reflect the message of occidental developmental psychology: An infant is a competent and sociable human being who deserves to be stimulated and loved. On the other hand, the immigrant mothers underestimated many infant competencies, with the exception of basic motor abilities and language which are judged to be more precocious by the Haitians. The Vietnamese mothers, just as the Haitians, stressed the importance of fostering moral and social development, but unlike the Haitians, they did not consider that parents can play a significant role in the psycho–affective development of the child. The importance of the child's formal education was more frequently expressed by the Vietnamese mothers. This is in keeping with the values of their culture of origin, but it also reflects an ideal shared by most immigrants who want their children to become successful members of their host country. Education and formal learning are important for Vietnamese; affective needs are important for Haitians and Québécois. In the Québécois society, as in most modern occidental cultures, it is considered important to help enhance the development of already present perceptual and cognitive competencies. Thus, the mothers introduce certain activities early. In addition, they surround their babies with toys and various objects aimed at improving cognitive development. Haitian mothers respond quickly to their infants. They consider it important to play with them at their request. They appear to be more "laissez–faire" concerning the necessity of introducing stimulation and activities at an early age. These observations are consistent with the cultural views of infant development in each group. Moreover, some of the differences in parental goals and conceptions between Western industrialized societies and Third–World countries could be related to the perceived vulnerability of the infant. In countries where infant mortality rate is high and life is threatened, mothers are centered on their infants' physical well–being more than on their psychological competencies (LeVine, 1988).

The above conclusions must be considered within the context of this study. Our conclusions are derived mainly from mothers' verbal responses to questions. Mothers can be incited to answer questions, and these answers may simply be transient, "newly constructed beliefs" (see Miller, 1988) and may not necessarily reflect pre–existing belief systems. There are many domains in which mothers might not have assimilated a cultural model of beliefs. This characteristic can vary across our groups. Also, the nuances that are more frequently expressed by Québécois mothers (for instance, the possibility of influencing the development of sitting and walking), and the variety of responses they give, may reflect their implicit cultural norms and values. But their responses could also be explained by a selection problem. Québécois mothers were more reluctant to participate in the study: Those who did accept may be more familiar with the research interview context, have a particularly positive attitude, or have special motivation for sharing their ideas.

Mother–Infant Interaction

Mother–infant interaction was observed in a learning context where mothers were asked to teach four different tasks to their infants. This paradigm provides insight into the various strategies used by the mothers, as well as the behaviors displayed by their infants. Although this data does not tell us how often such interactions occur in the daily life of the family, it does give a clue as to their specific ingredients when they do occur.

Some tasks were more effective than others at bringing to light cross–cultural variations in the behaviors of the mothers and infants. However, the age of the infants appeared to be the main factor in the increasing complexity and variability of behaviors of the dyads. The greater the diversity of possible behaviors, the greater the possibility of uncovering cross–cultural variations. However, from age to age, and even across tasks at a given age, it is difficult to trace a coherent line of culture–specific behaviors.

Four behavioral categories which distinguished cultural groups (demonstration, static restraint, stimulation, facilitation) appeared at two ages, but only two showed relative "cultural stability". First, demonstration behaviors were predominantly utilized by Québécois mothers with their 6–month–old infants and by Québécois and Haitian mothers with their 9–month–olds. The Vietnamese tended to use this type of teaching strategy the least. Second, static restraint was used predominantly by the Vietnamese at 3 and 9 months of age. In addition to these two categories, stimulation behaviors were evidenced at 3 and 6 months, and facilitation at 3 and

9 months, but the cultural differences varied from one age to the other and across tasks.

As for the infants, one behavioral category, deviation from task, appeared as a discriminator of cultural groups at all three ages. At two of these ages, the Vietnamese babies were the most "deviant" infants in two tasks. This predominant infant behavior coincided with the use of more static restraint on the part of their mothers.

Although our main goal was to identify cultural variations in behaviors, we are compelled to adopt the interpretation that maternal teaching strategies with young infants do not vary as drastically as certain researchers have reported. It can be argued, though, that our procedures and methods were not ecologically valid, or were not sufficiently sophisticated to allow for fine discrimination of behavioral repertoires. This is a complex issue which deserves further study. We must note, however, that we chose teaching tasks in order to observe mothers' behavioral strategies. This is different from most research in this area, where observations of spontaneous mother–infant interaction or of mothers' attempts to attract the attention of their infants, are the common procedures. This difference in choice of activity might explain our divergent results. Nevertheless, it is evident that the specific observational context, as well the age of the infant, will influence the repertoire of behaviors displayed by the mothers and consequently the opportunity to observe similarities and/or differences among groups. On the other hand, differential cultural reactivity to the observation context itself cannot be ruled out.

RELATIONS AMONG BELIEFS, INTERACTIONS, AND TEACHING

The examination of parental belief systems, infant daily stimulation, and maternal teaching strategies raises important questions concerning the relations among these clusters of variables. Much of the recent interest in parental beliefs has stemmed from the conviction that parents' conceptions about children mediate how they treat their own child. Parental beliefs and attitudes are regarded as filters through which their behavior is colored; they are interpreted as playing an important role in the mutual regulation between parent and infant. Some investigators consider that clarifying the attitude concept and the interplay of parental attitudes and behaviors will enhance our understanding of the parent–child relationship and its effects on child development. This knowledge, they suggest, can serve as a guideline for the creation of adequate social and health programs. However, one surprising feature of the literature on parental beliefs is the paucity of empirical work done to evaluate relations between beliefs and behavior. In fact, determining the extent and the nature of these relations has proven to be difficult.

The main goal of the present study was to establish an overview of the developmental niches of immigrant and Québécois babies. Up to now, there has been little information available on these populations. This research was not specifically designed to explore the nature of the relations between maternal beliefs and other aspects of the child's environment. The questionnaires and observations were constructed to identify similarities and differences among groups in each cluster of variables. Nevertheless, one can trace links between expressed maternal belief systems (what mothers know and expect of infants and their development) and the actual environment which they provide for their infants.

Some relations are obvious. For instance, Québécois mothers, more than the others, considered mouthing behaviors as a means to explore objects. In accordance with this point of view, they appeared to allow their 9–month–old infants to mouth the objects in the learning tasks more than the mothers of the other two groups. Québécois babies had longer durations of mouthing activity, and their mothers did not interrupt this activity by active or static restraint. In the same vein, our data indicate that Québécois mothers consider the infant as competent in the affective and cognitive domains. In accordance with this belief, they report introducing specific activities very early in order to stimulate development in this area.

In other domains, relations, if they exist, are not easy to determine. Two examples can illustrate the complexity of relations between beliefs and behavior. First, as mentioned previously, the Québécois babies, in contrast with the immigrants, are surrounded by toys, accessories, and miscellaneous objects. It is tempting to relate this difference in the physical environment of the infants to the mothers' belief concerning the course of development. However, the questions related to the function of play and of toys indicate that play is viewed by every mother, immigrant or not, as an important opportunity for learning, and that toys are appreciated for their educational properties. Furthermore, all mothers report that they play with their infants. We could thus conclude that there is no specific relation between maternal beliefs and the organization of the physical environment. Sigel (1986) has already discussed such results. He has shown that a point–to–point correspondence between beliefs and behavior can be misleading. In the present data, two alternative sources of influence can be postulated: The consumer habits of occidental societies and the need to be surrounded by many objects are certainly significant factors. In addition, while all mothers recognize the importance of play in the development of the infant, the Québécois mothers set the onset of most developmental abilities and stimulation activities much earlier than the others. This might put pressure on them and on the family to offer toys to the infant (even during the neonatal period). Since babies must be stimulated early, and the lack of stimulation could impair development, giving toys to the infant is seen as a sign, in our society, of a good parent–child relationship.

The second example bears on the relation between maternal beliefs and teaching strategies. We have seen that both Haitian and Vietnamese mothers stress the value of social conformity. Thus, one can expect that both groups of mothers would be more directive with their babies. However, in the teaching tasks, at 9 months there are differences between the two groups. Only Vietnamese mothers manifest directive behaviors with their infants. They guide and restrain more than the other two groups. We should consider here the consonance or co–effects of the two variables: maternal insistence on social conformity and maternal teaching strategies. Beyond simple correlations, these two variables can provide us with a more subtle understanding of the reality of maternal child–rearing practices. As Whiting and Edwards

(1988) have indicated, several types of mother interactions can be identified. Some mothers can be conceived as teachers, some as controlling, and others as liberal. Vietnamese mothers appear to fit into the first category: They value social conformity and at the same time they carefully supervise their babies' actions in order to control each of their movements. Québécois mothers value individuality, mainly in the affective and cognitive domains; they give their babies free reign to explore and to mouth objects. Haitians think that it is important to pay attention to the baby and to support the affective domain. At the same time, just as the Vietnamese, they value social conformity, but they are not as controlling as Vietnamese mothers in the observation context.

CONCLUSIONS

The present study illustrates the variety of child–rearing practices and conceptions to be found in a North-American metropolis. Cultural differences in maternal beliefs, in the organization of physical and social milieu, as well as in behavioral strategies in a teaching situation were identified. Our data also reveal cultural–consonance and disparity in these various components of the developmental context. One may expect that mothers born in Third–World countries, where parental goals are mainly centered around the survival and physical well–being of the baby, would share beliefs and practices in relation to child–rearing. Indeed, we found a number of similarities between our two immigrant groups. In other respects, however, the two groups are also quite different: Each has its own distinct way of raising children and its own vision of what their education should aim at. We explored the question of the possible relations between beliefs and the other components of the developmental context. Although these relations are not always obvious, they may best be considered as compound facets of the cultural context of development.

The disparities evidenced between the early developmental milieu of immigrant babies and of babies of the dominant cultural group raise the question of their future adaptation to day–care centers and schools. Children from minority groups will be confronted with the social norms of the Western world. At the same time, this brings to mind the question of the readiness of the host society to integrate immigrant children.

According to our data, Haitian and Vietnamese mothers express confidence in the medical world and in the physician as sources of information related to their infants. This apparent positive attitude might be an indication of their adaptation to the pediatric health services provided by the host country. Hopefully, with all the necessary adjustments to the specific needs and particular communication styles of the minority mothers, health and social programs can reach these populations.

ACKNOWLEDGMENTS

This work was supported by grants from the Conseil de Recherche en Sciences Humaines du Canada and the Conseil Québécois de la Recherche Sociale to G. Malcuit and A. Pomerleau. Louise Allard, Claudie Montpoint, Vinh Nguyen, Michèle Saint–Denis and Renée Séguin provided invaluable assistance with data collection and processing. Tibie Rome–Flanders made thoughtful comments on preliminary drafts. We thank the mothers and their infants who graciously participated in the study.

REFERENCES

Bastide, R. La socialisation de l'enfant en situation d'acculturation. *Carnets de l'enfance*, 1969, *10*, 26–35.

Bornstein, M.H. Cross–cultural developmental comparisons: The case of Japanese–American infant and mother activities and interactions. What we know, what we need to know, and why we need to know. *Developmental Review*, 1989, *9*, 171–204.

Bradley, R.H., Caldwell, B.M., Rock, S.L., Ramey, C., Barnard, K. E., Hammond, M.A., Mitchell, S., Gottfried, A.W., Siegel, L.S., & Johnson, D.L. Home environment and cognitive development in the first 3 years of life: A collaborative study involving six sites and three ethnic groups in North–America, *Developmental Psychology*, 1989, *25*, 217–235.

Bril, B., Zack, M., & Nkounkou–Hombessa, E. Ethnotheories of development and education. A view from different cultures. *European Journal of Psychology of Education*, 1989, *4*, 307–318.

Caldwell, B.M., & Bradley, R.H. *Home observation for measurement of the environment*. Little Rock: University of Arkansas, 1979.

Callaghan, J.W. A comparison of Anglo, Hopi and Navajo mothers and infants. In T. Field, A. Sostek, P. Vietze, & P.H. Leiderman (Eds.), *Culture and early interactions* (pp. 115–131). Hillsdale, NJ: Lawrence Erlbaum Associates, 1981.

Caudill, W., & Schooler, C. Child behavior and child rearing in Japan and the United States: An interim report. *The Journal of Nervous and Mental Disease*, 1973, *157*, 323–338.

Caudill, W., & Weinstein, H. Maternal care and infant behavior in Japan and America. *Psychiatry*, 1969, *32*, 12–43.

Chisholm, J.S. Biology, culture, and the development of temperament: a Navajo example. In J.K. Nugent, B.M. Lester, & T.B. Brazelton (Eds.), *The cultural context of infancy* (Vol. 1, pp. 341–364). Norwood, NJ: Ablex, 1989.

Dixon, S., Tronick, E., Keffer, C., & Brazelton, T.B. Mother–infant interaction among the Gusii of Kenya. In T. Field, A. Sostek, P. Vietze, & P.H. Leiderman (Eds.), *Culture and early interactions* (pp. 149–168). Hillsdale, NJ: Lawrence Erlbaum Associates, 1981.

Dixon, S., LeVine R.A., Richman, A., & Brazelton, T.B. Mother–child interaction around a teaching task: An African–American comparison. *Child Development*, 1984, *55*, 1252–1264.

Durand, Y. Structures familiales en Haïti. *Ethno–psychologie*, 1980, *35*, 47–51.

Fajardo, B.F., & Freedman, D.G. Maternal rhythmicity in three American cultures. In T. Field, A. Sostek, P. Vietze, & P.H. Leiderman (Eds.), *Culture and early interactions* (pp. 133–147). Hillsdale, NJ: Lawrence Erlbaum Associates, 1981.

Field, T., & Widmayer, S.M. Mother–infant interactions among lower S.E.S. black, Cuban, Puerto–Rican and South–American immigrants. In T. Field, A. Sostek, P. Vietze, & P.H. Leiderman (Eds.), *Culture and early interactions* (pp. 41–62). Hillsdale, NJ: Lawrence Erlbaum Associates, 1981.

Fogel, A., Toda, S., & Kawai, M. Mother–infant face–to–face interaction in Japan and the United States: A laboratory comparison using 3–month–old infants. *Developmental Psychology*, 1988, *24*, 398–406.

Holden, G.W., & Edwards, L.A. Parental attitudes toward child rearing: Instruments, issues, and implication. *Psychological Bulletin*, 1989, *106*, 29–58.

Johnson, D.L., Breckenridge, J.N., & McGowan, R.J. Home environment and early cognitive development in Mexican–American children. In A.W. Gottfried (Ed.), *Home environment and early cognitive development* (pp. 151–195). New York: Academic Press, 1984.

Keller, H., Miranda, D., & Gauda, G. The naïve theory of the infant and some maternal attitudes. A two country study. *Journal of Cross–Cultural Psychology*, 1984, *15*, 165–179.

Konner, M. Evolution of human behavior development. In R.L. Munroe, R.H. Munroe, & B.B. Whiting (Eds.), *Handbook of cross–cultural human development* (pp. 3–52). New York: Garland, 1981.

Laosa, L.M. Maternal behavior: Sociocultural diversity in modes of family interaction. In R.W. Henderson (Ed.), *Parent–child interaction: Theory, research and prospects* (pp. 125–167). New York: Academic Press, 1981.

Leiderman, P.H., Tulkin, S.R., & Rosenfeld, A. Looking towards the future. In P.H. Leiderman, S.R. Tulkin, & A. Rosenfeld (Eds.), *Culture in infancy* (pp. 599–607). New York: Academic Press, 1977.

LeVine, R.A. Human parental care: Universal goals, cultural strategies, individual behavior. In R.A. LeVine, P.M. Miller, & M.M. West (Eds.), *Parental behavior in diverse societies* (pp. 3–12). San Francisco: Josey–Bass, 1988.

LeVine, R.A., Miller, P.M., & West, M.M. (Eds.), *Parental behavior in diverse societies*. San Francisco: Josey–Bass, 1988.

Miller, S.A. Parents' beliefs about children's cognitive development. *Child Development*, 1988, *59*, 259–285.

Munro, D.J. The Chinese view of modeling. *Human Development*, 1975, *18*, 333–352.

Muret–Wagstaff, S., & Moore, S.G. The Hmong in America: Infant behavior and rearing practices. In J.K. Nugent, B.M. Lester, & T.B. Brazelton (Eds.), *The cultural context of infancy* (pp. 319–339). Norwood, NJ: Ablex, 1989.

Ninio, A. The naïve theory of the infant and other maternal attitudes in two subgroups in Israel. *Child Development*, 1979, *50*, 976–980.

Ninio, A. The effect of cultural background, sex and parenthood on beliefs about timetable of cognitive development in infancy. *Merrill–Palmer Quarterly*, 1988, *34*, 369–388.

Phan Thi Dac. *Situation de la personne au Vietnam*. Paris: Centre National de la Recherche, 1966.

Shand, N. Culture's influence in Japanese and American maternal role perception and confidence. *Psychiatry*, 1985, *48*, 52–67.

Sigel, I.E. *Parental belief systems: The psychological consequences for children*. Hillsdale, NJ: Lawrence Erlbaum Associates, 1985.

Sigel, I.E. Reflections on the belief–behavior connection: Lessons learned from a research program on parental belief systems and teaching strategies. In R.D. Ashmore & D.M. Brodzinsky (Eds.), *Thinking about the family: View of parents and children* (pp. 35–65). Hillsdale, NJ: Lawrence Erlbaum Associates, 1986.

Smith, S., & Freedman, D.G. *Mother–toddler interaction and maternal perception of child temperament in two ethnic groups: Chinese–American and European–American*. Paper presented at the meeting of the Society for Research in Child Development, Denver, Colorado, 1983.

Whiting, B.B., & Edwards, C.P. *Children of different worlds. The formation of social behavior*. Cambridge, MA: Harvard University Press, 1988.

Zeskind, Ph.S. Cross–cultural differences in maternal perception of cries of low– and high–risk infants. *Child Development*, 1983, *54*, 1119–1128.

Parenting in Cross–Cultural Perspective: The United States, France, and Japan

4

Marc H. Bornstein, Joseph Tal, and
Catherine Tamis–LeMonda
National Institute of Child Health and Human Development

INTRODUCTION

Parenting manifestly influences the course and outcome of children's cognitive and communicative achievements as well as their social and emotional adjustment. Further, "culture" presumably shapes systematic parenting practices. In this context, we compared and contrasted prominent characteristics of parenting in three different societies, the United States, France, and Japan. As part of parallel longitudinal studies, we have examined naturalistic interactions in mother–infant dyads in three comparable international urban locales, New York City, Paris, and Tokyo. Our observations revealed patterns of culture–specific parenting as well as some culture–general processes. We first review relevant aspects of maternal behaviors and provide a rationale for our West—West—East comparison, and then we report and comment on specific findings.

CULTURAL SIMILARITIES AND DIFFERENCES IN PARENTING

Parenting Activities

Mother–infant interaction is dynamic and transactional in the sense that one member of the dyad is always influencing the other (e.g., Sameroff, 1983; Stern, 1985). In this study of parenting, we report global estimates of activities of one member of the dyad, the mother, in terms of how often mothers engaged in a selected set of parenting activities. In addition, we focus particularly on responsive behaviors in mothers, viz. those actions of mothers that had identifiable, immediate, and direct antecedents in the behavior of their infants. General maternal activity is multiply determined; maternal responsiveness is specifiable to infant behavior.

Mothers act with and respond to their infants in many different ways. Certain activities predominate in the maternal repertoire, however, and in infancy three basic categories of maternal activities include nurturing, social exchange, and didactic stimulation (Bornstein, 1989a). This study focused on these three prominent interactive domains of visual and vocal exchange between mother and baby, examining their frequency of occurrence and patterns of covariation in three distinct cultures.

Mothers' activities harbor real consequences in the lives of their children. Whether the infants are normal, healthy, and term or at–risk preterms, whether they are lower, middle, or upper class, and even across diverse cultures, certain parenting activities have been documented to exert vigorous beneficial effects over major domains of development in children (e.g., Azuma, 1986; Beckwith & Cohen, 1989; Bee, Barnard, Eyres, Gray, Hammond, Spietz, Snyder, & Clark, 1982; Belsky, Gilstrap, & Rovine, 1984; Bornstein, 1985, 1989a, b; Bornstein, Miyake, & Tamis–LeMonda, 1985–1986; Bornstein & Tamis–LeMonda, 1990; Bradley, 1989; Bradley, Caldwell, & Rock, 1988; Carew, 1980; Goldberg, Lojkasek, Gartner, & Corter, 1989; Gottfried, 1984; Olson, Bates, & Bayles, 1984; Sigman, Neumann, Carter, Cattle, D'Sousa, & Bwibo, 1988; Tamis–LeMonda & Bornstein, 1989; Wachs & Gruen, 1982; Yarrow, Rubenstein, & Pedersen, 1975). Their concurrent and predictive validity indicate the significance of studying such maternal activities in child development. Of course, some other maternal characteristic, such as intelligence or socioeconomic status, could share variance with parental activities, and that variance could also be shared predictively with one or more developmental outcomes in children. However, the research studies cited above indicate that variance in specific maternal behaviors uniquely predicts a range of specific developmental outcomes in children. Further, the arrow of socialization is not unidirectional, mother → baby; infants in their own way also influence mother, infant → mother, and contribute to their own development, infant → mother → infant (Bell & Harper, 1977; Bornstein & Tamis–LeMonda, 1990; Lerner, 1989; Lewis & Rosenblum, 1974). In this study, as stated, we focussed on maternal behaviors directed toward infants.

Hypotheses about Parenting

At the most general level, a mother's behavior with her child may be considered a function of herself, her child, the situation, and interactions that obtain among these factors. For example, while nurturant diapering is often initiated by the demands of the child, the speed with which a mother responds to her infant's distress, the difficulty of the process for mother and infant, and the type of diapers used are likely influenced by multiple factors. The three main factors are themselves, in turn, influenced by multiple determinants. For example, a mother's behavior is a function of genetic inheritance, acculturation, SES, and so forth. Thus, a fruitful approach to understanding mother–infant interaction is to manipulate—in the most general sense of the word, since experimental manipulation of these factors is often impossible—variables that are thought to influence behaviors of interest while holding other possible influences constant. In the research reported here, our chief interest is in the effects of culture on parenting, and we have attempted to "manipulate" culture, holding other significant factors constant. In addition, we wished to examine two more specific hypotheses about parenting. Hypothesis 1 concerns itself with the frequency of certain basic parenting activities in different cultures, and Hypothesis 2 concerns itself with coherence among parenting activities across cultures. By comparing cultures, we aimed to find which, and to what degree, maternal behaviors vary and covary.

Hypothesis 1. Cross–cultural differences in parenting. New York City, Paris, and Tokyo represent an especially appealing and potentially informative comparative base on which to investigate specific as well as universal aspects of childrearing. These three locales are much alike in terms of modernity, urbanity, economics, ecology, and climate, and therefore it is possible to obtain roughly equivalent samples from the three. In the cultures of all three, mother is also normally the primary caregiver in the family setting, and parents share many of the same child–centered goals, notably educational achievement and economic security. However, substantial differences exist among the three cultures represented by these places in terms of history, beliefs, and values associated with childrearing. On this basis, mothers in these places are thought to have established different parenting styles in order to attain different central cultural goals. The American mother is believed to promote autonomy in her infant and to organize her interactions so as to foster physical and verbal independence in the child; the French mother is believed to share some of these characteristics, but also to see security and emotional support as natural and achievement stimulation as secondary; the Japanese mother is believed to see her infant as an extension of herself and to organize her interactions so as to consolidate and strengthen a mutual dependence between herself and her infant (see Befu, 1986; Caudill, 1973; Chen & Miyake, 1986; Clancy, 1986; Clarke, 1985; Dion & Pêcheux, 1989; Doi, 1973; Dolto, 1979; Fogel, Toda, & Kawai, 1988; Gramont, 1969; Hess, Azuma, Kashiwagi, Dickson, Nagano, Holloway, Miyake, Price, Hatano, & McDevitt, 1986; Hoffman, 1963; Kojima, 1986; Lamb & Bornstein, 1987; Maranda, 1974; Métraux & Mead, 1954; Miyake, Chen, & Campos, 1985; Morsbach, 1980; Triandis, 1989; Weisz, Rothbaum, & Blackburn, 1984).

On the basis of these reported differences in parental beliefs, we expected that mothers in these three cultures might differ in actual parenting practices. In specific, we expected that American mothers would favor active didactic stimulation of infant attention to the object world, and French and Japanese mothers social stimulation to themselves as well as tactile kinesthetic play. We also thought that French and Japanese mothers would favor use of the infant register in speaking to baby, whereas American mothers would favor using adult conversational tones. In terms of mothers' responses to infant signals, across this limited variety of cultural settings, mothers might reasonably be expected not to differ substantially in nurturant responsiveness, as for example in responding to infant distress. Indeed, responsiveness to distress may be universal and "infant driven" (Bowlby, 1969). The same might be true for responsiveness to infant nondistress vocalizations because of the significant and perhaps universal role of imitating, chorusing, and turn–taking in the early development of this form of dyadic interaction (e.g., Papoušek, Papoušek, & Bornstein, 1985; Stern, 1985). However, mothers in the different cultures might be expected to vary with respect to more discretionary forms of responsiveness vis–à–vis the object and social worlds. So, for example, we expected American mothers to emphasize object responsiveness by incorporating the environment outside the dyad into their interactions, and French and Japanese mothers to emphasize responsiveness oriented within the dyad.

Hypothesis 2. Coherence in parenting. Mothers naturally engage in a dynamic range of activities with their infants. Nevertheless, many theorists have conceptualized maternal caretaking as adhering to only one or a small number of dimensions, variously described as 'good,' 'sensitive,' or 'warm' (see Brody, 1956; MacPhee, Ramey, & Yeates, 1984; Rohner, 1985; Rothbaum, 1986). This view builds on the infrequently–tested assumption that parenting reflects a personality trait or traits, and predicts that parents behave in consistent ways across domains of interaction, time, and context. Such coherence among selected parenting activities implies consistency in rank–order status. Alternatively, frequently performed activities may not be linked psychologically, or individuals may vary in the pattern of their activities such that there is no unified organization to parenting. Finally, whether or not coherence in behavior patterning emerges depends in part on the activities chosen for study. We expected covariation among selected activities, and independence among others.

On the basis of prior study in the United States and United Kingdom (e.g., Bornstein & Tamis–LeMonda, 1990; Dunn & Richards, 1977), and the view that social and didactic forms of parental interaction are not necessarily coupled (Bornstein, 1989a), we expected that maternal encouragement of attention to the environment and to self would not covary, just as speech in the infant register and in adult conversational tones would be independent. On similar grounds, we expected that those mothers who more often engaged in tactile kinesthetic play would also encourage their infants' attention to themselves more often. Given the role that 'parentese' is thought to play in the recruitment of infant attention (e.g., D'Odorico & Franco, 1985; Papoušek et al., 1985), we hypothesized that speech in the infant register would covary with encouraging attention to objects and with encouraging attention to self in all three cultures. With respect to responsive parenting specifically, we expected (as above) that social and object responsiveness would be independent in different cultures, but that object responsiveness would covary with imitation of infant nondistress vocalization as both often share a language orientation.

Hypothesizing about culture and parenting. The implication of culture as an explanatory variable with regard to mean differences (Hypothesis 1) is different from examination of covariation with regard to coherence (Hypothesis 2). First, the implication of culture in mean differences is often causal (e.g., "A mother engages in active stimulation *because* she is American."). Hypothesizing that behaviors covary is another way of saying that the variance in one behavior is explained by the variance in the other behavior. In other words, mother behaviors can be used as culture is used—to explain mother behavior. The implication of a covariation structure, therefore, is often that another underlying latent structure is the cause of the covariation (e.g., "She nurses that infant *and* diapers him *because* she is his mother.").

Second, when culture is thought to be an influence, the implication is usually that it is a learned influence, assuming a more or less equivalent genetic pool (exceptions exist, of course; see, for example, Shand & Kosawa, 1985a, b). Thus, an infant born to American parents and raised in France by a French family can be expected to be as French as his step–siblings. However, covariation of behavior within a certain context (e.g., mothering, social situation) implies a "natural order." For example, an extraverted person can be expected to display a high frequency of many different social behaviors, and even if there is no heritable component to extraversion the same covariation pattern would be expected. So, for example, an extravert who converted to an introvert would now be expected to display uniformly low frequencies of social behavior. In other words, a constellation of behaviors labeled "social" ought to covary independent of the individuals selected for study.

THE UNITED STATES, FRANCE, AND JAPAN

Cultural generalization is implicit in most psychological reportage, even in spite of the monocultural character of most psychological investigation (e.g., Kennedy, Scheirer, & Rogers, 1984; Moghaddam, 1987; Triandis, 1980). Cross–cultural developmental comparisons are recommended by empiricists and theoreticians alike to meet the test of limits on cultural generalization, and they have long been recognized as requisite to a complete and accurate understanding of development (see Berry, 1983; Bornstein, 1980, 1989b; Brislin, 1983; Bruner, 1989; Campbell, 1964; Kessen, 1983; Nugent, Lester, & Brazelton, 1989; Piaget, 1966/1974; Russell, 1984; Sexton & Misiak, 1984; Super, 1981; Whiting, 1981).

American, French, and Japanese cultures constitute an especially attractive contrastive set for the several reasons reviewed earlier. Further, on more purely empirical grounds, the triad of contrasts undertaken in this study, including two Western and one Eastern culture, creates the possibility of evaluating generalities of childrearing patterns across a controlled diversity of culture. Culture has many facets, including economy and modernity, education and urbanity, and so forth (see Jahoda, 1980; Triandis, 1989). Cross–cultural research is often geared to evaluate the distinctiveness of some phenomenon in a setting that is exotic or unique; frequently, it is undertaken to compare samples from contrastive settings in order to maximize the potential of uncovering differences. However, such a strategy potentially confounds childrearing aspects of culture with other factors. For our research, we selected three samples that are similar on key variables (see below), given the constraint that they come from three still essentially distinct cultures. Thus, any potential differences ought to be ascribable to cultural factors.

Testing psychological theory provides additional motivation to undertake cross–cultural comparisons. Childrearing patterns are believed to differ between collectivist and individualist cultures in developmentally meaningful ways. Parents in collectivist cultures (as can be found in Japan) tend to emphasize obedient, reliable, and proper behavior in children, whereas parents in individualist cultures (as can be found in the U.S.) tend to emphasize self–reliant, independent, and creative behavior (Kohn, 1987; Triandis, 1989). In the one, children are encouraged to follow rules and conform to norms; in the other, children are allowed a good deal of autonomy and are encouraged to confront and engage in independent exploration of their environment. Our selection of locales nicely contrasts cultural collectivism and individualism (Hofstede, 1980), holding urbanity, complexity, and other global factors constant.

Finally, studies of behavioral similarities and differences in Japanese and American styles of parenting are few (e.g., Bornstein, 1989b; Bornstein et al., 1990a, b; Caudill & Weinstein, 1969; Otaki, Durrett, Richards, Nyquist, & Pennebaker, 1986; Sengoku, Davitz, & Davitz, 1982; Shand & Kosawa, 1985a, b; Ueda, 1985). Direct scientific, and more specifically developmental, comparisons between American and French, and between French and Japanese, are even more rare (see, e.g., Bertrand, 1986; Bornstein, Tamis–LeMonda, Pêcheux, & Rahn, 1991; Darnton, 1984; Dolto, 1955; Gramont, 1969; Hoffman, 1963; Maranda, 1974; Métraux & Mead, 1954; Wolfenstein, 1955).

In overview, some aspects of parenting in the United States, France, and Japan can be expected to be similar, and some different. Moreover, the three cultures provide an important contrastive set in which to explore similarities and differences in coherence among parenting activities. The chief purpose of the present study was, therefore, to evaluate cross–cultural specificity and universality of prominent types of parenting in mothers. We report nomothetic, group–based, across–culture comparisons.

A CULTURAL APPROACH TO PARENTING

Methods of Study

In its general organization, our study followed in the tradition of cross–cultural comparisons of home–based observations of typical ongoing family life (e.g., Bornstein et al., 1990a, b; Bornstein & Tamis–LeMonda, 1990; Caudill & Weinstein, 1969; Kaplan & Dove, 1987; Konner, 1977; Lewis & Ban, 1977; Sigman et al., 1988; Tulkin, 1977). In New York City, Paris, and Tokyo, dyads of infants and mothers were observed interacting as they normally do in the natural setting of the home. The study was designed to provide information about naturally–occurring behaviors of mothers and infants under everyday conditions, and not to standardize the context of data collection beyond what was ecologically valid. Thus, mothers were asked to behave in their usual manner and to disregard the observer's presence insofar as possible; beside the observer, only mother and baby were present; and observations took place at times of the day that were optimal in terms of individual babies being in awake and alert states (see Bornstein, 1985; Bornstein & Tamis–

LeMonda, 1990; Vibbert & Bornstein, 1989). A female observer, always a native of the country, visited the home to conduct the observation, and observations were conducted identically in the three locales. After a period of acclimation, mothers and infants were videotaped for 45 minutes.

In total, 72 primiparous mothers and their 5–month–old infants were observed; they had been recruited from patient populations of private obstetric and pediatric groups and included 24 Caucasian American dyads, 24 Caucasian French, and 24 Oriental Japanese. All infants were term at birth and healthy up to and at the time of the study. Mothers and babies in the American, French, and Japanese samples did not differ on central demographic characteristics: Babies were statistically the same age at the time of the home visits, 163 days on average, and their mothers were statistically the same age, 30 years on average, had statistically similar educational histories, 3.3 years post high school on average, and being primiparous had coextensive childrearing histories. The samples were each balanced for sex of baby and came from comparable middle to upper–middle class households. We focused on parenting in middle infancy because of the intentionality and flexibility in behavioral organization which infants demonstrate at this time (Emde, Gaensbauer, & Harmon, 1976; Wolff, 1984). By this age, the baby's scope of apperception includes both the dyad and the surrounding environment, and infants and their mothers often share the lead in turn–taking exchanges (Belsky et al., 1984; Bornstein & Tamis–LeMonda, 1990; Cohn & Tronick, 1987; Kaye & Fogel, 1980; Stevenson, Ver Hoeve, Roach, & Leavitt, 1986).

Nine maternal behaviors were scored from the videotapes. The codes used to quantify these activities and the procedures used for observation were extensively pretested and were found to transfer readily across cultural settings. Five codes concerned general maternal activity with infants. Two recorded the mother's active engagement and organization of her infant's attention to some property, object, or event in the environment ("object") or to the mother herself ("social"). In the one, a mother might demonstrate, point, name, or describe in order to facilitate the infant's visual and/or tactual exploration of some aspect of the environment; in the other, she might touch, gesture towards, or position her infant with the explicit purpose of engaging the baby to herself. Two codes assessed speech to the infant, either as infant register (characterized by extreme or fluctuating pitch commonly associated with "parentese") or as taking conventional adult conversational tones. One code assessed tactile kinesthetic play, that is maternal bids to nonverbal animated interaction with the infant. These maternal activities were sampled in partial intervals of alternating 30–second observation periods (Seitz, 1988; Suen & Ary, 1989). A behavior was scored one or zero for each interval depending on whether or not it appeared in that interval.

We also coded four types of maternal response having to do, respectively, with the object–world and the social–world (as above), nurturance (where mother engaged in feeding, pacifying, diapering, picking up to comfort), and imitation (specifically of infant vocalizations). To do this, we coded every occurrence of four infant activities—object visual attention, social visual attention, nondistress vocalization, and distress vocalization—and then coded the four maternal response types as they occurred to each infant act. In addition, we collected data on infant state and the time the infant was in view of mother in order to control for these factors within each dyad.

All maternal and infant behaviors were coded by individuals who were fluent in the language of the society. Coders established adequate reliability on all variables (for additional details, see Bornstein et al., 1990a, b; Bornstein et al., 1991).

The first set of analyses, related to the cross–cultural differences hypothesis, examined variation in the occurrence of maternal activities. Our interest in overall maternal behavior concerned the frequency of activity in the presence of the infant, and so the dependent measures were expressed as frequencies controlling for the amount of time mother was in view of her infant. Mothers' individual responsive behaviors were computed as proportions of total maternal responsive behavior and therefore were independent of overall infant activity (i.e., every mother's proportions summed to one, regardless of the amount of activity displayed by her infant). Our use of proportions in analyzing responsiveness was intended to provide information on the relative likelihood of mothers' different response types. (It is not appropriate to correct individual maternal response types for specific infant behaviors, because any response type can, by design, occur to any infant activity, with the exception of imitation which could occur in response to either vocal distress or nondistress. The propensity for a particular response type to occur to a specific behavior is, in part, what was being examined.) Error within each behavioral comparison was controlled using the Tukey Test.

The second set of analyses, related to the coherence hypothesis, examined relations among different maternal behaviors within cultures and compared these relations across cultures. Because there were nine behaviors, 36 different pairwise correlations were possible. Of these, hypotheses were originally developed for seven. These seven pairwise correlations were classified with respect to whether or not we expected covariation (as described earlier). Fisher z' transforms were used to compare correlation coefficients (r) between pairs of cultures; error was controlled using a modified Bonferroni for each of the seven correlations (Keppel, 1982). All correlations were conducted on frequencies rather than proportions. Because proportions are constrained to add to one, their variances are also constrained, leading to restriction of range. Restricting range would have reduced power to test coherence.

Hypothesis 1: Cultural Similarities and Differences

Table 4.1 displays means for mothers' individual parenting activities across the three cultures. For all but one, tactile kinesthetic play, ANCOVAs revealed significant main effects of culture. Subsequent pairwise comparisons showed, as hypothesized, that American mothers displayed significantly higher rates of object stimulation than French or Japanese mothers. American and Japanese mothers showed equal rates of social stimulation, and, contrary to expectations, American mothers engaged in more social stimulation than French mothers. American

TABLE 4.1
Means (Standard Deviations) of Parenting Activities in Three Cultures

	U.S.	France	Japan	p of Overall ANCOVA	Differences p < .05	Effect Size[a]
Stimulation						
Object	16.6	10.0	9.8	.05	US > F,J	.09
	(8.4)	(5.2)	(7.2)			
Social	10.0	3.4	7.8	.001	US > F	.27
	(5.1)	(2.8)	(4.7)			
Speech						
Infant register	14.0	6.8	5.2	.005	US > F,J	.15
	(9.4)	(6.3)	(4.6)			
Conversational tones	19.5	27.6	25.9	.001	F > US	.26
	(10.6)	(8.1)	(12.4)			
Tactile kinesthetic play	4.3	2.6	3.5	.25	—	—
	(2.9)	(2.6)	(2.9)			

[a]Proportion of variance explained by culture; computation follows Fliess (1969).

mothers showed the highest rates of speech in the infant register, and French mothers displayed higher rates of conversational speech than American mothers.

Table 4.2 isolates mothers' responsive parenting. Parallel patterns of results were found. Two responsive behaviors, object and social, showed significant culture main effects in the ANOVAs. As predicted, American mothers displayed the highest level of object responsiveness, but American and Japanese mothers displayed higher rates of social responsiveness than French mothers. As predicted also, mothers in the three cultures showed equivalent rates of nurturant and imitative responsiveness.

At least three important points emerge from these data: First, where significant differences in rates occurred, American mothers tended to display the highest levels; the one exception to this was French mothers' high levels of adult conversational speech to infants. Second, as hypothesized, maternal nurturant and vocally

TABLE 4.2
Proportions (Standard Deviations) of Response Types of Parenting in Three Cultures

	U.S.	France	Japan	p of Overall ANCOVA	Differences p < .05	Effect Size[a]
Object	.26	.06	.14	.001	US > F,J	.17
	(.20)	(.08)	(.21)			
Social	.04	.00	.06	.001	US,J > F	.16
	(.06)	(.01)	(.06)			
Nurturant	.02	.02	.03	.83	—	—
	(.03)	(.03)	(.05)			
Imitation	.17	.17	.19	.84	—	—
	(.16)	(.17)	(.15)			

[a]Proportion of variance explained by culture; computation follows Fliess (1969).

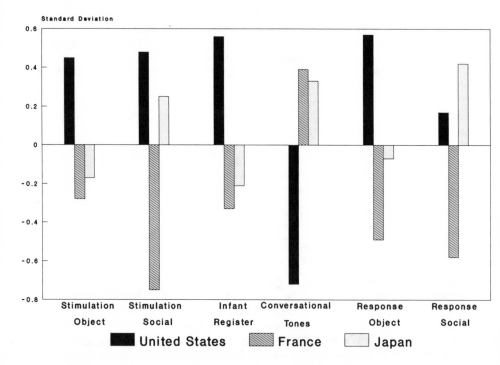

Figure 4.1. Cross-cultural differences in mother behaviors in SD units.

imitative responsiveness tended to occur equally across cultures. That is, these kinds of maternal responses appear less "free to vary" across culture. Finally, the expected differences between American and Japanese mothers with respect to object and social behaviors emerged in one direction only. American mothers displayed higher rates of behaviors than Japanese mothers where the object world was involved; however, no significant differences between American and Japanese mothers emerged where social behaviors were involved.

The last columns in Tables 4.1 and 4.2 provide effect sizes for the cultural differences that were found to be significant. These should be interpreted as proportions of variance explained by the cultural "manipulation." Figure 4.1 recasts mother behaviors for which significant cultural differences occurred in standard deviation units, and so provides more direct estimates of the effect of culture. In order to construct Figure 4.1, data were aggregated across cultures, a combined standard deviation computed, and group differences from the grand mean of 0 (in standardized units) were calculated. Such computations assume the standard ANOVA model, where each mother's mean is a function of a grand mean, a culture effect, and error (proportion of error = 1 − effect size). Theoretically, this is consonant with the initial conceptualization of our first hypothesis; that is, for the purposes of the current research, we view individual mothers' behaviors as consisting of an archetypical maternal behavior (grand mean) plus the effect of a culture manipulation. Of course, this is a simplistic assumption, and useful only to the degree that it provides information regarding the effect of culture. In order to investigate other effects on mothers' behaviors, we would need to manipulate other variables simultaneously controlling for the effect of culture (either statistically or by investigating variation among mothers within a single culture).

Hypothesis 2: Coherence among Parenting Activities

Table 4.3 displays Pearson correlation coefficients between pairs of maternal behaviors within and across cultures. The majority of the 15 within–culture correlations were not significant. Therefore, maternal behaviors appear largely independent in different cultures. As hypothesized, for example, object and social encouragement of infant attention were independent in mothers in all three cultures, and maternal speech in the infant register and in adult conversational tones were independent in two of the three cultures.

The five significant correlations occurred among either U.S. or Japanese mothers. Unexpectedly, social stimulation and tactile kinesthetic play covaried positively only in American mothers. As for cross–correlations between maternal stimulation and speech, object stimulation and speech in the infant register covaried positively in mothers in all three cultures, as predicted, but only significantly so among Japanese, and social stimulation and speech in the infant register covaried positively and significantly in American and Japanese, but not French, mothers.

Table 4.4 displays Pearson correlations among maternal responsive behaviors. As hypothesized, mothers' object responses were not related to their social responses in any of the three cultures. The hypothesized relation between object and imitative responsiveness did not materialize in any of the cultures.

The number of activities in mothers that covaried overall was small. Clearly, that number itself will vary with the maternal activities actually selected for measurement. Still, the number covarying in the United States and in Japan was greater than that in France. This suggests that any existing covariation among maternal behaviors is in part culturally specific. Such a result is particularly important because researchers often expect that, despite mean differences between groups, within–group covariation will remain similar across groups. Another implication of differences between cultures in covariation is that care must be exercised in generalizing from one culture to another, even when the cultures are relatively similar. Moreover, different cultural groups within a relatively pluralistic country (as the U.S.) may display different patterns of covariation.

Table 4.1 shows that Japanese and American mothers displayed generally higher variation than French mothers. Based on this information alone, it might be expected that French mothers display generally lower covariation than mothers in the other two cultures. Restriction of range attenuates the size of potential correlations (Cohen & Cohen, 1983). However, the fact that a result is expected statistically does not necessarily mean that it is simply a statistical artifact; that is, the result may still reflect a particular reality. Thus, assuming that the three groups of mothers

TABLE 4.3
Covariation Among Selected Maternal Activities in Three Cultures

	U.S.	France	Japan	Overall	Differences p < .05
Object with Social	.21	.20	.23	.33**	—
Infant register with Conversational tones	−.22	−.21	.55**	−.15	J > US,F
Social with Tactile kinesthetic play	.43*	.15	.35	.41***	—
Object with Infant register	.33	.29	.45*	.47***	—
Social with Infant register	.46*	−.16	.43*	.40***	US,J > F

*p < .05   ** p < .01   *** p < .001

TABLE 4.4
Covariation Among Selected Maternal Responsive Behaviors in Three Cultures

	U.S.	France	Japan	Overall	Differences p < .05
Object with Social	.21	−.15	.32	.32**	J > F
Object with Imitation	−.04	−.04	.25	.07	—

** p < .01

are more or less equally representative of their respective cultures, the generally lower variance among French mothers should be a function of the population sampled (rather than an artificial restriction of range).

As can be seen in Tables 4.3 and 4.4, correlations resulting from aggregation across cultures were sometimes different in magnitude, and often in significance, from within–culture correlations. This could happen because aggregating groups results in a greater n and, perforce, more power so that equivalent or lower aggregated correlations appear statistically significant, where intra–group correlations are not. This is a positive result of aggregation. However, when mean group differences exist, aggregation can be expected to yield different, and sometimes misleading, covariation patterns from those observed in individual groups. Figure 4.2 displays four of many possible scenarios. These four were chosen in order to illustrate the unpredictability of results that can emerge from aggregating heterogeneous groups.

It is also important in this context to note the contrast between comparisons of means and comparisons of covariations. As emerged in the discussion of Hypothesis 1, combining cultural groups in order to compute a grand mean can be informative. Further, it was consistent with our initial hypotheses regarding a culture "manipulation." However, there may be cases where combining cultural groups can be misleading. Here, combining cultural groups for the purpose of exploring covariation appears to distort findings.

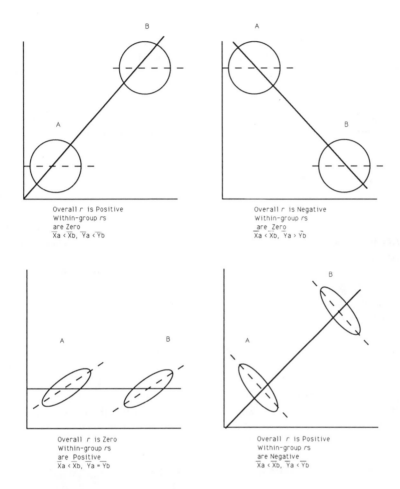

Figure 4.2. Effects of aggregating heterogeneous groups (A and B) on covariation: Four instructive scenarios.

RECAP

The purpose of this study was to compare and contrast maternal behaviors in two Western and one Eastern culture in order to understand better how patterns of parenting might be similar or vary cross–culturally. It is important to note that the samples we observed in these countries are comparatively restricted in terms of sociodemographic level, urban location, and educational history. This restriction actually aided the comparison we undertook, since the three samples are similar on these variables. However, this restriction and others have clear implications for the generalizability of the findings. First, different results could emerge in mothers coming from other regions of the SES scale, from less metropolitan environments, or from less educated families. Moreover, we concentrated on a small and selected number of activities; analyses of other activities in mothers may give rise to similar or different patterns of findings. Also, our results might apply uniquely to the open style of interaction we studied, but not to other more constrained situations. Discontinuities characterize infant development in the first year of life (e.g., Emde et al., 1976; Fischer, 1980); if our observation time had straddled a period of reorganization in infancy, presumably other patterns of results might have emerged. Nonetheless, the activities we defined appear to be common in mothers in these countries, and we observed considerable individual variation in them within cultures.

The findings point to several areas of cultural similarity and difference in maternal approaches to parenting, and submit to cross–cultural evaluation the universality versus particularity of certain parenting processes. With respect to the frequency data, mothers in these different cultures were mostly unalike in the degree to which they stimulated and spoke to their infants and responded to their infants vis–à–vis the object and social worlds. However, mothers in these different cultures were mostly alike in terms of how much they engaged their infants in tactile kinesthetic play and in responding nurturantly and imitatively. In general, too, mothers in the three cultures produced similar patterns of independence among their activities (see, too, Sigman & Wachs, in this volume). In the United States, in France, and in Japan, only a minority of mothers' activities positively covaried, even if the degree of relatedness among activities sometimes varied. That is, mothers who do more of one activity do not necessarily or automatically do more or less of others. The finding of independence among maternal activities in such disparate cultural settings casts into doubt a unitary or monistic view of parenting. Although some activities covary, mothers in different cultures were typically observed to engage in patterns of individualized and differentiated parenting.

SOURCES OF VARIATION IN CULTURAL APPROACHES TO PARENTING

What are the prominent sources of similarity and difference in the expression of maternal activities? Since parenting behaviors were observed in the context of mother–infant interaction, systematic influences could arise if mothers in these cultures spent different amounts of the observation period in the company of their infants or if infants were in different states of alertness. Similarly, the behavior of infants could be responsible, at least in part, for differences in mothers' responsiveness. Statistical comparisons controlled for the total duration of the session mothers spent with their babies; further, the times mothers and babies were observed were selected to provide for an optimal assessment of dyadic interaction in terms of the babies' state, and babies in the three cultures were observed to be in equivalent and high states of alertness throughout the course of the observation. Further, effects of infant activity on maternal responsiveness were eliminated through our use of proportions.

Thus, variation and covariation in parenting among mothers in these three cultures cannot be ascribed to maternal availability or infant state or behavior. Nor, can the variation and covariation readily be ascribed to differences among strictly maternal variables. We attempted to "equate" mothers who participated in these studies on factors like age, parity, SES, as well as years of education. Mothers were the same age, and they were all primiparous with babies the same age. Of course, socioeconomic class may not indicate exactly similar standings in the United States, France, and Japan, or necessarily within any country. Further, even though the Japanese educational system is modeled on the American and the two show rough comparability with the French, what curricula these mothers followed in school and more particularly what they learned (in and out of school) obviously also vary considerably.

There are at least three general ways in which cultures might be "equated" with respect to the conduct of investigations such as this one. One consists of matching groups with regard to their relative standing within each group's respective culture (e.g., $50,000/year income in one country is the same percentile ranking as $4,000/year in another country). A second refers to actual equality, that is matching groups on observable measures (e.g., same number of rooms in the home owned in each of two countries). A third method requires equating groups in different cultures on key latent, rather than observed, variables (e.g., 13 years of education in one country is equivalent, with respect to childrearing practices, to 10 years of education in another country). Each of these methods presents some difficulty. Equating relative standing in very different cultures (e.g., industrialized versus developing nations) may result in groups that are, in reality, markedly different. Literal equality across cultures assumes that observable variables relate to latent variables in the same way in different cultures (e.g., 12 years of education in two cultures have identical implications for childrearing practices). In order to equate groups on latent variables, additional study is required. Although these difficulties exist in any cross–cultural comparison, they are greatly reduced when societies that possess roughly equivalent standards of living are compared, as here among the United States, France, and Japan. In such cases, observed variables in different cultures (e.g., years of education) relate similarly, though certainly not identically, to latent variables. In other words, using observable equivalence in similar cultures is akin to combining the second and third methods noted above. Ours is a rough equation on these factors.

With respect to additional sources of variation, it could also be the case that mothers in different cultures hold differing views on being observed. New Yorkers, Parisians, and Tokyo people are normally reticent to invite strangers into the home. Nonetheless, mothers in all three locales volunteered participation, and all expressed interest in the study and cordiality toward the observers. To examine the possibility that entering the home to videotape ongoing maternal behavior would selectively alter activity, we conducted a demonstration control experiment using portions of each of the American and French videotapes. The American—French comparison was selected because it reflected empirically extreme differences. Native French and native Americans rated each French and American mother and baby on seven separate dimensions: embarrassment at being filmed, awareness of camera, expression of different emotions, extent of baby/mother orientation to partner, degree of comfort and naturalness, activity level toward infant/mother, and spontaneity. Specifically, two segments were selected from each of the videotapes: The first segment was randomly selected with the only stipulation being that mother and infant appeared together in the tape for the full segment, and the other segment consisted of the first instance in the observation when the mother encouraged her infant to attend to a property, object, or event in the environment. These random and didactically–oriented interaction sequences were presented to raters in random order (except that segments from the same culture, the same infant, the same sex of infant, and the same category of random or didactic activity never occurred more than twice in a row). Raters used a semantic differential, and ratings were submitted to multivariate analysis of variance. One of the seven dimensions, maternal activity toward the infant, served as a manipulation check on the raters. In keeping with expectations, judges rated mothers in didactic interactions as significantly more active toward infants than they were in random conditions ($p = .006$), regardless of the culture of the dyad or the culture of the rater. Analyses of the balance of maternal and infant ratings showed no systematic differences between cultures. Country of rater was not a meaningful factor in the ratings either.

Finally, factors external to childrearing style per se could play a part in shaping activities of mothers with their infants, and some specific ones—prominently urban–rural locale or differing physical layouts of homes in different cultures—could conceivably influence parenting differentially. In several respects, however, this New York City—Paris—Tokyo comparison overcomes these potential shortcomings. These three cities are among the most cosmopolitan metropolitan areas in the world. Moreover, participating families in these three cities lived in comparable apartments in multistory buildings. These considerations tend to diminish the possibility that general location or structural differences in dwellings systematically affected at least these aspects of parenting.

CONCLUSIONS

For new parents, the first months with an infant are thought to constitute a period of adjustment and transformation; for the infant, parents' activities in the same time frame are thought to constitute experiences critical to development. The present study aimed to learn more about the nature of maternal behaviors in the period of the dyad's initial accommodation, early in the infant's first year of life, by examining representative and common interactions of mothers with their infants in several different cultures. Taken together, our results support findings of cross–cultural universals as well as culturally–specific differences in parenting behaviors in American, French, and Japanese mothers.

Having ruled out several sources of variation, we suspect that components of culture to do with parental beliefs and childrearing philosophy might be responsible for varying patterns of maternal behavior toward young infants. Of course, genetic and ecological factors could still play a part in generating cultural differences. Presumably, universal parenting activities occur automatically in mothers, and mothers are not consciously aware of them; they are "intuitive" (see Papoušek & Papoušek, in this volume). It may even be the case that parenting activities that are culture–specific are intuitive by the time individuals reach parenting age. Our current research concerns itself with unravelling aspects of maternal beliefs, values, and motives particular to each culture as well as those that may be universal across cultures, for it may be the case that these factors mediate between culture and behavior. In follow–up studies, we are interviewing mothers about their goals for their infants, their sense of responsibility and their beliefs about their own role in helping their infants reach those goals, as well as about their understanding of the meaningfulness and role of parenting activities in development. The central tasks that face future comparative multicultural research will be to document individual behavioral differences and mutual influences in infants and their parents, to examine how and why parents in different societies set different social agenda, and to explicate precisely the processes by which parents in different societies succeed at their respective socialization goals. Given both the similarities and, especially, the provocative differences observed among mothers in these three settings, it seems promising also to trace the differential developmental course and predictive validity of differences in parenting that appear already to have emerged early in the first year of life. We are presently doing so in the realms of child cognitive and communicative competencies, as well as social and emotional adjustment.

ACKNOWLEDGMENTS

M.H.B. was supported by research grants (HD20559 and HD20807) and by a Research Career Development Award (HD00521) from the National Institute of Child Health and Human Development and by a Guggenheim Foundation Fellowship. C.T.–L. was supported by an IRTA Fellowship to the National Institute of Child Health and Human Development. We thank the Laboratoire de Psychologie du Développement et de l'Éducation de l'Enfant of the Sorbonne and the Faculty of Education of the University of Tokyo for gracious hospitality in providing bases for data collection, and H. Azuma, H. Bornstein, P. Ludemann, M. Ogino, K. Painter, M.–G. Pêcheux, C. Rahn, J. Ruel, J. Suwalsky, S. Toda, D. Vardi, and B. Wright for assistance. Certain formulations in this work appear in Bornstein et al. (in preparation).

REFERENCES

Azuma, H. Why study child development in Japan? In H. Stevenson, H. Azuma, & K. Hakuta (Eds.), *Child development and education in Japan* (pp. 3–12). New York: W. H. Freeman, 1986.

Beckwith, L., & Cohen, S. E. Maternal responsiveness with preterm infants and competency at age twelve years. In M. H. Bornstein (Ed.), *Maternal responsiveness: Characteristics and consequences* (pp. 75–87). San Francisco: Jossey–Bass, 1989.

Bee, H. L., Barnard, K. E., Eyres, S. J., Gray, C. A., Hammond, M. A., Spietz, A. L., Snyder, C., & Clark, B. Prediction of IQ and language skill from perinatal status, child performance, family characteristics, and mother–infant interaction. *Child Development*, 1982, *53*, 1134–1156.

Befu, H. Social and cultural background for child development in Japan and the United States. In H. W. Stevenson, H. Azuma, & K. Hakuta (Eds.), *Child development and education in Japan* (pp. 13–27). San Francisco: W. H. Freeman, 1986.

Bell, R. Q., & Harper, L. *Child effects on adults*. Hillsdale, NJ: Lawrence Erlbaum Associates, 1977.

Belsky, J., Gilstrap, B., & Rovine, M. The Pennsylvania infant and family development project, I: Stability and change in mother–infant and father–infant interaction in a family setting at one, three, and nine months. *Child Development*, 1984, *55*, 692–705.

Berry, J. W. The sociogenesis of social sciences: An analysis of the cultural relativity of social psychology. In B. Bain (Ed.), *The sociogenesis of language and human conduct* (pp. 449–454). New York: Plenum, 1983.

Bertrand, M. (Ed.). *Popular traditions and learned culture in France, 17th–20th centuries*. Stanford, CA: Stanford University Press, 1986.

Bornstein, M. H. Cross–cultural developmental psychology. In M. H. Bornstein (Ed.), *Comparative methods in psychology* (pp. 231–281). Hillsdale, NJ: Lawrence Erlbaum Associates, 1980.

Bornstein, M. H. How infant and mother jointly contribute to developing cognitive competence in the child. *Proceedings of the National Academy of Sciences*, 1985, *82*, 7470–7473.

Bornstein, M. H. Between caretakers and their young: Two modes of interaction and their consequences for cognitive growth. In M. H. Bornstein & J. S. Bruner (Eds.), *Interaction in human development* (pp. 197–214). Hillsdale, NJ: Lawrence Erlbaum Associates, 1989a.

Bornstein, M. H. Cross–cultural developmental comparisons: The case of Japanese—American infant and mother activities and interactions. What we know, what we need to know, and why we need to know. *Developmental Review*, 1989b, *9*, 171–204.

Bornstein, M. H., Azuma, H., Tamis–LeMonda, C. S., & Ogino, M. Mother and infant activity and interaction in Japan and in the United States: I. A comparative macroanalysis of naturalistic exchanges. *International Journal of Behavioral Development*, 1990a, *13*, 267–287.

Bornstein, M. H., Miyake, K., & Tamis-LeMonda, C.S. A cross-national study of mother and infant activities and interactions: Some preliminary comparisons between Japan and the United States. *Annual Report of the Research and Clinical Center for Child Development* (1-12). University of Hokkaido, Sapporo, Japan, 1985–1986.

Bornstein, M. H., & Tamis–LeMonda, C. S. Activities and interactions of mothers and their firstborn infants in the first six months of life: Covariation, stability, continuity, correspondence, and prediction. *Child Development*, 1990, *61*, 1206–1217.

Bornstein, M. H., Tamis–LeMonda, C. S., Pêcheux, M.–G., & Rahn, C. Mother and infant activity and interaction in France and in the United States: A comparative study. *International Journal of Behavioral Development*, 1991, in press.

Bornstein, M. H., Toda, S., Azuma, H., Tamis–LeMonda, C. S., & Ogino, M. Mother and infant activity and interaction in Japan and the United States: II. A comparative microanalysis of naturalistic exchanges focused on the organization of infant attention. *International Journal of Behavioral Development*, 1990b, *13*, 289–308.

Bowlby, J. *Attachment and loss* (Vol. 1). New York: Basic Books, 1969.

Bradley, R. H. HOME measurement of maternal responsiveness. In M. H. Bornstein (Ed.), *Maternal responsiveness: Characteristics and consequences* (pp. 63–74). San Francisco: Jossey Bass, 1989.

Bradley, R. H., Caldwell, B. M., & Rock, S. L. Home environment and school performance: A ten–year follow–up and examination of three models of environmental action. *Child Development*, 1988, *59*, 852–867.

Brislin, R. W. Cross–cultural research in psychology. *Annual Review of Psychology*, 1983, *34*, 363–400.

Brody, S. *Patterns of mothering: Maternal influence during infancy.* New York: International Universities Press, 1956.

Bruner, J. *Culture and human development: A new look.* Invited address to the Annual Meeting of the Society for Research in Child Development, Kansas City, Missouri, 1989.

Campbell, D. T. Distinguishing differences of perception from failures of communication in cross–cultural studies. In F. S. C. Northrop & H. H. Livingston (Eds.), *Cross–cultural understanding: Epistemology in anthropology* (pp. 308–336). New York: Harper and Row, 1964.

Carew, J. V. Experience and the development of intelligence in young children at home and in day care. *Monographs of the Society for Research in Child Development*, 1980, *45* (67, Serial No. 187).

Caudill, W. A. The influence of social structure and culture on human behavior in modern Japan. *Journal of Nervous and Mental Disease*, 1973, *157*, 240–257.

Caudill, W., & Weinstein, H. Maternal care and infant behavior in Japan and America. *Psychiatry*, 1969, *32*, 12–43.

Chen, S.–J., & Miyake, K. Japanese studies of infant development. In H. Stevenson, H. Azuma, & K. Hakuta (Eds.), *Child development and education in Japan* (pp. 135–146). New York: W. H. Freeman, 1986.

Clancy, P. The acquisition of communicative style in Japanese. B. Schieffelin & E. Ochs (Eds.), *Language socialization across cultures* (pp. 213–250). Cambridge: Cambridge University Press, 1986.

Clarke, E. V. The acquisition of Romance, with special reference to French. In D. I. Slobin (Ed.), *The crosslinguistic study of language acquisition: The data* (Vol. 1, pp. 686–782). Hillsdale, NJ: Lawrence Erlbaum Associates, 1985.

Cohen, J., & Cohen, P. *Applied multiple regression/correlation analysis for the behavioral sciences.* Hillsdale, NJ: Lawrence Erlbaum Associates, 1983.

Cohn, J. F., & Tronick, E. Z. Mother–infant face–to–face interaction: The sequence of dyadic states at 3, 6 and 9 months. *Developmental Psychology*, 1987, *23*, 68–77.

Darnton, R. *The great cat massacre.* New York: Vintage, 1984.

Dion, F., & Pêcheux, M.–G. *Parental beliefs about cognitive development and their role in this development.* Unpublished manuscript, 1989.

D'Odorico, L., & Franco, F. The determinants of baby talk: Relationship to context. *Journal of Child Language*, 1985, *12*, 567–586.

Doi, T. [*The anatomy of dependence*] (J. Bester, trans.). Tokyo: Kodansha International, 1973.

Dolto, F. French and American children as seen by a French child analyst. In M. Mead & M. Wolfenstein (Eds.), *Childhood in contemporary cultures* (pp. 408–423). Chicago: University of Chicago Press, 1955.

Dolto, F. *Lorsque l'enfant paraît.* Paris: Seuil, 1979.

Dunn, J. D., & Richards, M. P. M. Observations on the developing relationship between mother and baby in the neonatal period. In H. R. Schaffer (Ed.), *Studies in mother–infant interaction* (pp. 427–455). New York: Academic Press, 1977.

Emde, R. N., Gaensbauer, T. J., & Harmon, R. J. Emotional expression in infancy: A biobehavioral study. *Psychological Issues X* (Monograph 37). New York: International Universities Press, 1976.

Fischer, K. W. A theory of cognitive development: The control and construction of hierarchies of skills. *Psychological Review*, 1980, *87*, 477–531.

Fleiss, J. L. Estimating the magnitude of experimental effects. *Psychological Bulletin*, 1969, *72*, 273–276.

Fogel, A., Toda, S., & Kawai, M. Mother–infant face–to–face interaction in Japan and the United States: A laboratory comparison using 3–month–old infants. *Developmental Psychology*, 1988, *24*, 398–406.

Goldberg, S., Lojkasek, M., Gartner, G., & Corter, C. Early maternal responsiveness and social development in low–birthweight preterm infants. In M. H. Bornstein (Ed.), *Maternal responsiveness: Characteristics and consequences* (pp. 89–103). San Francisco: Jossey–Bass, 1989.

Gottfried, A. W. (Ed.). *Home environment and early cognitive development.* New York: Academic Press, 1984.

Gramont, S. E. *French, portrait of a people*. New York: Putnam, 1969.

Hess, R. D., Azuma, H., Kashiwagi, K., Dickson, W. P., Nagano, S., Holloway,S., Miyake, K., Price, G., Hatano, G., & McDevitt, T. Family influences on school readiness and achievement in Japan and the United States: An overview of a longitudinal study. In H. W. Stevenson, H. Azuma, & H. Hakuta (Eds.), *Child development and education in Japan* (pp. 147-166). New York: W. H. Freeman, 1986.

Hoffmann, S. *In search of France*. Cambridge, MA: Harvard University Press, 1963.

Hofstede, G. *Culture's consequences*. Beverly Hills, CA: Sage, 1980.

Jahoda, G. Cross–cultural comparisons. In M. H. Bornstein (Ed.), *Comparative methods in psychology* (pp. 105–148). Hillsdale, NJ: Lawrence Erlbaum Associates, 1980.

Kaplan, H., & Dove, H. Infant development among the Ache of Eastern Paraguay. *Developmental Psychology*, 1987, *23*, 190–198.

Kaye, K., & Fogel, A. The temporal structure of face–to–face communication between mothers and infants. *Developmental Psychology*, 1980, *16*, 454–464.

Kennedy, S., Scheirer, J., & Rogers, A. The price of success: Our monocultural science. *American Psychologist*, 1984, *39*, 996–997.

Keppel, G. *Design and analysis: A researcher's handbook*.Englewood Cliffs, NJ: Prentice–Hall, 1982.

Kessen, W. The child and other cultural inventions. In F. S. Kessel & A. W. Siegel (Eds.), *The child and other cultural inventions* (pp. 16–39). New York: Praeger, 1983.

Kohn, M. L. Cross–national research as an analytic strategy. *American Sociological Review*, 1987, *52*, 713–731.

Kojima, H. Child rearing concepts as a belief-value system of the society and the individual. In H. W. Stevenson, H. Azuma, & K. Hakuta (Eds.), *Child development and education in Japan* (pp. 39-54). New York: W. H. Freeman, 1986.

Konner, M. J. Infancy among the Kalahari Desert San. In P. H. Leiderman, S. R. Tulkin, & A. Rosenfeld (Eds.), *Culture and infancy: Variations in the human experience* (pp. 287–328). New York: Academic, 1977.

Lamb, M. E., & Bornstein, M. H. *Development in infancy: An introduction*. New York: Random House, 1987.

Lerner, R. M. Developmental contextualism and the life–span view of person–context interaction. In M. H. Bornstein & J. S. Bruner (Eds.), *Interaction in human development* (pp. 217–239). Hillsdale, NJ: Lawrence Erlbaum Associates, 1989.

Lewis, M., & Ban P. Variance and invariance in the mother–infant interaction: A cross–cultural study. In P. H. Leiderman, S. R. Tulkin, & A. Rosenfeld (Eds.), *Culture and infancy: Variations in the human experience* (pp. 329–356). New York: Academic, 1977.

Lewis, M., & Rosenblum, L. *The effect of the infant on its caregiver*. New York: Wiley, 1974.

MacPhee,, D., Ramey, C.T., & Yeates, K.O. Home environment and early cognitive development: Implications for intervention. In A.W. Gottfried (Ed.), *Home environment and early cognitive development* (pp. 343-370). Orlando, FL: Academic Press, 1984.

Maranda, P. *French kinship structure in history*. London: Mouton, 1974.

Métraux, R., & Mead, M. (Eds.), *Themes in French culture: A preface to a study of French community*. Stanford, CA: Stanford University Press, 1954.

Miyake, K., Chen, S.-j., & Campos, J. J. Infant temperament, mother's mode of interaction, and attachment in Japan: An interim report. In I. Bretherton & E. Waters (Eds.), *Growing points of attachment theory and research. Monographs of the Society for Research in Child Development, 50* (Serial No. 209). Chicago: University of Chicago Press, 1985.

Moghaddam, F. M. Psychology in three worlds. *American Psychologist*, 1987, *42*, 912–920.

Morsbach, H. Major psychological factors influencing Japanese interpersonal relations. In N. Warren (Ed.), *Studies in cross–cultural psychology* (Vol. 2, pp. 317–342). London: Academic Press, 1980.

Nugent, J. K., Lester, B., & Brazelton, T. B. (Eds.). *The cultural context of infancy* (Vol. 1). Norwood, NJ: Ablex, 1989.

Olson, S. L., Bates, J. E., & Bayles, K. (1984). Mother–infant interaction and the development of individual differences in children's cognitive competence. *Developmental Psychology, 20*, 166–179.

Otaki, M., Durrett, M. E., Richards, P., Nyquist, L., & Pennebaker, J. W. Maternal and infant behavior in Japan and America: A partial replication. *Journal of Cross–Cultural Psychology*, 1986, *17*, 251–268.

Papoušek, M., Papoušek, H., & Bornstein, M. H. The naturalistic vocal environment of young infants: On the significance of homogeneity and variability in parental speech. In T. M. Field & N. Fox (Eds.), *Social perception in infants* (pp. 269–297). Norwood, NJ: Ablex, 1985.

Piaget, J. [Need and significance of cross–cultural studies in genetic psychology] (C. Dasen, trans.). In J.W. Berry & P. R. Dasen (Eds.), *Culture and cognition*. London: Methuen, 1974. (Originally published, 1966.)

Rohner, R. P. *They love me, they love me not*. New Haven, CT: HRAF Press, 1975.

Rothbaum, F. Patterns of maternal acceptance. *Genetic, Social, and General Psychology Monographs*, 1986, *112*, 435–458.

Russell, R. Psychology in its world context. *American Psychologist*, 1984, *39*, 1017–1025.

Sameroff, A. Developmental systems: Contexts and evolution. In W. Kessen (Ed.), *Handbook of child psychology: History, theory, and methods* (Vol. 1, pp. 237–294). New York: Wiley, 1983.

Seitz, V. (1988). Methodology. In M. H. Bornstein & M. E. Lamb (Eds.), *Developmental psychology: An advanced textbook* (pp. 37–79). Hillsdale, NJ: Lawrence Erlbaum Associates, 1988.

Sengoku, T., Davitz, L., & Davitz, J. *Mother-infant interaction: A cross-cultural study of behavior in Japan and the United States*. Unpublished manuscript, Japan Youth Research Institute, 1982.

Sexton, V. S., & Misiak, H. American psychologists and psychology abroad. *American Psychologist*, 1984, *39*, 1026–1031.

Shand, N., & Kosawa, Y. Japanese and American behavior types at three months: Infants and infant-mother dyads. *Infant Behavior and Development*, 1985a, *8*, 225-240.

Shand, N., & Kosawa, Y. Culture transmission: Caudill's model and alternative hypotheses. *American Anthropologist*, 1985b, *87*, 862-871.

Sigman, M., Neumann, C., Carter, E., Cattle, D. J., D'Souza, S., & Bwibo, N. Home interactions and the development of Embu toddlers in Kenya. *Child Development*, 1988, *59*, 1251–1261.

Stern, D. *The interpersonal world of the infant*. New York: Basic Books, 1985.

Stevenson, M., Ver Hoeve, J., Roach, M., & Leavitt, L. The beginning of conversation: Early patterns of mother–infant vocal responsiveness. *Infant Behavior and Development*, 1986, *9*, 423–440.

Suen, H. K., & Ary, D. *Analyzing quantitative behavioral observation data*. Hillsdale, NJ: Lawrence Erlbaum Associates, 1989.

Super, C. M. Behavioral development in infancy. In R. H. Munroe, R. L., Munroe, & B. B. Whiting (Eds.), *Handbook of cross–cultural human development* (pp. 181–270). New York: Garland STPM Press, 1981.

Tamis–LeMonda, C. S., & Bornstein, M. H. Habituation and maternal encouragement of attention in infancy as predictors of toddler language, play, and representational competence. *Child Development*, 1989, *60*, 738–751.

Triandis, H. C. (Ed.). *Handbook of cross–cultural psychology*. Boston: Allyn & Bacon, 1980.

Triandis, H. C. The self and social behavior in differing cultural contexts. *Psychological Review*, 1989, *96*, 506–520.

Tulkin, S. R. Dimensions of multicultural research in infancy and early childhood. In P. H. Leiderman, S. R. Tulkin, & A. Rosenfeld (Eds.), *Culture and infancy: Variations in the human experience* (pp. 567–586). New York: Academic, 1977.

Ueda, R. A comparison of home environment between Japanese and American children through the HSQ (the Home Screening Questionnaire). *The Japanese Journal of Health and Human Ecology*, 1985, *21*, 52–61.

Vibbert, M., & Bornstein, M. H. Specific associations between domains of mother–child interaction and toddler referential language and pretense play. *Infant Behavior and Development*, 1989, *12*, 163–184.

Wachs, T. D., & Gruen, G. E. *Early experience and human development*. New York: Plenum, 1982.

Weisz, J. R., Rothbaum, F. M., & Blackburn, T. C. Standing out and standing in: The psychology of control in America and Japan. *American Psychologist*, 1984, *39*, 955-969.

Whiting, J. W. Environmental constraints on infant care practices. In R. H. Munroe, R. L. Munroe, & B. N. Whiting (Eds.), *Handbook of cross–cultural human development* (pp. 155–179). New York: Garland STPM Press, 1981.

Wolfenstein, M. French parents take their children to the park. In M. Mead & M. Wolfenstein (Eds.), *Childhood in contemporary cultures* (pp. 99–117). Chicago: University of Chicago Press, 1955.

Wolff, P. H. Discontinuous changes in human wakefulness around the end of the second month of life: A developmental perspective. In H. F. R. Prechtl (Ed.), *Continuity of neural functions from prenatal to postnatal life* (pp. 144–158). Philadelphia, PA: Lippincott, 1984.

Yarrow, L. J., Rubenstein, J., & Pedersen, F. *Infant and environment: Early cognitive and motivational development.* New York: Halstead, 1975.

Parenting and Child Development in The Efe Foragers and Lese Farmers of Zaïre

5

Gilda A. Morelli
Boston College
Edward Z. Tronick
Children's Hospital—Boston

INTRODUCTION

In previous work, we have described an extensive pattern of multiple caretaking for a group of foragers, the Efe, living in the Ituri Forest of Zaïre (Tronick, Morelli, & Winn, 1987). This pattern of caretaking begins at birth with community members typically holding and nursing the infant for several hours before returning him or her to the mother (Morelli, Winn, & Tronick, 1987). This level of non–maternal involvement continues for the infant's first six months of life, and provides the majority of daytime caretaking the infant receives. The Efe multiple caregiving pattern calls into question existing models of child care. These models, referred to as the *continuous care and contact* models (CCC; Tronick, Morelli, & Winn, 1987), are based on Western industrialized and technologically simple agricultural societies, and argue that the mother is the infant's primary caretaker during the first year of life. Cognizant of the inconsistency between CCC models and Efe parenting, we developed a position on the nature of caretaking informed by cultural psychology and evolutionary biology (Tronick, Winn, & Morelli, 1985).

The major tenet of our position is that childrearing practices, which we refer to as parental investment strategies[1], are shaped by proximal (e.g., ontogenetic) and distal factors (e.g., evolutionary history) operating on people within a community. Proximal factors include the sociocultural system and the individual's social and psychological history within the system, current social interactions, and ecological factors. Distal factors include the individual's biological heritage. The parental investment strategy that caregivers employ represents their understanding (no conscious intent implied) of how to raise their children to engage in the behaviors,

---

[1] Caregiving practices are referred to by us as parental investment strategies. We recognize that parental investment strategies have traditionally included all mechanisms by which parents attempt to insure the survival of their offspring, and consequently the perpetuation of their genes in future generations.

and to have the psychological representations necessary to become a member of the community.

According to our view, mental processes (e.g., psychological representation of attachment figures) and emotional and cognitive functioning develop in the context of the child's active participation in daily social engagements with other culturally more sophisticated members of the community (see, too, the Rogoff chapter, in this volume). These engagements are shaped by fitness maximizing (i.e., evolutionary) processes and by proximal factors such as value and belief systems, and economic work routines.

Parental investment strategies, thus, are shaped by a matrix of factors. They function to maximize the infant's survival and the development of culturally appropriate ways of thinking, feeling, and behaving; both of these ultimately serve to enhance the infant's success as an adult member of the community.

To illustrate our perspective, consider the Efe and their system of care. The Efe are a short–statured people living in the Ituri rainforest of northeastern Zaïre. Efe women give birth to infants whose average weight is 2.4 kg. and average length 43.4 cm (Winn, Morelli, & Tronick, 1989). U.S.–born infants born at this weight/length would be considered at risk for medical complications. This also may be the case with Efe neonates, however, we believe that the caregiving strategy adopted by the Efe mitigates against threats to infant survival and, at the same time, communicates cultural messages to the infant and to community members alike.

Efe childrearing practices must deal with immediate hazards to survival, such as dehydration, and long–term hazards to social functioning, such as anti–social behaviors. How is this accomplished? Nursing the infant by individuals in addition to the mother may increase the infant's fluid balance, reducing the small infant's vulnerability to dehydration. Multiple nursing may also foster the development of social capacities for relating to many different individuals, and the development of multiple secure bases for attachment. The competencies emerging from these social experiences serve the infant well throughout his or her life time. Infants and toddlers are often left in the camp in the care of others while their mothers forage for forest foods (Morelli, 1987), a practice unlike that observed among foraging communities such as the !Kung (Draper, 1976). Further, mortality is high among the Efe, leaving many infants motherless or parentless. Thus, the ability to form trusting relationships with a variety of individuals is likely to be important for the Efe infant. Further, Efe adults and children alike are almost always in social and often physical contact with one another, and are largely dependent on each other for their survival. The ability to get along with community members appears to be an essential part of Efe living, and their parental investment strategy fosters this ability.

CULTURAL COMMUNITY, SOCIAL PARTNERS, AND DEVELOPMENT

The description of Efe lifestyle suggests one of the more important ways in which people of a community create the contexts that foster the development of culturally appropriate thought and behavior: guiding infants' and young children's active participation in activities with community members (Rogoff, 1990; Whiting &

Edwards, 1988). The cultural arrangement of infants' activities with community members is one mechanism for shaping the development of social and cognitive competencies. The Efe infant will form representations of his or her social world in a way unlike the infant whose life is differently arranged. A North American infant, for example, who is in almost constant contact with only one or a few individuals, and for whom other individuals are unfamiliar or occasionally contacted as novel "events", will most likely think and behave differently than an Efe infant. Participation in cultural routines shapes the way an individual thinks, and the way he or she behaves. Thus, the study of children in day–to–day activities with community members helps us understand the emergence of mental processes and behavior, and provides us with a way of examining the similarities and differences existing among children living in different cultural communities.

Our thinking about the importance of children's participation in cultural activities as a way to understand development owes much to the work of Whiting and her colleagues (see Whiting & Edwards, 1988), to Rogoff (1990), and other cultural psychologists (for example, Cole, 1985; Rogoff & Morelli, 1989; Wertsch, 1985), who have expanded on the sociohistorical perspective advanced by Vygotsky (Vygotsky, 1978; Wertsch, 1985). The essence of their perspective is that children's construction of reality emerges from their participation in the day–to–day activities of the community. In the context of daily culturally important engagements and routines with more competent individuals, children's understanding about themselves develops, as do the social and cognitive skills needed to engage in culturally appropriate activities.

An important feature of cultural activity identified by Whiting and her colleagues is the social partners with whom children are involved. Whiting and Edwards (1988) argue that by interacting with different 'categories' of people (classified on the basis of gender, age, and kinship) children learn and practice certain patterns of behavior. Each category of companion shares certain behavioral qualities, and as a result models and teaches specific behaviors to, and elicits specific behaviors from children. For example, children given the responsibility of caring for infants are likely to practice nurturant behaviors because infants elicit nurturance from those with whom they interact. Mothers, by comparison, elicit dependent behaviors. The opportunity to be involved with different categories of people is instrumental in guiding development. The category of people with whom children are engaged is structured by the settings children frequent, which is influenced by sociocultural features.

The role siblings (and peers) play in shaping the social, emotional, and cognitive development of children is currently the focus of much research (see, for example, Zukow, 1989a). Watson–Gegeo and Gegeo (1989) argue that in the Kwara'ae, a Melanesian people of Malaita in the Solomon Islands, adult guidance of siblings in activity with children fosters children's understanding of classificatory kinship, seniority, and sibling cooperation. Further, the infant's physical and social mobility, and therefore knowledge of others, is increased when cared for by siblings who often range outside their village. Caregivers, however, are more than babysitters. They facilitate the development of infants' interactional and language skills, and in the context of being with infants and young children appropriate a variety of competencies themselves.

The sibling relationship also fosters social understanding in children. In the course of witnessing or participating in social conflict with siblings, British children's knowledge of social rules and responsibilities, intentions, and feelings develop (Dunn, 1989). Further, in the context of playing with siblings, children often engage in symbolic representation of the social world, an event that rarely takes place in playful interactions with adults.

The contribution of both siblings and mothers to young children's understanding of social events is noted by Zukow in her study of families living in urban and rural Central Mexico (Zukow, 1989b). Siblings and mothers guide young children's understanding of ongoing activities. But siblings differ from mothers in that they are more likely to proclaim their competence and, at the same time, their siblings' incompetence in the activity. Zukow argues that explicitly displaying one's competence has the effect of making known to the young child exactly what event is taking place and what is needed to be successful at it. Concludes Zukow (1989b, p. 98) "... knowing what you are doing incorrectly may be quite as informative as gradually getting it right."

Integrating the research reported with our perspective on parenting leads us to the following. First, children's participation in the routines of their community is shaped by proximal and distal factors, and is mediated by parental investment strategies. Second, mental processes, and ways of behaving and feeling, develop in the course of actively participating in sociocultural activity. Finally, the competencies children develop are shaped by their social partners who vary in the way they guide children in activity. The perspective outlined above moves us forward in our understanding of the child as a biological being living in a social world.

RESEARCH ON THE EFE FORAGERS AND LESE FARMERS

In this chapter we want to extend our earlier work on the Efe foragers in two ways. First, we want to examine in detail with whom Efe 12– to 15–month–olds participate in activity because of the role different social partners play in guiding children's understanding of their social world. The activities chosen for analysis are childcare and play. One–year–olds are the focus of study for several reasons. At this age most Efe children are able to move about their environment with little or no assistance from others, and are therefore able to involve themselves in various types of activities (Morelli, 1987). Further, this age is identified as an important time for the development of social representations, including children's representation of attachment figures. Thus, how children spend their time with different community members might shed light on the nature of their developing relationships.

As noted earlier, features of the sociocultural system play an important role in arranging children's day–to–day activities. And it is in the context of sociocultural activity that children appropriate cultural knowledge. Thus, a second goal of this paper is to examine the activities of 1–year–olds living in two cultural communities, foragers and farmers. By studying children of two communities we are in a better position to understand how differently their lives are arranged, and how through those arrangements the child's social and psychological world is constructed.

The specific questions examined in this chapter are how do Efe forager and Lese farmer 1–year–olds allocate their time, and how much time (measured in intervals per hour) do they spend in care and play with their mothers and fathers, and with adult females, adult males, and juveniles/children.

Given our view that the child's mental processes emerge out of shared activity with community members, we have developed an analytic approach that we think provides a more accurate measure of the child's social experience[2] than approaches more commonly used. Typically, questions on with whom the child spends his or her time are addressed by taking the proportion of total time (often measured in intervals per hour) the child is with mother, father, other adults, and juveniles/children. Such a measure might indicate that the infant is with mother 30% of the intervals observed, father 20%, other adults 25%, and so on. But obviously these categories are not equivalent from either an analytic or psychological perspective. There is only one mother and father, but there are many adults, juveniles, and children. It is possible, for example, for a child to spend less time with mother compared to other women, but nonetheless to spend more time with mother compared to an individual woman. This raises the question of how the infant experiences his or her mother relative to another and others. The infant may perceive his or her mother as a distinct individual compared to another individual woman, even though the infant spends more time with other women. Thus, traditional measures of time with community members compares singular (e.g., mother) with multiple classes of social partners (e.g., women), and provides us with one way to make sense of the child's experience of community members. But traditional measures may not capture critical aspects of this experience.

In an attempt to deal with problems arising from traditional analytic approaches, we developed a measure that compares the time (measured in intervals per hour, and referred to as a rate score) the infant spends with mother and father, and the time he or she spends with the average woman (man, child). The *average person score* is simply generated by computing the total time the infant is with some category of person (e.g., men or women) and dividing it by the number of *different* individuals belonging to that social category who are involved with the child. By comparing the infant's experience of mother and father with their experience of the average man, woman, and juvenile/child we are able to evaluate the relative distinctness of the child's experience of these individuals.

The amount of time a child spends with mother, father, other adult men and women, and juveniles/children (*total person score*) is also calculated because the measure provides another way of conceptualizing the child's experience of others. We believe that while the two measures reflect meaningful differences for the child,

---

[2] Infants' experience of different categories of people is measured only by the amount of time (i.e., the number of 1–minute intervals per hour) infants spend in care and play with them.

when considered together they provide more inclusive information about the nature of children's partnership with different community members.

THE FORAGER AND FARMER COMMUNITY

The Efe foragers and Lese farmers are sympatric communities living in the Ituri forest of northeastern Zaïre, and are involved in a complex exchange relationship that has been going on for generations. They play an important role in the lives of one another, and inhabit and exploit a similar ecosystem (Bailey & Devore, 1989; Wilkie, 1988).

Efe Foragers

The Efe are a short–statured people who acquire forest foods by gathering and by hunting with bows and mainly metal–tipped arrows. Cultivated foods are also an important part of the Efe diet, and are obtained from the Lese in exchange for forest foods and/or services.

The majority of Efe live in transient camps established in small, forested areas cleared of vegetation. In this study, camp membership ranged from 7 to 21 people, and was made up of one or several extended families. Descent and resident patterns are patrilineal and virilocal. Each family consists of brothers and their wives, children, unmarried sisters, and parents. The Efe build leaf huts which are primarily used for sleeping, food storage, and protection from inclement weather. The huts are typically arranged around the camp's perimeter creating a large, open communal space. Since most day–to–day in–camp activities take place outside, within this communal space, they are in clear view of other camp members.

Camp members do not regularly synchronize their day–to–day activities. During the mid–morning and early afternoon hours when most out–of–camp activities take place, one or several individuals are likely to be found in the camp resting, taking care of children, preparing food, or socializing. The almost continual presence of people in the camp provides mothers with an opportunity to leave their children in the camp while, for example, foraging for food; an opportunity often taken advantage of by them.

Cultural guidelines concerning the social and physical arrangement of community members make it easy for men and women to work together, usually side–by–side, in clear view of children. Cultural guidelines also make it more acceptable for fathers to eat with their families, even though each family is never far away from any other family. Indeed, it is quite common for families to carry on conversations with one another while sitting in front of their respective huts. Many camp activities are shared by men and women, although some activities are considered more appropriate for members of one gender. It is not unusual, for example, to see a man involved in some economic household routine such as preparing food for consumption. However, women rarely accompany men on hunts, and when they do accompany them, they do not kill forest game with bows and arrows.

Since the amount of time young forager children spend in the camp is considerable, ranging from 80 to 95% of daytime hours (Morelli, 1987), they are developing in a community where men, women, boys, and girls are physically and visually available to them. Young children also have the opportunity to be involved in varied ongoing camp activities, and to practice a variety of skills.

Lese Farmers

The Lese are slash–and–burn horticulturalists whose work cycle is entrained to seasonally appropriate tasks such as clearing and burning fields, planting, weeding, and harvesting. The Lese rely on the Efe for labor in their fields.

All Lese farmers live in roadside villages that rarely change location. Each village generally contains several families, but each family's living quarters are often spatially and sometimes visually isolated from one another. In this study, membership ranged from 8 to 36 people. Descent is patrilineal, and residency virilocal, with some exceptions. Farmer houses are arranged so that small communal areas are created for members of only one or a few households. A village is more accurately described as a collection of homesteads, that vary in social composition and accessibility to others living in the village.

Village houses are primarily used for sleeping, storage, and protection from inclement weather. Most of the activities of women and their children such as cooking, eating, and socializing, take place near the house and the cooking area, called the *mafika,* both of which are often set back from the only road in the area. Men's activities, by comparison, take place in a semi–enclosed sitting area, called the *baraza,* where it is customary for them to wash, eat, socialize, and relax. The men's *baraza* is often located near the road, and separate from the house and *mafika.* As a result, in–village activities of farmer men and women are often physically separated, a separation that is promoted by cultural guidelines concerning the social and physical arrangement of men and women in the village.

Women are generally found in their fields or *shamba* when not in the village, as fieldwork is essentially a woman's responsibility. During active agricultural periods they spend most of their day in the *shamba,* leaving only men and elderly people in the village. Children accompany their mothers to the fields. Fieldwork is not a communal activity, except during short periods around planting and harvesting. Women are not able to easily socialize with one another when involved in fieldwork because of the distance separating fields. As a result, women are often isolated from each other's company, and from the company of men, when laboring in the field.

Men work hard 3 months of the year when land is cleared for planting. During this 3–month period, women may visit their relatives or spend time in the village making or repairing sleeping mats, baskets, and the like. Men work very little for the remaining portion of the year, and only occasionally help their wives with fieldwork. More often than not, men are found relaxing in their *baraza,* or visiting friends in a nearby village.

The economic responsibilities of men and women, their scheduling of work, and the cultural guidelines concerning their physical and social arrangement when in the village influence the amount of time spent in each other's company. Since Lese farmer children spend about 2/3 of the day in the village, and about 1/3 in the *shamba*, time in the company of men including their fathers, and the activities in which they engage when with men, is limited in scope.

THE STUDY

Children Observed

Data on the social activities of 12– to 15–month–olds were collected over a 2–year period. Eight forager and eight farmer children, four boys and girls in each community, were observed.

Behavioral Observations

Data collected. Children were observed using a focal subject sampling technique (Altmann, 1974). Each child was observed for six, 1–hour observation sessions evenly distributed throughout the daylight hours. Data were recorded continuously using prepared data sheets. All occurrences of a behavior were coded, and the sequence in which behaviors occurred was preserved. Time was marked at 1–minute intervals.

Behaviors recorded. Two specific activities were selected for detailed analysis: caregiving and social play. Caregiving includes dressing, washing, or feeding the infant, and supporting the infant in his or her attempt to stand or walk. Caregiving does not include nursing which is done almost exclusively by the mother until the infant's first birthday. Social play includes activities that are recreational in scope, usually engaged in for pleasure, joy, or amusement. Included in this category are singing, use of musical instruments, games, object play, and pretend play. A third measure, social contact, was created to examine the amount of time children are engaged with camp members. Social contact combines caregiving, comforting, social play, and watching people in routine economic or social activity. These behaviors were selected from amongst a larger list of coded behaviors, and have been shown to be critical in the formation of early social and attachment relationships, and in the development of culturally appropriate behavior.

Social partners. Children's partners are divided into five classes of individuals: mother, father, adult women (excluding mother), adult men (excluding father), and juveniles/children (referred to as children for ease of writing). Social partners are examined for the behaviors caregiving and play, but not for the composite measure social contact.

Behavioral Data Management and Analysis

Mean hourly *behavioral* rate scores (i.e., care, play, social contact) were created for each child by calculating the number of intervals a behavior occurred, and dividing the summed score by the number of hours the child was observed.

Mean hourly *social partner* rate scores were created for each child by calculating the number of intervals in which mother, father, adult women, adult men, girls and boys, were coded as partners in the different activities. The summed score was divided by the number of hours the child was observed. Using this procedure the *average* and *total* person scores were determined.

Our primary interest is in understanding how features of the sociocultural system shape children's involvement with community members, and how, through their involvement, they appropriate cultural knowledge. Thus, our strategy is to describe forager children's involvement with different categories of people, and farmer children's involvement with different categories of people using paired *t*-tests. Statistical significance is reported at $p \leq .05$.

RESULTS OF BEHAVIORAL STUDY

Allocation of Time in Activity

Figure 5.1 presents the amount of time 1–year–old forager children are engaged in childcare, play, and social contact. Young forager children spend, on average,

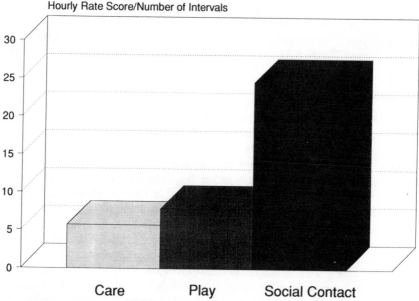

Figure 5.1. Average number of intervals forager 1–year–olds are in care, play, and social contact.

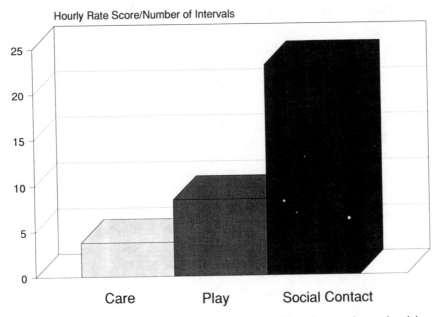

Hourly Rate Score/Number of Intervals

Figure 5.2. Average number of intervals farmer 1-year-olds are in care, play, and social contact.

approximately 10% of their time (6 of the 60 hourly intervals) in childcare, 13% in play (8 of 60 intervals), and 40% in social contact (24 of the 60 hourly intervals). Farmer 1-year-olds are similar in the amount of time they spend in each of the three activities (Figure 5.2).

Partners in Childcare

Efe community members' and mothers' involvement in childcare is illustrated in Figure 5.3. It is clear that community members share care-related activities with mothers, providing one-half of the total care received by 1-year-olds. But what is mothers' role relative to different individuals? Does the child's experience of mother as caregiver depend on whether her involvement is compared to all individuals of a social category or to the average person of a social category? Data presented in Figure 5.4 help us answer this question.

When the time mothers spend in care is compared to the time fathers, women, men and children spend (total person score, Figure 5.4, left hand side of graph) we immediately see that mothers provide significantly more care (see Table 5.1 for *p* values for care). Thus, forager 1-year-olds' experience of their mothers as caregivers is different from their experience of other social classes of individuals. By comparison, fathers, men, women, and children are experienced similarly by 1-year-olds in the care they provide.

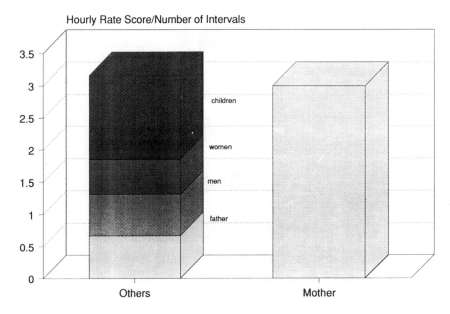

Figure 5.3. Forager 1–year–olds: Care by mother and other community members.

Mothers are also unlike the average man, woman, and child in the care they provide (average person score, Figure 5.4, right–hand side of graph). Mothers spend significantly more time in care than the average person—man, woman, or child. However, similar to the total person score, fathers, and the average man, woman, and child are alike in the time spent caring for 1–year–olds.

Childcare in the foraging community is clearly an activity in which mothers are seen as distinct by their children, and mothers are distinct relative to the average

TABLE 5.1

	\multicolumn{4}{c}{Forager Community: Partners in Care (p values)}				
	\multicolumn{4}{c}{Total Person Score}	\multicolumn{4}{c}{Average Person Score}
	Father	Men	Women	Children	Father	Man	Woman	Child
Mother	.02	.00	.01	.04	.02	.00	.01	.02
Father		.83	.91	.19		.77	.78	.44
Men			.74	.11			.89	.33
Women				.24				.26

	\multicolumn{4}{c}{Farmer Community: Partners in Care (p values)}				
	\multicolumn{4}{c}{Total Person Score}	\multicolumn{4}{c}{Average Person Score}
	Father	Men	Women	Children	Father	Man	Woman	Child
Mother	.01	.01	.02	.13	.01	.01	.02	.08
Father		.31	.70	.01		.31	.70	.03
Men			.15	.00			.15	.01
Women				.01				.04

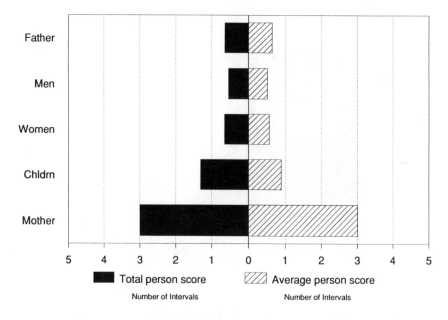

Figure 5.4. Forager 1–year–olds: Total and average person score for care.

caregiver. Yet, fathers, men, women and children are similar in the care they provide whether the total person or the average person score is chosen as the unit of analysis. This finding, in and of itself, suggests that the caregiving pattern embracing the 1–year–old may be different from that embracing the infant (Tronick, Morelli, & Winn, 1987).

Who are farmer children's partners in care? Are there similarities between forager and farmer 1–year–olds in who accepts caregiving responsibilities? Data on the farming community, presented in Figures 5.5 and 5.6, suggest that differences exist between children of the two communities in their experience of community members as caregivers.

Farming mothers are more involved in care than other community members, providing over 60% of the care 1–year–olds receive (Figure 5.5). Examination of mothers' role relative to other classes of individuals reveals, however, that farmer mothers and children are similar in the extent to which they are involved in care, and are significantly more involved in care than men, women, and fathers (total person score, Figure 5.6, left–hand side). Fathers, women and men, by comparison, do not differ significantly in the amount of care they provide.

Does this pattern of findings shift when the average person score is considered? No (average person score, Figure 5.6, right–hand side of graph)! Mothers are still observed as similar to the average child in the care they provide; and mothers and the average child still provide more care than fathers, and the average man and woman. Thus, childcare in the farming community is clearly an activity in which

Hourly Rate Score/Number of Intervals

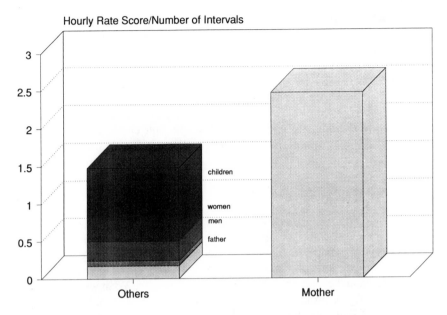

Figure 5.5. Farmer 1–year–olds: Care by mother and other community members.

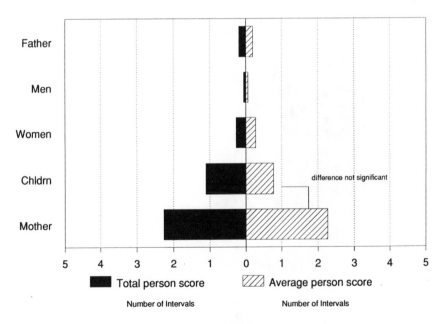

Figure 5.6. Farmer 1–year–olds: Total and average person score for care.

mothers AND children are like one another, but different from fathers, and the average woman and man. Yet, fathers, men, and women are similar as partners in care regardless of whether the total person or the average person score is considered.

Thus, mothers in the forager community occupy a special position with respect to care. They are experienced as distinct by their children, and are distinct from other community members. Foraging fathers, men, women, and children, on the other hand, are similar to one another. Mothers and children in the farming community, by comparison, share a special position because they are experienced similarly by 1–year–olds, and are distinct from fathers, men, and women.

Partners in Social Play

A somewhat different pattern of findings emerges when forager and farmer children's partners in social play are examined. Forager mothers play little with their 1–year–olds compared to community members, about 20% of the time (Figure 5.7). Furthermore, forager 1–year–olds' experience of their mothers as caregivers is not repeated in their experience of them as play partners. What we see instead is that children figure prominently in the social play of 1–year–olds (total person score, Figure 5.8, left–hand side). Children are more involved in play than women, men, fathers, and mothers (Table 5.2 presents *p* values for play). Keeping in mind

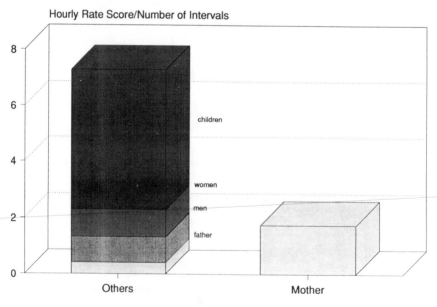

Figure 5.7. Forager 1–year–olds: Play by mother and other community members.

TABLE 5.2

Forager Community: Partners in Play (p values)

| | Total Person Score | | | | Average Person Score | | | |
	Father	Men	Women	Children	Father	Man	Woman	Child
Mother	.00	.05	.12	.02	.00	.03	.11	.35
Father		.19	.02	.00		.28	.03	.01
Men			.89	.00			.72	.03
Women				.01				.03

Farmer Community: Partners in Play (p values)

| | Total Person Score | | | | Average Person Score | | | |
	Father	Men	Women	Children	Father	Man	Woman	Child
Mother	.03	.01	.03	.00	.03	.01	.03	.08
Father		.24	.47	.00		.24	.47	.00
Men			.05	.00			.05	.00
Women				.00				.01

the prominent role of children as play partners, what are adult roles relative to one another?

Mothers and women are similar in their involvement, as are fathers and men. However, 1–year–olds are more likely to play with their mothers than with fathers and men; and are more likely to play with women than fathers. Women and men are experienced the same as play partners.

Does this pattern shift when we consider the average person in play with 1–year–olds? Yes, in a rather interesting way (average person score, Figure 5.8,

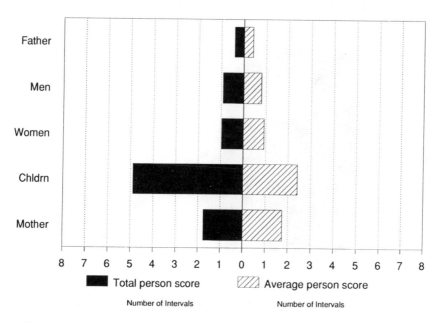

Figure 5.8. Forager 1–year–olds: Total and average person score for play.

right–hand side of graph). While children are experienced by 1–year–olds as playing more often with them than their mothers, the average child was as likely to play with 1–year–olds as mothers. Nevertheless, the average child still occupies a distinct role as play partner because the average child played more with 1–year–olds than the average woman and man, or fathers. Other than the changes noted in the mother's role relative to the child's role as play partner, no other changes were observed as a result of shifting our focus from a study of the total person score to the average person score.

As a social class, Efe children are experienced more often as play partners by 1–year–olds than mother, father, and all other classes of individuals; on an individual basis, however, the average child and mother are experienced equally often. The mother and the average child do not occupy distinctive roles insofar as duration of play is concerned. Nor does mother and the average woman.

Who are farmer 1–year–olds' partners in play, and how do their experiences compare to those of young forager 1–year–olds? Farmer mothers' involvement in play is overshadowed by other community members (Figure 5.9), an observation made for the foraging community. Children's role as play partners was as impressive in the farmers as it was in the foragers (total person score, Figure 5.10, left–hand side of graph). Farmer 1–year–olds were more likely to experience children in play than mothers, fathers, men, and women.

Does this pattern shift when the average person is considered? Yes, in a way similar to that observed for the forager community (average person score, Figure

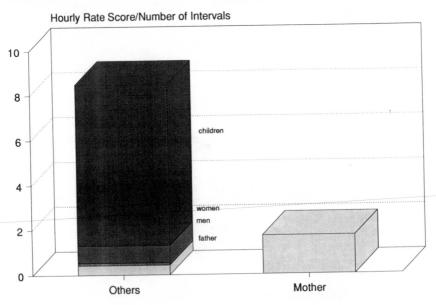

Figure 5.9. Farmer 1–year–olds: Play by mother and other community members.

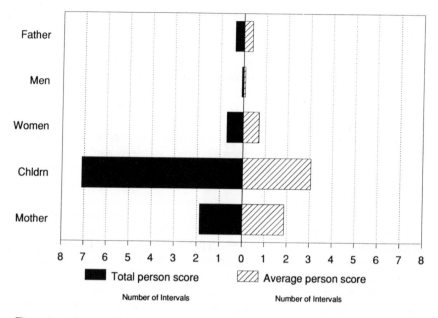

Figure 5.10. Farmer 1–year–olds: Total and average person score for play.

5.10, right–hand side of graph). Mothers were seen by 1–year–olds as playing less often with them than other children, but mothers played as often with their 1–year–olds as the average child. Other than the change noted, no other changes are observed when mothers, fathers, and the average man and woman are compared as play partners.

There are similarities in forager and farmer 1–year–olds' experience of community members as play partners, but there are important differences as well. Forager and farmer 1–year–olds are alike in that their mothers play less often with them than other children, but as often with them as the average child. They are not alike in that farmer 1–year–olds' mothers are more involved in play than fathers, men, AND women. Forager 1–year–olds' mothers, by comparison, are as involved in play as are women. This is true whether women are viewed as a class of individuals or as an average person. Thus, the special relationship existing between farmer 1–year–olds and their mothers and children in care is repeated to a large extent in play. The relationship between forager 1–year–olds and their mothers in care, on the other hand, is not repeated in play.

SUMMARY AND CONCLUSIONS

The skills and competencies appropriated by a child are shaped by the particular community members with whom he or she is involved, and by the nature of their involvement. Seemingly small differences among childrens' social activities may have rather substantial psychological and behavioral consequences because of their literally daily and yearly reiteration. It may, therefore, be more appropriate to view the structuring of children's activities with others as having a cumulative effect on development. Examining the sociocultural activities of the 1–year–old Efe forager and Lese farmer with this perspective in mind is particularly helpful in understanding relations among cultural community, social partners in activity, and appropriation of cultural knowledge.

The Efe forager mother clearly provides more care than any other class of individual, or any other average person. Forager community members—including fathers—in contrast, are indistinguishable from one another with respect to the amount of care they provide. This is true whether we compare classes of individuals, or average people.

What type of cultural knowledge is appropriated by the Efe 1–year–old with respect to the pattern of care received? One message is that caregiving is a responsibility shared by men, women, and children. One–year–olds are therefore learning about people's roles in the community, and learning that they can rely equally on community members (who provide about 50% of childcare) to care for them. Participating in care–related activities with different people may foster the emergence of close and trusting relationships with a variety of community members. This may be particularly important in a community where young children are often left in the camp while their mothers engage in subsistence–related, and other activities. Furthermore, 1–year–olds may be appropriating varied competencies in the context of being cared for by different classes of individuals each of whom brings to the interaction a particular set of behaviors and experiences.

The Efe foraging community is structured in a way that facilitates the pattern of care observed. Communities members, males and females, clearly perceive caregiving as a shared responsibility. This is certainly consistent with the loose adherence to a gender–based division of labor. Further, Efe community members are available to young children as caregivers because of their physical and social arrangement in camp. Although availability, per se, is not a sufficient condition for involvement with 1–year–olds.

In the farming community, care is a responsibility shared equally by mothers and children. Mothers provide as much care as children, and as much care as the average child. Given our knowledge of the Lese community, we believe that the children providing most of the care are siblings, in particular female siblings. Siblings often stay in and around the homestead, and often accompany their mothers to the field.

The importance of children as caregivers is noted for African agricultural societies (Weisner & Gallimore, 1977; Whiting & Edwards, 1988), and the Lese are no exception. Fieldwork is an arduous task; it involves laboring under the hot equatorial sun, often for many hours a day. One–year–olds cannot tolerate these extreme conditions for long periods of time, and it is the responsibility of children to care for infants in shaded areas while their mothers work. In our experience, women without child caregivers often work fewer hours each day in the fields, at a considerable expense to the family's food supply. The importance of child caregivers is so keenly felt that women with infants and young children often recruit their relatives' children from distant villages to help with caregiving.

Farmer men, women, and fathers are alike in the amount of time they care for 1-year-olds. In this way they are similar to members of the foraging community. However, closer inspection of Figures 5.4 and 5.6 suggests that this similarity is more apparent than real. The amount of care provided by the three classes of individuals in the farming community is negligible compared to that of the foraging community. So while farmer 1-year-olds may be learning that they can rely equally on men, women, and fathers for care, they also learn that they can do so only infrequently.

The farmer 1-year-olds' experience of community members as caregivers is understandable in terms of community life. Women tend to be around infants more than men, and therefore have more of an opportunity to help as caregivers. Further, caregiving is perceived more of a woman's responsibility in the Lese farming community. The data are consistent with these practices: women provide more care than men.

But why don't women provide as much care as mothers? Once again, reference to the Lese community helps us understand the arrangement of 1-year-olds' social partners. Women are kept busy because of the demands of farming life. When in the fields, women work most of the time, often without the assistance of other women. Socializing in the village is also an uncommon event, occurring primarily when a woman is on her way to the fields or marketplace. Thus, when farming women are in the presence of children they are often involved in activities that compete with childcare, especially the care of another woman's child.

Play was the second activity selected for analysis because of its recognized importance in social and cognitive development. As Dunn's (1989) research shows, the opportunity to practice social rules and regulations is related to one's partner in play, with mothers and siblings providing different opportunities. Children were clearly the primary play partners of Efe forager 1-year-olds, playing with them more often than any other class of individual—mothers and fathers included. Given the social composition of the average Efe camp, and our knowledge of the Efe community, it is reasonable to assume that play partners were of mixed ages and gender. Konner (1976) made similar observations of play in the !Kung bushman of Botswana. Interestingly, mothers and women played as frequently with Efe 1-year-olds, as did women and men. Once again, adults in the foraging community appear to share activities with children, and in this way are like one another. However, when the number of children are taken into consideration (i.e., average person score) we found that Efe mothers played as often with 1-year-olds as the average child. Mothers are like the average child in terms of time spent in play—there are just many children and only one mother available as play partners. One reason why a mother plays with her infant is that play at this age is often used as a way to quiet a fussy infant, or to shift the infant's attention away from nursing. If this is the case, then play with mother may have a different flavor to it than play with children, or for that matter than play with other community members. We are presently looking at the contexts framing play episodes between mothers and their infants. While 1–year–olds' experience of mothers and the average child is similar with respect to time in play, in matters of play no adult truly occupies a distinctive role—mother is like the average woman, and the average woman is like the average man who is like the father.

Children were also clearly the primary play partners of Lese farmer 1–year–olds. Thus, children are important as partners in play as well as in care. Second to children, mothers spent the most time in play, sharing this position with no other category of adult. This is in contrast to what was noted in the foraging community. Farmer maternal involvement in play may occur for reasons similar to that offered for forager mothers, and because fewer other adults are available to play with the infant.

The cross–cultural record shows quite convincingly that social composition is related to setting. Whether a person is available as a partner in activity with 1–year–olds depends, therefore, on the extent to which they share settings. Consider our data on people within 3 meters of 1–year–olds recorded 5 minutes before and 5 minutes following each hour of observation (Figure 5.11). For mothers and fathers, Figure 5.11 indicates the *average number of times* they were recorded in 3–meters; for women, men, and children it indicates the *average number of people* of a social class within 3–meters. There were significantly more forager men and women within 3 meters of 1–year–olds. The contrast between forager and farmer men is particularly striking, and helps us understand the differences in their role as

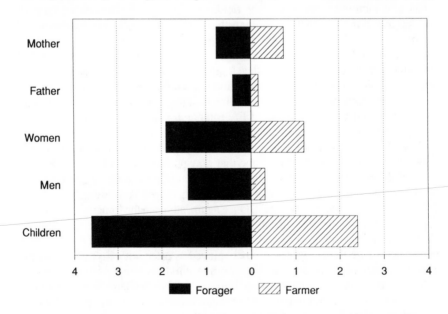

Figure 5.11. Community members within 3 meters of forager and farmer 1–year–olds (Mother, Father: Avg. # times present. Women, Men, Children: Avg # people present.)

partners in care and play relative to other community members. Yet, it is important to remember that although availability is necessary in determining partnership, it alone is not sufficient. Cultural rules guiding the physical and social arrangement of people, and perceived responsibilities are among the factors playing a role in determining how community members will be involved with the young child.

If asked to identify the important, recurrent themes emerging from the data we would emphasize the similarity among foraging community members in time spent in care and play. While mothers are more involved in care, there is little difference in the involvement of others. And while children are more involved in play, other social classes of individuals are more similar than different, regardless of whether the total or average person score is considered. A second important feature of Efe forager 1–year–olds' social experience is their involvement with men of the community. In many ways, men are like women. What impresses us about young forager children's experience is the relative lack of distinction among community members in their activities with them.

In regard to the farming community one re–occurring theme is the similarity between mothers and children in their roles as social partners. As far as adults are concerned, mothers are seen by their 1–year–olds as different, and, indeed, they are different. Finally, men play a relatively minor role in the life of farmer 1–year–olds.

What might this mean in terms of Efe forager and Lese farmer 1–year–olds' representation of their social world? Efe forager 1–year–olds are more likely to "see" a greater number of individuals belonging to different social classes as available to them than do Lese farmer 1–year–olds. Men figure prominently in the way young forager children represent reality. This broadly based representation serves young children well throughout their development by preparing them for the intensely social world in which they participate now, and in which they will participate as adults. As infants, and perhaps as adults, these contacts provide them with many more secure bases for attachment, and foster their exploration of the environment.

Lese farmer 1–year–olds, by comparison, "see" fewer individuals as available. Indeed, relative to other community members men are infrequent social partners. Young Lese 1–year–olds' representation may be more focused on mother and children as the responsive individuals. This more narrowly focused representation may serve to prepare the Lese 1–year–olds for a more nuclear, family–based social ecology.

We have shown that who the infant is with and what they do together is influenced by a variety of factors. These factors include the nature of men's and women's work, the physical layout of the homesteads, and the relations among adults. But one factor that has yet to be emphasized is the child's role in activity. Children are active participants in activity, guiding their own and their partner's involvement in sociocultural routines (see Rogoff, 1990, for a discussion of guided participation). In the course of social activity, the child appropriates particular ways of representing the world and reacting to it. The child in the community helps to create his or her social environment. This process of mutual creation means that there is an increasing reciprocity between parental investment strategies and behavioral strategies developed by children, allowing them to function in their communities.

In this chapter we introduced two ways of examining a child's experience of his or her partner's in activity; the total person score and the average person score. We believe that each measure taps into a different way of conceptualizing the child's experience, and these differences are meaningful to the child. The measures may be particularly useful when the number of people with whom the child is involved varies, as it does in the forager and farmer community. Finally, we want to emphasize that the measures chosen to examine 1-year-olds' activity with community members, mean number of intervals in care and play, is but one approach that helps us understand the child's sociocultural experiences. Other measures, such as the contexts in which activities are embedded or the shared affective state of child and partners, play a role in shaping the meaning emerging from the child's social activities.

ACKNOWLEDGMENTS

This research was supported by grants from the National Science Foundation (BNS–8609013), the National Institute of Child Health and Development (1–R01–HD22431), The Spencer Foundation, and Faculty Research Funds from Boston College. The authors would like to thank David S. Wilkie for his critical reading of this manuscript and Cathy Angelillo for assisting with its preparation.

REFERENCES

Altmann, J. Observational study of behavior: Sampling methods. *Behaviour*, 1974, *49*, 227-267.
Bailey, R. C., & Devore, I. Research on the Efe and Lese populations of the Ituri Forest, Zaire. *American Journal of Physical Anthropology*, 1989, *78*, 459-471.
Cole, M. The zone of proximal development: Where culture and cognition create each other. In J. V. Wertsch (Ed.), *Culture, communication, and cognition: Vygotskian perspectives* (pp. 146-161). Cambridge: Cambridge University Press, 1985.
Draper, P. Social and economic constraints on child life among the !Kung. In R. B. Lee & I. DeVore (Eds.), *Kalahari hunter-gatherers: Studies of the !Kung San and their neighbors* (pp. 199-217). Cambridge, MA: Harvard University Press, 1976.
Dunn, J. Siblings and the development of social understanding in early childhood. In P. G. Zukow (Ed.), *Sibling interaction across cultures: Theoretical and methodological issues* (pp. 106-116). New York: Springer-Verlag, 1989.
Konner, M. J. Maternal care, infant behavior and development among the !Kung. In R. B. Lee & I. DeVore (Eds.), *Kalahari hunter-gatherers: Studies of the !Kung San and their neighbors* (pp. 218-245). Cambridge, MA: Harvard University Press, 1976.
Morelli, G. A. *A comparative study of Efe (Pygmy) and Lese one-, two-, and three-year-olds of the Ituri Forest of northeastern Zaire: The influence of subsistence-related variables, and children's age and gender on social-emotional development* (Doctoral dissertation, University of Massachusetts, 1987). Dissertation Abstracts International, 48/02B, p. 582, (8710487). 1987.

Morelli, G. A., Winn, S., & Tronick, E. Z. Perinatal practices: A biosocial perspective. In H. Rauh & H-Ch. Steinhausen (Eds.), *Psychobiology and early development* (pp. 13-22). North Holland: Elsevier Scientific Publication, 1988.

Rogoff, B. *Apprenticeship in thinking: Cognitive development in social context.* New York: Oxford University Press, 1990.

Rogoff, B. & Morelli, G. A. Perspectives on children's development from cultural psychology. Special issue children and their development: Knowledge base research agenda and social policy application. *American Psychologist*, 1989, *44*, 343-348.

Tronick, E. Z., Morelli, G. A., & Winn, S. Multiple caretaking of Efe (Pygmy) infants. *American Anthropologist*, 1987, *89*, 96-106.

Tronick, E. Z., Winn, S., & Morelli, G. A. Multiple caretaking in the context of human evolution. Why don't the Efe know the western prescription of child-care? In M. Reite & T. Field (Eds.), *Psychobiology of attachment and separation* (pp. 293-322). New York: Academic Press, 1985.

Vygotsky, L. S. *Mind in society: The development of higher psychological processes.* Cambridge, MA: Harvard University Press, 1978.

Watson-Gegeo, K. A., & Gegeo, D. W. The role of sibling interaction in child socialization. In P. G. Zukow (Ed.), *Sibling interaction across cultures: Theoretical and methodological issues* (pp. 54-76). New York: Springer-Verlag, 1989.

Wertsch, J. V. *Vygotsky and the social formation of mind.* Cambridge, MA: Harvard University Press, 1985.

Whiting, B., & Edwards, C. *Children of different worlds: The formation of social behavior.* Cambridge, MA: Harvard University Press, 1988.

Weisner, T. S., & Gallimore, R. My brother's keeper: Child and sibling caretaking. *Current Anthropology*, 1977, *18*, 169-190.

Wilkie, D. Hunters and farmers of the African forest. In J. S. Denslow & C. Padoch (Eds.), *People of the Tropical Rain Forest* (pp. 111-126). California: University of California Press, 1988.

Winn, S., Morelli, G. A., & Tronick, E. Z. The infant and the group: A look at Efe care-taking practices. In J. K. Nugent, B. M. Lester, & T. B. Brazelton (Eds.), *The cultural context of infancy* (pp. 86–109). Norwood, New Jersey: Ablex Publishing Corp, 1989.

Zukow, P. G. (Ed.). *Sibling interaction across cultures: Theoretical and methodological issues.* New York: Springer-Verlag, 1989a.

Zukow, P. G. Siblings as effective socializing agents: Evidence from Central Mexico. In P. G. Zukow (Ed.), *Sibling interaction across cultures: Theoretical and methodological issues* (pp. 79-105). New York: Springer-Verlag, 1989b.

6 Discussion: Cultural Attitudes and Actions

T. Berry Brazelton

These chapters, written by leading child developmental researchers, address many reasons for doing cross–cultural research. Most of them try to cope with extant all–too–simplistic empirical models. Our research models tend to limit our data as well as our observational techniques. If we had better ways to document complexity, we would be freer to collect the variables necessary to understand their interactions. In cross–cultural research, we are made aware of the contribution of many variables to the complex interactions we observe. In cross–cultural research, it may be even more critical to look for a multivariate interactional approach. We need to document and evaluate as many differences in each culture as we can.

The Papoušeks' chapter, for example, addresses an interactional model for analysis of communication between parents and infants. The qualitative aspects contained in a dyadic interaction shape the significance of the interaction. These qualitative aspects may be "nonconscious," but they dominate the quality of the interaction. Their study, aimed at defining the universality of the parameters of speech, brings to light the importance of the melodic contours, elevated pitch, slowed tempo, frequent repetitions of "motherese." These aspects of a mother's communication account appropriately for the immaturity of the infant's linguistic equipment. A higher–pitched, slow voice captures the attention of a brand–new neonate. These universal variables lead the mother to share the baby's future speech production. This cross–cultural study elegantly highlights the universals which are present in both baby and mother, as well as the variability in differences across cultures. More subtle differences in "motherese" began to show up in each culture. These later developments were utilized to shape the older baby's speech toward the cultural goals. They were built on top of the universals. On the basis of these elegant, detailed studies, we see subtle values and emotions which parents in each culture transmit. This kind of empirical window into Chinese and U.S. differences gives us insight into the early shaping for cultural values.

In my experience, the main reason for doing cross–cultural research has been to better understand my own biases. Our cultural values are so deep–seated that they dominate our observations and the weighting of the variables we collect. I found that my values were difficult to give up in another culture. I could feel the dissonance long before I could objectify it. In my own work, I found that I adapted my examination of the newborn (Lester & Brazelton, 1982) in subtle ways before I understood that my changed behavior was an adaptation to the differences in neonatal behavior *and* to the differences in expectations in the other culture. We now use this insight after we have trained a researcher to reliability, and then s/he will have adapted the neonatal assessment to the average neonatal behavior in the other culture. Rather than viewing these changes as error variables, we use them to help us understand the culture. We ask returning researchers to perform the NBAS as we observe them. As they do, we note carefully any slight changes in administration and scoring. These changes become the subtlest window into differences in behavior and expectations within the culture they have studied. For, although our own values are difficult to relax, our behavioral adaptations may not be. After such an exam, we ask the researcher to identify his or her conscious changes, such as any necessary adaptations to maternal expectations. The less conscious changes become the subtler adjustments. Each has significance. In our experience, the qualitative evaluations of such an experience contribute a valuable dynamic insight into cross–cultural research. Why are we unsettled in another culture? Why do we yearn for more familiar child–rearing practices? Facing such uncomfortable questions openly may help us to begin to objectify our data.

We have added nine items to the new version of the Neonatal Behavioral Assessment Scale (NBAS, 1984) in an attempt to account for the subtle differences in newborn babies' performance and our adaptation to them. For, we are sure now that these qualitative items are more predictive than are the objective scores of the items in the NBAS. These nine items contain three dynamics, which are scoreable and may give insight into these subtle differences. How much does it cost the examiner to bring the baby to optimal performance? How much does it cost the baby to produce such a performance (this is a valuable insight into fragile infants)? What is the level of this best performance? These concepts might be applied to our work in other cultures. What biases do we have to face in ourselves to join the other culture's values? What do they have to do to include us in an understanding of their value system? The subtle differences need not remain as biases if they can be identified and quantified. The most valuable reason for cross–cultural research is a personal one. It can force us to adapt our goals and our research to a different set of values. In the process, we gain deep personal insights.

Most of the chapters in this book seem to have been motivated by a common goal—to identify relative contributions of the inborn genetic processes, as they interact with environmental or experiential factors. In our own experience with the NBAS across cultures, the newborn's behavior already reflects this interaction. The intrauterine environment with its auditory, tactile, kinesthetic experiences is shaping the fetal organism in powerful ways for nine months. Neonates in Tokyo are already slightly different from those in the remote fishing villages of the Goto Islands. Their scores on the NBAS are comparable, but the quality of their performances differ. Can we find ways to score and value these differences, for they are likely to shape the parent–infant interaction we will observe? Does the newborn influence his environment? I certainly believe the baby does. But how?

Cross–cultural differences must be studied in terms of group differences as well as of individual differences, since the behavioral phenotype we see at birth is already affected by synergistic relationships among intrauterine variables. These changes in behavior give us insight into the most recent adaptations to cultural demands. The universals of neonatal behavior, such as the reflexes which occur across cultures, are those which are necessary for survival. Those which lend themselves to the individual differences in neonatal behavior, which are more easily influenced by intrauterine variables, are more recent in the historical hierarchy of behaviors. In our use of the Neonatal Behavioral Assessment Scale, the qualitative differences reflect the precursors for individual differences. These subtle differences in neonatal behavior at birth influence the quality of the parent–infant interaction. In turn, the interaction is shaped by the neonate's responsiveness (Lester & Brazelton, 1982).

We may study variations in behavior within a local population to learn what are the determinants of behavior in that setting. The inclusion of other independent variables can be used to provide additional explanations, to help sort out interactions, and to widen the window on behavioral processes. They become expounding, rather than confounding, variables. Comparisons across local populations and between cultures enable us to look for patterns of differences and commonalities. Patterns of differences between populations may suggest how common processes are expressed and shaped by a culture.

Differences or similarities in behavior between groups are entirely separate from (and statistically independent of) patterns of individual differences for that behavior. For example, we might find that two ethnic groups do not show significant mean differences on the social interactive items of the Brazelton scale. The two distributions of social interactive behavior overlap to have similar means, but there is still a range of social interactive behavior, and we need to ask what accounts for this variability in the two groups. By studying individual differences we may learn why some infants perform better than others within each group. Individuals may have differential susceptibility to obstetrical effects, and obstetrical effects may interact with other variables that affect behavior.

Because it is often used as a methodology, much cross–cultural work suffers from a lack of theoretical focus. The investigation of patterns of differences and their replication among populations rests on the articulation of at least a set of a priori hypotheses. A theoretical model serves as a guide toward deciding which variables to measure, how they should be measured, which are plausible confounding variables, and which differences and patterns of relationships to investigate. An atheoretical approach may result in simply cataloging behaviors that differ between two cultures, calculating mean differences between the cultural groups, and then generating post hoc explanations for those differences. This can be especially dangerous when the lack of a theoretical model results in the projection of one's own cultural biases and prejudices onto the beliefs and mores of another culture.

We view the infant as a biological–psychological system that proceeds developmentally from less complex to increasingly higher and more differentiated levels of organization. Organization refers to the biological tendency to coordinate and integrate processes into systems or structures that are both biological and behavioral—or "biobehavioral." These biobehavioral systems are dynamic and are accessible for investigation through the study of the process by which they develop; that is, we focus on the *how*, rather than the *what* or *why*, of development. Thus, infant behavior becomes a way of documenting biological processes of organization and development.

Implicit in this model is also the assumption that much, if not all, behavior is adaptive, and that the neonate emerges with a preprogrammed response repertoire that is designed to maximize the survival of the individual and of the species. The form of adaptation as evidenced in neonatal behavior reflects both the evolutionary, or phylogenetic, history of the species and the particular, or ontogenetic, history of the individual's development. The neonate is viewed as a competent organism that is skilled, selective, and socially influential, who actively interacts with and makes demands on the caretaking environment. This organization is the product of the synergistic relationship among several classes of variables. These include the obstetrical and reproductive history of the mother, the genetic endowment of the child, and the prenatal environment (which includes the conditions and complications associated with pregnancy and delivery—directly, such as nutrition, and indirectly, such as the effects of maternal attitude).

These forces act to produce a behavioral phenotype, the expression of genetic endowment in a particular environment. This behavioral phenotype is predisposed to act on and respond to the caregiving environment in ways that represent the phylogenetic adaptation of the species to a given cultural setting. Although basic organizational processes may remain constant from culture to culture—for example infants universally become more alert and develop increasing interactive skills in the first few weeks of postnatal life—the range and form of adaptation for a particular culture will depend upon the demands of that culture. The behavioral repertoire of the individual newborn represents an adaptation, with the limits set by adaptation of the species to a particular culture and the ontogenetic history of that individual. Thus, in the neonate, we see already a blend of cultural practice and biological predisposition.

The subtle differences in maternal responsiveness to infant cues which Bornstein et al., for example, have defined are fascinating. The shared and heightened responsiveness to vocalizing compared to looking demonstrates the universality of the importance of vocalizations to mothers in early infancy. The adaptation of the mother's behaviors to different kinds of vocalization contained cross–cultural universality. This universality points to "mother's interpretations" and to their sensitive and appropriate responses to small infants across cultures. As infants progress through the first year, the Japanese–American differences emerge. Their cultural goals become evidenced in these differences. This study points to the importance of repeated evaluations of a culture over time, in order not to miss the evolution of important differences which emerge and which lead to cultural value–setting in later infancy. Similarly Shatz's study in Part II brings out significant differences in language teaching and language learning in 2–year–olds. These two studies together convey a sense of the longitudinal trends which influence language development in other cultures.

Pomerleau, Malcuit, and Sabatier exemplify a different perspective. They describe the adaptations of three cultures to Montréal, using three clusters of variables (the physical and social environment, the mother's perceptions about infant development, and mother–infant interaction patterns). Their study attempts to identify cultural variations in behavior as they are adopted from the parents' own culture to another. They have provided us with a set of tasks in which we can uncover the changes which parents must make as they give up a known set of values. This view deserves much further study as we ask strong cultures to join our "melting pot" society. In Washington, D.C., we followed a group of inner–city African–American families as they reared their babies. At 4 months, mothers could tell us that they had two sets of standards—one to fit the baby for his role in a middle–class white society; the other contained the African–American values which "really mattered." Any such study would need to account for this kind of complexity in order to uncover "what really matters."

Morelli and Tronick have studied a remote group of pygmies in the Ituri Forest of Africa. Their multiple caregiving in infancy was first seen as a model for us to observe in order to understand its effect on infant development in our own culture as we entered an era of working parents and multiple caregiving. The question was raised of how does a baby establish the intense parent–infant relationship that we value in this country. "How do fathers in such a culture establish themselves as integral to a child's life?" This study gives us insights into such questions.

It also leaves others unanswered. For example, I feel that studies which sample daytime behavior tend to overlook a very integral part of an infant's experience— the nighttime experience. When a baby sleeps with parents in these cultures, there are major opportunities for cementing attachment processes and for transmitting affective cues which serve the parent–infant bond.

We have learned an enormous amount from such studies which we can apply to our reasons for doing cross–cultural studies —i.e., understanding ourselves and our own culture better. But they also point out how inadequate our research techniques are to answer our burning question—the relative contributions of nature and nurture to a child's development.

As I studied the first chapters in this volume, I felt the need for urging more uniformity in assessment, recording, and evaluation techniques in cross–cultural research. The variables are many. Our ability to rid ourselves of our own cultural biases and of variables beyond our control are too easily overlooked. For example, we can never really account for the influence of our observational techniques on the behaviors we are observing. Certainly, across cultures, they are likely to be more influential and less easily understood. We know that gaining informed consent in subjects in our own culture can be complex and difficult.

I would suggest that we retain and include careful records on how we collected our data as well as what our observations can tell us about their influence on the subjects we study. I call this recording and retaining the "bath water" as well as the baby. In our work in other cultures, we can learn a great deal from subjective observations of the problems of doing complex cross–cultural research (Brazelton, 1990).

In our prediction systems, we could include a concept first advocated by Benjamin (1968). As we make a prediction from one time to the next, we could evaluate our correct predictions and our missed predictions separately. In the case of accurate predictions, we can use the empirical models with which we are familiar. The missed predictions needn't be considered as errors, but as opportunities for learning. When we are doing longitudinal research, we have an especially valuable opportunity for re–evaluation at each change point in our research. The missed opportunities contain three sets of information: (1) the defenses of the subjects, which protect them from the intrusiveness of our observations and which are necessary as they attempt to comprehend our study requirements; (2) our own biases, which can interfere with the objectivity with which we observe and evaluate their behaviors; and (3) the extent of the transference of our subjects to us as observers. Over time and within our relationship, these three will change and give us an increasing opportunity to understand ourselves and our subjects in more depth. In constructing theories across cultures, this is critical.

We are all looking for a more satisfactory model for research, embodying systems theory. The all–too–simplistic models we have now of stimulus $\rightarrow$ response do not lend themselves satisfactorily to probing the complexity of human interaction and human development.

REFERENCES

Benjamin, J. D. Uses of prediction. In E. Pavenstedt (Ed.), *Prediction and outcome*. New York: International Universities Press, 1968.

Brazelton, T. B. *Neonatal Behavioral Assessment Scale*. Philadelphia: J. B. Lippincott, 1984.

Brazelton, T. B. On saving the bathwater. *Child Development*, 1990, *61*, 1661-1671.

Caudill, W. A. The influence of social structure and culture on human behavior in modern Japan, *Journal of Nervous and Mental Disease*, 1973, *157*, 240–257.

Lester, B. M., & Brazelton, T. B. Cross–cultural assessment of neonatal behavior. In D. Wagner & H. Stevenson (Eds.), *Cultural perspectives on child development*. San Francisco: Freeman, 1982.

II CONSEQUENCES

Structure, Continuity, and Nutritional Correlates of Caregiver Behavior Patterns in Kenya and Egypt

7

Marian Sigman
University of California
Theodore D. Wachs
Purdue University

INTRODUCTION

One of the primary areas of focus for developmental psychologists has been the study of factors governing the socialization of the child. The socialization process is typically defined as the means through which children acquire the knowledge base, skills, and attitudes that allow them to function as effective members of a given society (Brim, 1966). One major means through which knowledge, skills, and attitudes are transmitted is through specific patterns of caregiver child relations as the child develops (Bornstein, 1989; Maccoby & Martin, 1983). In studying the relevance of caregiver child relations for subsequent socialization, cross–cultural studies of parenting have been viewed as a critical area of research. Cross–cultural studies are important as a means of testing the generalizability of theories about the nature and influence of different patterns of caregiver child relations formulated within a given culture (Kagitcibasi & Berry, 1989). Further, by looking only within a given culture the range of potential caregiver patterns is often restricted to those that are characteristic of the culture under study. Thus, cross–cultural studies are also important as a way of generating new hypotheses about how variability in caregiver — child behavior patterns translates into variability in socialization (Kagitcibasi & Berry, 1989).

Much of the available research on the nature or influence of caregiver behaviors across cultures has involved either preschool or school age children (e.g., Bornstein, 1980; Childs & Greenfield, 1980; Tapp, 1981; Whiting & Edwards, 1988; Winata & Power, 1989). However, the relevance of caregiver — child relations for

123

socialization is not restricted only to older children. Rather, caregiver influences in different cultures can be seen to be salient even during the first years of life (Wachs & Gruen, 1982), perhaps even as early as the first six months of life (Bornstein, Azuma, Tamis–LeMonda, & Ogino, 1990). Hence, there is also a need for cross–cultural study on the nature and influences of caregiver behaviors upon development across the first years of life as well.

While existing cross–cultural studies on caregivers' behavior toward their infants and toddlers have yielded some valuable insights, certain methodological problems can be seen as limiting the ability of existing studies to answer questions about the nature and influence of caregiver behavior patterns for infant development in different cultures. First, many of the available studies are cross–sectional in nature, making it difficult to determine if age changes in caregiver behaviors within or across cultures are real or ascribable to sample differences at the different ages studied (e.g., Dixon, LeVine, Richman, & Brazelton, 1984; Keller, Scholmerich, & Eibl–Eibesfeldt, 1988; Otaki, Durrett, Richards, & Nyquist, 1986; Whiting & Edwards, 1988).

Second, many of the available studies report only mean differences between cultures on indices of caregiver behavior (e.g., Dixon et al., 1984; Otaki et al., 1986; Winata & Power, 1989). Such a strategy ignores the possibility that similar behaviors may have totally different meanings in different cultures (Dixon et al., 1984; Super & Harkness, 1986). To assess whether discrete caregiver behaviors across different cultures share a common underlying meaning requires looking at the covariance or factor structure of different caregiver behaviors within and across cultures.

Finally, in terms of looking at the etiology of differences in caregiver behaviors across cultures, most researchers have investigated what might be called psychocultural determinants, such as culturally–based parent belief systems and values (Kagitcibasi & Berry, 1989; Super & Harkness, 1986), or culturally–based differences in maternal work load or support (Whiting & Edwards, 1988). Some studies have related aspects of the physical ecology to caregiver behaviors in different cultures, with physical ecology defined either at a macroenvironmental level (e.g., geographic features: McSwain, 1981) or at a microenvironmental level (e.g., physical setup of the home: Woodson & DaCosta–Woodson, 1984). There has been relatively little detailed research on the possibility that individual biological factors may also influence patterns of caregiver behavior across cultures (Pollitt, 1988). Potential biological factors that have been suggested include nutritional status of the toddler or caregiver (Chavez & Martinez, 1984) and incidence or severity of infant or toddler morbidity (Pollitt, 1983). Not only has there been relatively little research in this area, but interpretation of available findings often tends to be post–hoc in nature. For example, Whiting and Edwards (1988) suggested that the *similarity* of caregiver nurturance patterns seen across the cultures they studied reflects parents innate reactivity to the infantile physical features of their young child. In contrast, Shand and Kosawa (1985) hypothesized that cultural *differences* in caregiver behavior patterns are driven by culturally–based gene differences in infant behavior, which in turn influence caregiver behaviors. In neither case is the hypothesized underlying casual mechanism (innate releasers or genes) assessed or directly related to differences in caregiver behavior patterns. In other studies, where direct measurements have been used, existing methodological problems make cross–cultural comparisons hazardous. For example, Kermoian and Leiderman (1986) concluded that differences in nutritional history among Kenyan infants influences the patterns of caregiver behavior directed toward these infants. However, their measure of caregiver behavior (infant attachment) and their nutritional history measure (weight for height) are only indirect proxy measures of the critical predictor and outcome variables they are discussing. Other studies utilizing direct measures are hampered by small sample sizes (e.g., Chavez, Martinez, & Yashine, 1975).

The research reported in this chapter looks at patterns of caregiver—toddler interaction across cultures in a way that minimizes the problems noted above. Our concern is with the structure of caregiver interaction patterns within and across cultures, rather than with mean differences. Our focus is on age changes in patterns of caregiver—child interaction, within the same sample in each culture. Finally, we directly relate toddler nutritional status to measures of caregiver behavior patterns, utilizing two large samples in two cultures.

PERFORMANCE SITES IN KENYA AND EGYPT

This study took place in two performance sites. The performance sites were chosen on the basis of meeting ten entry conditions, including different cultural traditions, population stability at each site and the degree to which the populations at each site were representative of rural populations in each culture. One site was in the Embu district in Eastern Kenya. The study area included 2059 households, all of which belonged to the Embu tribe. Families in the study were primarily small landhold farmers, who produce subsistence and cash crops and keep some livestock. Households in the district are primarily monogamous and nuclear, with an average of between six to seven people per family. Most houses are small two room structures, consisting mostly of mud with thatch or tin roofs. There is no electricity in the houses.

The second study site was in the village of Kalama, Egypt. Kalama has a population of 8,000 individuals and is located 25 kilometers north of Cairo. Over half of the families obtain their income primarily from nonfarming activities (working in Cairo, skilled labor), and the remainder obtained at least part of their income from farming. Again, the family unit was primarily nuclear in nature, with the average household size consisting of six individuals. Most houses are one to two stories, built either of brick or adobe, and containing two to three rooms. All houses have electricity, but only 10% of the houses have an indoor water supply.

Sample Characteristics in Kenya and Egypt

In both study sites children in the age ranges needed wereidentified by a census of the village. In Kenya, the original sample consisted of 119 toddlers, who were 18 months of age at the time of entry into this study. Attrition rate over the course of the Kenya study was 8%, leaving a total sample of 110 toddlers (53 boys). In Egypt, 179 toddlers were originally identified, with an attrition rate of 17%; thus, the total sample size consisted of 153 toddlers (77 males). In both cultures preliminary hearing and vision screening ensured that none of the toddlers seen in the study had auditory or vision problems.

Caregivers in both cultures included mothers, adult relatives, and older sibs. However, in both cultures the primary caregiver for toddlers remained the mother (75% of the caregiving activities in Egypt were done by the mother versus 60% in Kenya). In terms of the adults themselves, in Egypt about 26% of the families were rated as high SES (technical, working in Cairo, craftsman, farmers owning more then 10 acres); 38% were rated as intermediate SES (skilled laborers, street vendors, farmers who owned some land); the remaining 36% were rated as low SES (unskilled laborers, farm hands). In Kenya the overwhelming majority of the families (70%) derived their subsistence primarily from farming, hence the usual socioeconomic indices do not easily apply. Survey data indicated that 32% of the families cultivated (which does not necessarily mean ownership) less than 2 acres of land, 49% cultivated between 2 and 5 acres of land, 16% cultivated between 5 to 8 acres, and only 4% of the families cultivated over 8 acres of land.

Based on parent interview, 52% of the Egyptian fathers were fully literate (able to read and write), however only 10% of Egyptian mothers were fully literate. The mean age of the mothers in Egypt was 25.9 years, with a range from 17–45 years. Literacy was assessed in Kenya using a test of reading and writing skills. Performance on this test was scored in terms of school standards (grade levels). For the men, 75% were able to read and 68% were able to write at the first grade level or better; 51% of the women were able to read at a first grade level, but only 40% of the women were able to write at this level. The mean age of the mothers in Kenya was 30.6 years, with a range from 20 to 54 years.

Research Procedures in Kenya and Egypt

Standard nutritional procedures for obtaining measures of food intake were utilized. A similar procedure was used in each culture. Specifically, in both cultures trained dieticians obtained information on food preparation and consumption for two consecutive days each month when the toddlers were between 18 and 30 months of age. Dieticians weighed available food in the household that was consumed over each two–day period, and food intake was recorded. For mixed dishes the amount of ingredient in each recipe was obtained. Since observers left before sundown, on each day mothers were asked to recall *what* was consumed by each toddler the previous evening. Mothers were also asked to estimate how much was consumed, using the mothers' estimate of toddler consumption in relation to her own portion. Dietary recall methods were validated by direct observations and food weighing in pilot research prior to the actual study itself. Details on validation procedures for the food intake measures can be found in Calloway, Rosberg, Horan, Murphy, Balderston, Selvin, and Beaton (1988).

Energy composition of available nutrients was estimated through use of food composition tables based on local norms, plus laboratory analyses of common foods. The primary food intake variable calculated for the toddler was *energy* (kilocalories per day - K–cal). Nutritional data were aggregated across the 18– to 30–month period to obtain an average energy intake variable for each toddler.

Home observations were used to measure characteristic caregiver—child interactions in each culture. Differences in the study sites in each country (close proximity to Cairo in Egypt; distance from Nairobi in Kenya) necessitated different observational techniques. In Kenya observations were carried out for 120 minutes every other month from 18 to 30 months. One minute time–sampling procedures were used, with 30 seconds devoted to observation of behavioral occurrences and the following 30 seconds used for recording. Behaviors that occurred more than once in a specific 30–second interval were scored only once. Observers in Kenya were 16 recent secondary school graduates. These observers had been trained previously on observational coding techniques. Mean interobserver reliability (Pearson correlations) across interaction codes in Kenya was $r = .90$, with a range from .69 to .98.

In Egypt, measures of caregiver—child interaction were obtained twice a month between 18 and 30 months using 30–minute observation periods. Toddlers were observed starting at 17 months to get the family used to being observed, but only data from 18 months on were counted. Direct coding was utilized, such that every time a specific behavior occurred it was recorded. Observers were dieticians in the Egypt Nutrition Institute. The Egyptian scientist in charge of the coding was trained in the U.S. by the American senior scientist in charge of psychological measures (TDW); the Egyptian senior scientist then trained her field director who in turn trained field workers. Reliability was checked by the U.S. senior scientist during each of four visits to Egypt. Mean interobserver reliability (Pearson correlations) across interaction codes in Egypt was $r = .93$, with a range from .58 to 1.00.

Although different methods were used in the two countries, there was a common set of caregiver variables measured in each culture. Specifically, in each country we recorded the percent of toddler vocalizations that were either not responded to or were responded to either nonverbally or verbally, the number of spontaneous vocalizations by the caregiver to the child, the percent of time there was a response to the toddler's distress, and the total number of times the toddler was picked up or held by a caregiver. These core variables were chosen partly on the basis of ease of measurement, and partly on the basis of previous usage in cross–cultural studies of caregiver–infant interaction patterns (Werner, 1988). In both cultures, caregiver behaviors were aggregated across the study period from 18–30 months.

To assess the structure of caregiving in each culture, the aggregated scores for caregiver behaviors from 18 to 29 months were intercorrelated, and the correlational matrix was factor analyzed using a principal components solution with Varimax rotation. Both a minieigen criterion of 1.00 and scree plots were used to determine which factors would be considered for interpretation.

To assess continuity, individual caregiver behaviors were grouped into non–overlapping 2–month time blocks (e.g., 18–19 months, 20–21 months, 28–29 months), and changes across the six time blocks between 18 and 29 months were analyzed utilizing the SAS GLM repeated–measures analysis of variance, testing for the existence of both linear and nonlinear trends. Continuity data were analyzed using individual caregiver behaviors rather than factors because of the possibility that unique time changes for a specific caregiving behavior might be lost when this specific behavior was combined in a single factor score with other behaviors having different developmental trajectories.

To assess the relation of toddler K–Cal to caregiver behaviors, the principal components solutions were used to develop a set of factor scores for each subject on each of the factors that was identified. Individual factor scores were then correlated with the aggregated K–Cal values.

STRUCTURE OF CAREGIVER BEHAVIORS

The factor structure of caregiver behaviors for Egypt is shown in Table 7.1. As can be seen, two factors are defined by the minieigen criteria of 1; however, inspection of the scree plot suggested that a three–factor solution might yield a better fit. For completeness, all three factors in the Egypt data are presented. Results indicate that Factor 1 is defined primarily by verbal response to the child's vocalization and spontaneous caregiver vocalizations, which are positively loaded, as well as by strong negative loadings for nonresponse to child's vocalization and amount of physical contact. This pattern suggests a verbal interaction factor. Factor two is bipolar, defined primarily by a positive loading for nonverbal response to child's vocalization and by a negative loading for nonresponse to child's vocalization. This pattern suggests a structure characterized by patterns of response to the child's vocalization. Factor three is defined almost totally by response to the child's distress.

The three factors in the Kenya data are presented in Table 7.2. The first factor is very similar to that found in the Egyptian data. This factor is defined primarily by verbal response to child's vocalizations and spontaneous caregiver vocalizations which are positively loaded, as well as by a strong negative loading for nonresponse to child's vocalization. This pattern suggests a verbal interaction factor. The only difference from the Egyptian data is that amount of physical contact is not loaded on this factor. It is loaded positively on Factor 2 which also reflects response to the child's distress, so that the loading is positive for greater response to distress. The

TABLE 7.1
Factor Structure of Project-Comparable Cargiver Behaviors: Egypt

Variables	I.	II.	III.
		Factor	
Non-response to child vocalization (%)	−.50	−.84	−.06
Non-verbal response to child vocalization (%)	−.27	.91	−.04
Verbal response to child vocalization (%)	.84	.19	.11
Spontaneous caregiver vocalization (#)	.69	−.00	.02
Response to child distress (%)	.06	−.00	.99
Physical contact (amount)	−.73	.12	−.00
Factor Label	Verbal Interaction	No or Non-verbal Response to Vocalization	Response to Distress
Eigenvalue	2.21	1.50	0.96
Variance accounted for	36%	25%	16%

TABLE 7.2
Factor Structure of Project-Comparable Cargiver Behaviors: Kenya

Variables	I.	II.	III.
		Factor	
Non-response to child vocalization (%)	−.93	−.14	−.24
Non-verbal response to child vocalization (%)	−.05	.05	.96
Verbal response to child vocalization (%)	.94	.17	.08
Spontaneous caregiver vocalization (%)	.68	.24	−.23
Response to child distress (%)	.49	.60	.15
Physical contact (%)	.12	.92	.12
Factor Label	Verbal Interaction	Physical Contact	No or Non-verbal Response to Vocalization
Eigenvalue	2.92	1.06	.85
Variance accounted for	49%	18%	14%

third factor is quite like the second factor in the Egyptian data set in that nonverbal responsiveness to the child's vocalization is positively loaded; this factor appears to reflect the pattern of response to vocalizations.

Overall, the factor structures for the two cultures are *similar* in terms of yielding factors reflecting amount of verbal interaction and patterns of responsiveness to child vocalizations. The factor structures are *different* in that amount of physical contact is an independent factor in the Kenyan data but is not in the Egyptian data, and responsiveness to distress is an independent factor in the Egyptian data but is not in the Kenya data.

CONTINUITY OF CAREGIVER BEHAVIORS

A summary of the changes in Egyptian caregiver behaviors from 18 to 29 months is shown in Table 7.3. Two caregiver behaviors basically decline across this age period. These include no response to child's vocalizations, and nonverbal response to child's vocalization. In contrast, caregiver verbal response to the child's vocalization shows a steady increase across time. For the remaining three variables the pattern is somewhat more complex. As shown in Table 7.3, for the number of spontaneous caregiver vocalizations to the child, both the linear and cubic components are significant. Inspection of changes across time indicates a slight decline in number of spontaneous caregiver vocalizations to the child from 18 to 21 months, followed by a sharp increase from 21 to 27 months, and then a decline from 27 to 29 months. For amount of physical contact, both the linear and quadratic components are significant. Inspection of the time change pattern indicates a decline in amount of physical contact from 18 to 27 months, followed by an increase from 27 to 29 months. Finally, as shown in Table 7.3, we were unable to find a satisfactory fit for either the linear, quadratic, or cubic components for percent of time the caregiver was responsive to the child's distress. Inspection of changes across time indicates an essentially flat pattern from 18 to 29 months.[1]

A summary of the changes in Kenyan caregiver behaviors from 17 to 30 months is shown in Table 7.4. There was much greater continuity in caregiving in Kenya than in Egypt. There are cubic trends in response to distress and vocalization which are not easily interpretable. The main trend is a significant decline in physical contact over time, which is also found in the Egyptian data. It is also evident from the means given in Tables 3 and 4 that there are some differences in responsiveness in the two cultures. Non–verbal responsiveness to toddler vocalizations and response to distress are higher in Egypt than in Kenya.

NUTRITION AND CAREGIVER BEHAVIORS

The energy status of Egyptian toddlers (K–Cal) is significantly correlated with the amount of verbal interaction they receive from their caregivers, Factor I: $r = .24$, $p < .01$. In contrast, the energy level of Egyptian toddlers is negatively related to caregiver behaviors as defined by Factor II (no or nonverbal response to vocalization), $r = -.16$, $p < .05$. Inspection of the two individual items defining Factor two (nonresponse to vocalization and nonverbal response to child vocalization) shows that the relation between K–Cal and Factor II scores is defined primarily by nonverbal response, suggesting that more well–fed toddlers received fewer nonverbal responses to their vocalizations from their caregivers, $r = -.21$, $p < .05$. The correlation of toddler energy intake with response to distress (Factor III) was nonsignificant, $r = .08$, ns.

---

[1] Transforming the response to distress data by means of square–root transform did not yield a more interpretable pattern.

TABLE 7.3
Changes in Caregiver Behaviors from 18-29 Months: Egypt

Variable	Time Blocks						Total
	18-19	20-21	22-23	24-25	26-27	28-29	
Non-response to vocalization (%)	28	30	30	26	25	20	Linear: $F = 14.66**$
Non-verbal response to vocalization (%)	34	30	29	28	26	24	Linear: $F = 22.70**$
Verbal response to vocalization (%)	37	39	40	46	48	54	Linear: $F = 68.47**$
Vocalizations (#)	9.49	9.33	10.36	12.12	12.59	11.87	Linear: $F = 21.99*$ Cubic: $F = 5.14*$
Response to distress (%)	98	98	98	98	98	98	NS
Physical contact (amount)	553.91	279.62	147.72	80.69	29.38	41.46	Linear: $F = 249.53**$ Quadratic: $F = 56.51**$

$*p < .05$
$**p < .01$

TABLE 7.4

Changes in Caregiver Behaviors from 18-29 Months: Kenya

Variable	Time Blocks							Total
	17-18	19-20	21-22	23-24	25-26	27-28	29-30	
Non-response to vocalization (%)	46	37	39	42	38	38	39	Cubic: $F = 4.35*$
Non-verbal response to vocalization (%)	4	7	5	5	5	6	4	NS
Verbal response to vocalization (%)	52	61	58	56	60	59	59	NS
Spontaneous vocalizations (%)	36	39	37	37	38	36	38	NS
Response to distress (%)	67	71	68	71	68	64	74	Cubic: $F = 5.13*$
Physical contact (%)	36	29	20	26	19	15	14	Linear: $F = 131.57**$

$*p < .05$
$**p < .01$

Figures for % non-response, non-verbal response, and verbal response to vocalization add up to more than 100% because simultaneous non-verbal and verbal responses were both scored, allowing multiple scores for a single toddler vocalization.

The major relation between caregiver behavior and energy intake is a negative association between the energy intakes of Kenyan toddlers and the amount of physical contact they have with their caregivers, Factor II, $r = -.22, p < .05$. Toddlers who are fed less are carried and held more by their caregivers. The association between verbal interaction and energy intake approaches significance and is also negative, unlike the relation in the Egyptian data, $r = -.16, p < .10$. When we examine the individual behaviors that load on this factor in relation to energy intake, significant associations emerge between both the amount that the toddler is not responded to when he or she vocalizes, $r = .25, p < .05$, and the percentage of vocalizations that are responded to by adult verbalizations, $r = -.29, p < .01$. There is no association between energy intake and the amount of spontaneous caregiver vocalization and responsiveness to toddler distress. Thus, the Kenyan toddlers who are fed poorly are carried and held more, and their vocalizations are responded to more, particularly by a verbal response. This pattern is quite unlike the Egyptian data where better fed infants are talked to and attended to more with verbal responses.

CONCLUSIONS

Three major findings emerge from the present project. First, their are similarities in the structure of caregiver behaviors across the two cultures observed in this project, Egypt and Kenya. Second, depending upon the culture we find either stability or instability in caregiver behaviors across time. Third, although cultural differences moderate the relation between toddler energy intake and caregiving, the relation of toddler nutrition to caregiver behaviors does seem to be verified in the present project.

In terms of the structure of caregiving, the present results point to a surprising number of similarities between the two different cultures studied in this project. These findings could be used to support an ethological hypothesis developed by Keller et al. (1988), who suggest that there may be certain "intuitive" patterns of caregiver behavior which have a high probability of maximizing optimal development for offspring, and thus are likely to replicate across cultures (also see chapter by Papoušek & Papoušek, in this volume). Given the existence of universals in language acquisition (Bornstein, 1980), the present results suggest that vocalization and responsivity to toddler vocalization may be prime candidates for inclusion among a listing of "intuitive" caregiver behaviors. However, in suggesting that our results lend support to a notion that some aspects of caregiving may be "intuitive", we realize many of the problems inherent in this type of statement. First, as noted by Campbell (1964) and by Jahoda (1980), we recognize that we are making comparisons only across two cultures. Making generalizations about intuitive caregiver patterns based on a sample of two cultures is akin to making generalizations about the nature of human development based on a sample consisting of two different individuals. Further, there is an increasing amount of evidence that suggests that certain acculturation processes such as urbanization or education may be breaking down many traditional cultural differences (Jahoda, 1980; Otaki et al., 1986). Thus, one cannot assume different cultures based simply on the fact that a researcher has samples from two different countries. Rather, the nature of the cultures studied must be specified in greater detail before the researcher can distinguish between true similarities across distinct cultures, as opposed to cross–cultural similarities based on a common acculturation process such as urbanization. Finally, while there were similarities in the factor structures of caregiver behaviors there were also differences across cultures, particularly in terms of the meaning of physical contact and responsiveness to distress.

Overall, given the available evidence, we would argue that there may be a small subset of caregiver behaviors which are more or less universal, and a larger subset of caregiver behaviors which are culture specific. "Universal" caregiver behaviors would be those which would have the greatest chance of optimizing the offspring's development across a wide variety of environments, whereas culture specific caregiver behaviors would be those which yield the greatest probability of optimizing offspring adjustment within the specific ecological conditions of a given culture. At a cultural level, this distinction between universal and culture specific caregiver behaviors is equivalent to the distinction between *experience expectant* and *experience dependent* stimulation made by Greenough, Black, and Wallace (1987) as a means of explaining the nature of environmental contributions to central nervous system development.

In terms of continuity of caregiver behaviors, if we use the Egyptian data as a guide, it seems clear that we cannot automatically assume that caregiver behaviors will be stable across the child's second to third year of life. In contrast, in Kenya age changes in caregiver behavior toward children appear to be more continuous. One possible reason for these cultural differences in continuity may involve changes in the primary caregiver as toddlers develop. In Kenya, as toddlers get older we find less caregiving is provided by the mother and more by older sisters. Thus to the extent that older sisters maintain the caregiver patterns established by their mothers it would not be surprising to find continuity of caregiver behaviors across the toddler period in Kenya. In contrast, in Egypt amount of direct maternal caregiving declines as toddlers get older, but there is no corresponding increase in level of sib caregiving. Hence, the cultural context of Egyptian caregiving provides less support for continuity of caregiving activities across the toddler period.

In terms of biological factors the present results indicate a relation between toddler energy intake and patterns of caregiver behavior. However, results also indicate that the relation between nutrition and caregiving is moderated by cross–culture country differences, with the relation suggesting a positive correlation between toddler nutritional status and adequacy of caregiver behaviors in Egypt and a negative correlation in Kenya. The pattern of results for Egypt are congruent with data from other countries, such as Mexico, which also indicate that children who are adequately nourished receive more developmentally faciliative interactions from their primary caregivers (Chavez & Martinez, 1984). However, cultural differences in the pattern of relations between nutritional status and caregiving behaviors have also been reported in the literature (e.g., Graves, 1978). Assuming that the cross–cultural differences in relations between toddler K–Cal and caregiver behavior do not represent random variations, the critical question is what processes are underlying these differences.

Several possible interpretations could be invoked to explain these cultural differences in nutritional status and caregiver interaction patterns. One possibility involves the relation between the child's nutritional status and amount of physical contact. In Kenya, poorly nourished children were carried more and spent more time in proximity to their caregivers. These children also tended to be smaller, lighter, and more ill. Thus, infants who are more at risk (malnourished) are more likely to be carried in Kenya; at least in Kenya, infants who are carried more are also more likely to be verbalized to. Thus, the negative covariance between low food intake and carrying and the positive covariance between carrying and verbalization may explain the negative relation between food intake and verbal interactions in Kenya (lower food intake means more carrying; more carrying means more vocalization; hence lower the food intake the more the verbalization to the toddler). In contrast, in Egypt toddlers who were ill were more likely to be isolated from their caregivers (e.g., Egyptian toddlers with more gastrointestinal illness are less likely to have an adult or sib caregiver available to the child, $r = -.18, p < .05$. Thus, in Egypt, infants who are at risk, either from morbidity or poorer nutrition would receive less verbal interaction from their caregivers.

The second explanation has to do with the fact that the level of nutrition between the two countries is markedly different. The average caloric intake for toddlers in Egypt was 1119 K–Cal, as opposed to 848 K–Cal in Kenya. Based on current nutritional standards (Recommended Dietery Allowance, 1989) the Egyptian toddlers would be classified as having energy intakes below what is recommended but are not malnourished, while the Kenyan toddlers would be classified as moderately malnourished. Thus, the poorly fed Kenyan toddlers are more deprived than the poorly fed Egyptian toddlers, suggesting that a different process may be operating depending upon the level of nutritional intake of the toddler. That is, Kenyan caregivers may be more responsive with their children as a way of compensating for the inability of the family to feed them. In contrast, poorly–fed Egyptian toddlers may come from families that have less ability to provide for them in all areas.

A third possible explanation has to do with the physical ecology of the home situation in the two countries. In Kenya, children spend very little time inside dwellings. Thus, a child who is not carried on the back of the mother or older sister is not likely to be in close proximity to an adult. As noted earlier, in Kenya physical contact appears to increase caregivers responsiveness to toddler vocalizations. In contrast, in Egypt the spaces occupied by mothers and children are smaller; for nearly 75% of the observations Egyptian toddlers were found inside or in front of the family dwelling. Thus, the mobile Egyptian toddler may not wander off as far from the caregiver, and may thus be more likely to be responded to verbally because of the close proximity of the caregiver, even if the child is not carried by the caregiver.

In spite of the cultural differences, our results suggest that biological factors such as child nutritional status can influence the patterns of caregiver child relations. These results do not negate the importance of social or physical–ecological determinants of caregiving, but they suggest that greater attention needs to be given to child biological variables which may also impact upon caregiver behavior patterns. Nutritional status may be one important variable. Another potentially significant biological parameter may be morbidity, based on evidence suggesting that deformed or seriously ill children are more likely to be rejected by their caregivers (Whiting & Edwards, 1988). The critical point to note is that caregiver behavior must not be viewed in isolation, but must be seen as a larger system including the physical ecology and the biological status of the toddler.

ACKNOWLEDGMENTS

The research reported in this paper was supported by the Agency for International Development (grant DAN–1309–G–55–1070–00). The authors gratefully acknowledge the collaboration of a number of colleagues in this interdisciplinary project; they include Zeinab Bishry, Osman Galal, Gail Harrison, Norge Jerome, Nell Kirksey and Wafaa Moussa in Egypt and Nimrod Bwibo, Susan Weinberg, and Charlotte Neumann in Kenya.

REFERENCES

Bornstein, M. Cross–cultural developmental psychology. In M. Bornstein (Ed.), *Comparative methods in psychology* (pp. 231–282) Hillsdale, NJ: Lawrence Erlbaum Associates, 1980.

Bornstein, M. Cross cultural developmental comparisons: The case of Japanese – American infant and mother activities and interactions. *Developmental Review*, 1989, *9*, 171–204.

Bornstein, M., Azuma, H., Tamis–LeMonda, C., & Ogino, M. Mother and infant activity interaction in Japan and the United States. *International Journal of Behavioral Development*, 1990, *13*, 267–287.

Brim, D. Socialization through the life cycle. In D. Brim & S. Wheeler (Eds.), *Socialization after childhood* (pp. 1–50). New York: Wiley, 1966.

Calloway, D., Roseberg, C., Horan, H., Murphy, S. Balderston, J., Selvin, S., & Beaton, G. *Collaborative research support program on food intake and human function. Final report.* Agency for International Development: Washington, D.C., 1988.

Campbell, D. Distinguishing differences of perception from failures of communication in cross–cultural studies. In E. Northrup & H. Livingston (Eds.), *Cross–cultural understanding: Epistemology in anthropology* (pp. 308–336). New York: Harper and Row, 1964.

Chavez, A., & Martinez, C. Behavioral measurements of activity in children and their relation to food intake in a poor community. In E. Pollitt & P. Amante (Eds.), *Energy intake and activity* (pp. 303–322). New York: Liss, 1984.

Chavez, A., & Martinez, C., & Yaschine, T. Nutrition, behavioral development and mother child interaction in young rural children. *Federation Proceedings*, 1975, *34*, 1574–1582.

Childs, C., & Greenfield, P. Informal modes of learning and teaching: The case of Zinacanteco Weaving. In N. Warner (Ed.), *Studies in cross cultural psychology*. (Vol. 2, pp. 269–316). New York: Academic Press, 1980.

Dixon, S., LeVine, R., Richman, A., & Brazelton, T. Mother child interaction around a teaching task: An African American comparison. *Child Development*, 1984, *55*, 1252–1264.

Graves, P. Nutrition and infant behavior. *American Journal of Clinical Nutrition*, 1978, *31*, 541–551.

Greenough, W., Black, J., & Wallace, C. Experience and brain development. *Child Development*, 1987, *58*, 539–559.

Jahoda, G. Cross–cultural comparisons. In M. Bornstein (Ed.), *Comparative methods of psychology* (pp. 105–148). Hillsdale, NJ: Lawrence Erlbaum Associates, 1980.

Kagitcibasi, C., & Berry, J. Cross–cultural psychology: Current research and trends. *Annual Review of Psychology*, 1989, *40*, 493–532.

Keller, H., Scholmerich, A., & Eibl–Eibesfeldt, I. Communication patterns in adult infant interaction in Western and Nonwestern cultures. *Journal of Cross Cultural Psychology*, 1988, *19*, 427–445.

Kermoian, R., & Leiderman, P. Infant attachment to mother and child caretaker in an East African community. *International Journal of Behavioral Development*, 1986, *9*, 455–469.

Maccoby, E., & Martin, J. Socialization in the context of the family. In E. Hetherington (Ed.), *Socialization, personality and social development* in *Mussen's handbook of child psychology* (Vol. 4, pp. 1–101). New York: Wiley, 1983.

McSwain, R. Care and conflict in infant development. *Infant Behavior and Development*, 1981, *4*, 225–246.

Otaki, M., Durrett, M., Richards, P., Nyquist, L., & Pennebaker, J. Maternal and infant behavior in Japan and America. *Journal of Cross Cultural Psychology*, 1986, *17*, 251–268.

Pollitt, E. Morbidity and mental development: An hypothesis. *International Journal of Behavioral Development*, 1983, *6*, 461–475.

Pollitt, E. A critical view of three decades of research on the effects of chronic energy malnutrition on behavioral development. In B. Schurch & N. Scrimschaw (Eds.), *Chronic energy deficiency: Consequences and related issues* (pp. 123–142). IDECG–Nestle Foundation. Lausanne Switzerland, 1988.

Recommended Dietary Allowance 10th Edition, National Academy of Sciences: Washington, D. C., 1989.

Shand, N., & Kosawa, Y. Cultural transmission: Caudill's model an alternative hypothesis. *American Anthropologist*, 1985, *87*, 861–871.

Super, C., & Harkness, S. The developmental niche. *International Journal of Behavioral Development*, 1986, *9*, 545–570.

Tapp, J. Studying personality development. In H. Triandis & A. Heron (Eds.), *Handbook of cross cultural psychology* (Vol. 4, pp. 343–424). Boston: Allyn & Bacon, 1981.

Wachs, T. D., & Gruen, J. *Early experience and human development*. New York: Plenum, 1982.

Werner, E. A cross cultural perspective on infancy. *Journal of Cross Cultural Psychology*, 1988, *19*, 96–113.

Whiting, B., & Edwards, C. *Children of different worlds*. Cambridge: Harvard University Press, 1988.

Winata, H., & Power, T. Child rearing and compliance. *Journal of Cross Cultural Psychology*, 1989, *20*, 333–356.

Woodson, R., & DaCosta–Woodson, I. Social organization, physical environment and infant caregiver interactions. *Developmental Psychology*, 1984, *20*, 473–476.

Using Cross–Cultural Research to Inform Us about The Role of Language in Development: Comparisons of Japanese, Korean, and English, and of German, American English, and British English

8

Marilyn Shatz

The University of Michigan

INTRODUCTION

Talking is certainly one of the most frequent, if not the most frequent, parental behavior children experience. Whether they are interacting with their parents or observing them interacting with others, children regularly hear their parents using the language customary in their community. In fact, language is a powerful tool of parenting. Because language both reflects and expresses cultural values, parents convey those values when their children hear them speak. Not only do parents use language to tell their children directly what is acceptable social behavior, but their language also includes indirect information about social values.

Despite the pervasiveness of language behavior, we know little about the subtle ways in which parental language practices affect child development. There is, of course, work suggesting that certain language experiences enhance children's cognitive and linguistic development. Reading picture books with children, for example, results in such benefits (Whitehurst, Falco, Lonigan, Fischel, DeBaryshe, Valdez–Menchaca, & Caulfield, 1988). The present concern, however, is with those aspects of language use reflecting a culture's view of how individuals relate to each other and to social institutions, for it is these that should be most informative with regard to how one grows up to be an accepted member of a particular cultural community.

We know that cultures differ importantly in the world views they construct and pass on to their children. For example, Shweder (1989) suggests that cultures can be categorized according to a tripartite system as centered on individualism, community, or other–worldliness, and Triandis (1989) makes a related distinction between cultures emphasizing individualism versus collectivism. Although little is presently known about how language use reflects such differences or when and how differences in use affect children, the claim that language use is a central source of socialization differences is so reasonable that it demands further study. As Givon (1985, p. 1026) argues, "...when one compares language acquisition across cultural boundaries, one ought to keep in mind that different *manners* of acquisition are not necessarily different manners of acquiring the same end results. Rather, they may be different manners of acquiring strikingly different communicative *modes*. And as may be often observed elsewhere, style is not always separable from substance, but may turn out on occasion to be substance itself."

Earlier Studies of Language and Development across Cultures

The sorts of language and culture questions raised by this orientation are very different from those addressed by the earlier cross–cultural work on language acquisition. There were two main foci of the earlier efforts. One was on the acquisition of grammar, where grammar was taken to mean a largely autonomous syntax, uninfluenced by possible variations in semantic systems. Indeed, the basic assumption underlying the autonomous syntax approach was that, as cognitions developed, children would look for those understandings to be expressed in their language. To the extent that they appeared at different times in children learning different languages, one could conclude that the grammatical forms carrying them differed in their grammatical complexity. Thus, cross–cultural work was useful in that it was presumed to be informative about the relative difficulty of acquiring different kinds of syntactic constructions (Slobin, 1973, 1985).

In her critique of such work, Bowerman (1985) makes the important point that this approach ignores the possibility that the mapping between underlying cognitive distinctions and the partitioning of semantic space in a language is not necessarily isomorphic, and that this mapping itself can be an additional source of complexity and, indeed, difference between languages. Differences in the ways semantic space is partitioned, then, might well be a fruitful area of investigation for future cross–cultural studies on language development and might have important implications for our understanding of aspects of cognitive development such as categorization, problem solving, and decision making.

The second focus of the earlier work was on the role that others in the child's environment play in the process of acquisition, again with an emphasis on syntactic acquisitions. Work on parent–child linguistic interactions in the 1970s focused on the nature of the input to the child and whether and how it might facilitate grammar acquisition. Because the early studies on the topic were done primarily on American speakers of English, cross–cultural work followed in order to examine the generality of the use of motherese, a child–directed speech register that had been claimed to facilitate language acquisition. These studies showed that the patterns of parental speech in non–Western cultures did not conform to the description of motherese provided for middle–class American speakers (Ochs, 1982; Schieffelin, 1979). One important implication of this work was that the American style was not necessary for normal language acquisition to occur. (Whether it is nonetheless more facilitative is another issue that was not addressed in the early work, in part because direct cross–cultural comparisons of cultures and languages as different as Samoan and American are difficult indeed.)

Language as a Medium of Cultural Transmission

Related to this second focus on motherese is more recent work on parent–child interactions that takes as its primary goal not the description of input to a grammar acquisition device, but the description of the language practices that expose children to the principles of social order and the worldviews of their culture (Ochs, 1986). Such work is motivated not by the question of how a grammar is learned but by questions of how cultural values are transmitted and acquired in the process of the child's learning of a language. Anthropologists, rather than psychologists, have typically investigated such questions. Most of the work to date has not utilized direct comparisons between cultures, but rather has focused on the description of communicative behaviors in a single culture, drawing comparisons where possible only informally to what is known about American culture. Rather than doing experiments, researchers in this area have done field studies, using ethnographic methods and sociolinguistic techniques of careful transcription and analysis of spontaneously occurring conversations. A good example of this is Clancy's work on Japanese mothers interacting with their 2–year–olds (Clancy, 1986).

Two of the most prominent researchers in this new field of language socialization, Ochs and Schieffelin, argue on the basis of their findings that language practices are an essential carrier of information about how to function appropriately in a society (Ochs & Schieffelin, 1984; Schieffelin & Ochs, 1986). The relational model shown in Figure 8.1 is my interpretation of their proposal.

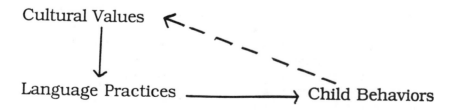

Figure 8.1. Relations among cultural values, language practice, and child behavior.

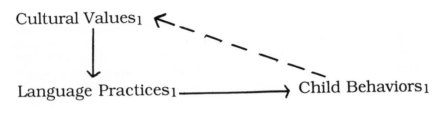

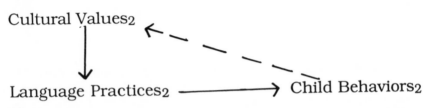

Figure 8.2. Framework for cross-cultural research on the role of language in development.

The solid lines in Figure 8.1 show that cultural values have a direct effect on a community's language practices. These in turn influence child behaviors. To the extent that the values must be acquirable by children from the language practices, the child behaviors themselves both reflect and constrain cultural values (dotted line).

Obviously such a model is incomplete. A full explanatory model would have to include biological constraints on cultural values as well as ecological and historical influences. Nonetheless, such a model can be useful as a framework for comparative research. Figure 8.2 illustrates that framework. Two cultures differing in cultural values can be compared by considering whether and how their language practices differ in particular ways and whether and how those practices affect child behaviors.

To date there has been very little research that directly compares the language practices of different cultures and then investigates their influences on developmental outcomes. Thus, we have no idea how truly pervasive language practices are as mediators of either cognitive or social functioning. The studies reported here begin to bridge that gap in our knowledge. They are direct comparisons across cultures, they involve language use, and they deal both with differences in language practice and with the possible consequences of such practices.

The two studies are very different, however. The first study examines behavioral outcomes directly and then makes inferences about the possible differences in language practice that might account for the observed outcomes. The second study examines language practices directly and then makes inferences about their relation to differences in cultural values and outcomes. In both cases, there is independent, corroborating evidence for differences in cultural values that supports the plausibility of the inferences made.

Rather than using ethnographic techniques, my collaborators and I have done controlled comparisons, utilizing quasi–experimental and experimental methods. To do so, we had to select our comparison groups with care and to focus on specific sets of dependent measures. Although we did not solve all the control and design problems involved in doing this sort of research, our successes lead me to believe that such research is not only possible, but extremely informative. It has the potential to corroborate, extend, and clarify ethnographic work on single cultures. Thus, the studies are offered as examples of the kinds of direct, cultural comparative work that can be done using this research framework to understand better the role of language in development.

THE EFFECT OF LANGUAGE USE ON SENTENCE VERIFICATION: JAPANESE, KOREAN, AND ENGLISH

Cognitive psychologists have investigated the relative degree of difficulty adults and children have in judging the truth or falsity of affirmative and negative sentences. Two kinds of tasks have been used, one in which subjects are asked to compare pictures to the sentences they hear (e.g., "This is not an apple." when viewing a picture of an apple) and one in which they are asked to compare the sentences to knowledge they already have (e.g., "You are not a baby."). Generally, English–speaking children find it easiest to judge true affirmative sentences (e.g, "You are a child."), followed by false affirmatives, ("You are a baby."), false negatives ("You are not a child."), and then true negatives ("You are not a baby.") This pattern conforms to what English–speaking adults do.

When processing models were first proposed to account for such verification data, the assumption was that the proposed verification processes would be universal. However, using the knowledge verification task, Akiyama (1984) discovered that Japanese children found true negative sentences easier than false negatives (Akiyama, 1984). The models proposed to account for the English speakers' data could not account for the data from Japanese–speaking children. Akiyama argued that the differences between Japanese speakers and English speakers were based on differences between the Japanese and English languages, having to do with some general characteristics such as the placement of the verb, placement of the negative, and the way questions are answered.

Korean is a language that shares many structural similarities with Japanese. For example, they are both primarily subject–object–verb languages, whereas English conforms to a subject–verb–object order. One might expect, then, if language structure were the determinant of processing differences as Akiyama (1984) had proposed, that Korean–speaking children would perform like Japanese–speaking children on sentence verification tasks. Yet, Kim (1985) reported that, on a picture verification task, the Korean speakers she studied had produced the same order of difficulty as English–speaking children. Jeansue Lee Kim, Michael Akiyama, and

I decided to examine whether the tasks were responsible for the differences between the Japanese and Korean studies (as Akiyama, 1986, suggested they might be), or whether, indeed, Korean–speaking children conformed to English speakers' patterns, regardless of task (Kim, Shatz, & Akiyama, 1990). In that case, the differences in processing between speakers of Japanese and speakers of English that Akiyama had found would no longer be attributable to characteristics of the Japanese language that Korean shared.

Our study included 32 Korean monolinguals and 24 monolingual English speakers. Both groups had a mean age of 4 years, 5 months. Half the children in each group were given a picture verification task and the other half a knowledge verification task. Each task involved the children listening to 40 sentences that exemplified true affirmative, false affirmative, false negative or true negative relations to pictures or some knowledge; thus, there were 10 trials for each type of relation. The child's task was simply to say "right" or "wrong" after each presentation. Our measures included the rate of errors, the mean time to respond overall (computed from audiotapes of the sessions), and the mean time to respond correctly.

For all three measures, there was no significant main effect of language or task. That is, the Korean speakers and the English speakers did not differ, nor did the particular task (comparisons to pictures or to knowledge) affect their performance. Both groups of children showed the same pattern of difficulty. They made significantly more errors on true negative sentences than on the others, and it took them longer to verify negative sentences than affirmatives. Thus, the structural similarities that the Korean and Japanese languages share cannot account for why Japanese speakers and English speakers differ in their performance on the knowledge task.

What, then, are the characteristics that English and Korean, but not Japanese, might share that could influence the way children process such sentences? Despite our combined native knowledge of these languages, we were initially stumped by this question. Only gradually, after many conversations about how our languages differed in their uses, did we conclude that there were indeed several reasons why Japanese–speaking children might be primed to process true negative sentences more easily than Korean or English speakers. For one, Japanese puts the negative marker in sentence final position. Although Korean also has such a form, there is a "short" form of the negative as well, one that places the negative preverbally, as does English, and it is this form that children apparently learn first (Choi & Zubin, 1985). Thus, Japanese children seem to have more expertise earlier with the postverbal negative placement that Akiyama argued would be facilitative of the true negative verifications (see Akiyama, 1984; Kim et al., 1990, for details).

More relevant to our present interest in cultural differences and their consequences for cognitive processing and socialization is the second difference between Korean and Japanese, one involving language use. In Japan, it is considered appropriate for speakers to use their interlocutors' words in formulating their replies (Makino, 1980). When confronted with an inaccurate statement from a speaker, then, a listener would still tend to use the speaker's original words while denying the truth of the statement, thus producing a response that, from the speaker's perspective, would be a true negative. Clancy (1986) notes that, even though they are generally indirect in refusing their children, Japanese parents often use such direct negative forms when correcting child misspeakings, first negating the child's statement, and then providing an appropriate correction.

Evidence that young Japanese–speaking children have acquired the strategy of using negatives like this in discourse denial comes from a study by Akiyama (1985) in which Japanese–speaking and English–speaking children were asked to give the opposite of sentences like "A car is little." The Japanese–speaking children made significantly more negative denial statements ("A car is not little.") than did the English–speaking children, who regularly produced affirmative denials ("A car is big.").

Apparently Korean speakers do not share the tendency of Japanese speakers to repeat interlocutors' words, which fosters the use of the negative denial form. In fact, we found in an experiment eliciting denials that Korean children again looked more like English speakers than Japanese speakers, producing more affirmative denials than negative ones (Kim et al., 1990).

In sum, children's exposure to and acquisition of true negatives differs in the cultures we studied as a function of pragmatic concerns. That difference seems to affect sentence processing as early as the age of 4 years. Specific patterns of language use, even socially motivated ones exemplified early on by parents, apparently are more influential than general typological similarities between languages in determining shared patterns of language processing. Thus, we have found a culturally sanctioned language practice that seems to affect a cognitive process originally assumed to be universal.

PARENTAL SPEECH STYLES AND CULTURAL VALUES: GERMAN, AMERICAN ENGLISH, AND BRITISH ENGLISH

Comparing German and American Mothers

As noted earlier, cultures can be categorized as more or less oriented toward the needs and interests of the individual. Western, industrialized cultures, and particularly the United States, are typically said to be more individualistic than others. Whereas middle–class American mothers assign intentionality and will to infant behaviors, anthropologists tell us that in other cultures there is often more concern with making the child respond appropriately in conventional ways to the utterances of others than in helping the child express her own intentions. Saying what is situationally appropriate is more central to language use than is the expression of individual desires and beliefs, and it is this that parents train their children to do. Parental language style, then, reflects cultural values; differences in style lead to understandings of different cultural values in children.

This parental style hypothesis has not yet been tested directly; the cultural groups anthropologists have studied, such as the Kaluli in New Guinea, or the Athapaskan Indian, differ on so many dimensions from American culture that it is difficult to make direct comparisons of language style and its consequences for socialization. In carrying out a direct test of the parental style hypothesis, we selected two countries that we had reason to believe would differ with regard to socialization practices and cultural values about the role of children, but where there would be relatively fewer other differences, either in language typology, economic status, or social organization.

A comparison between the United States and West Germany seemed to fit these criteria. They both are industrialized, have a large middle class and a basically nuclear family structure, and they share some common linguistic ancestry. Yet, despite these similarities, educated observers of both cultures from Lewin (1948) to the Grossmans (1985) have noted differences in child rearing behaviors between German parents and American parents. German parents are observed to be more authoritative, dominating, and rejecting, whereas Americans are observed to be more egalitarian and attentive to child desires and intentions. Although both cultures apparently value independence in their children, the Germans also value obedience, and independence for them apparently is often taken to mean self–reliance as opposed to freedom of action.

If these sorts of observations of differences in parental styles are correct, then we should be able to find specific evidence in speech directed to children of how these values are conveyed. Hannelore Grimm and Karin Niemeier–Wind (of the University of Bielefeld), Sharon Wilcox, and I hypothesized that we would be able to find such differences even in speech directed to 2–year–olds, because, as Dunn's work shows, the process of socialization begins very early (e.g., Dunn & Munn, 1985). We then looked for an aspect of the languages that we could identify readily in both German and English and could code reliably for uses related to socialization. We selected the modal verb system (with expressions in English such as *must, may, might, can, could, would, should, ought, shall, will, hafta, wanna, gonna, needta, getta*, and *gotta*, and in German, *müssen, können, mögen, dürfen, werden, wollen, sollen*, and *nicht brauchen*). These words, in both languages, encode a variety of meanings having to do with necessity, possibility, obligation, permission, and related concepts such as volition, intention, and ability.

In both epistemic matters (those having to do with knowledge) and deontic ones (those having to do with will), modal expressions allow speakers to express their beliefs about propositions to others. Modals, then, are a large part of how both the German and English languages transmit information about complex social systems, via comments about permission, obligation, willingness, and intentions. However, as noted earlier, a common semantic space may be partitioned differently in two different languages, and we could not assume identical meanings for any two word pairs such as *müssen* and *must*. Moreover, even within a language, such words can have several different meanings. Thus, we coded for the semantic functions of the words in context, rather than just the counting the frequencies of the words themselves.

The subjects we studied were all middle–class, monolingual mothers and their children, eight German and eight American pairs, living in their native countries. The German families had been studied by Hannelore Grimm previously, and the transcripts of their conversational interactions were used for this study. Similarly, the data on the American families had been collected by me earlier as part of a larger study, with the particular families included here selected so that the children would be most comparable in age and language ability to the sample of German children. Overall, the children had a mean age of 2 years, 5 months and a mean length of utterance in words of 3.25 at the time of the first comparison, with no significant differences in age or MLU between the two groups of children.

For both groups, the families had been observed at home twice, 4 months apart, as they played with toys and books provided by the experimenters. The parents had been told to talk to their children as they normally would under such informal interaction circumstances. The main difference in procedure between the samples was that the German interactions had been longer, roughly about an hour, compared to the American ones, which were about half that.

Using transcriptions of the family conversations, we examined the use of modals in the two languages by coding each occurrence of modal words for the type of word and the semantic function it served in an utterance (see Table 8.1). We also counted the number of modal utterances that were questions and negatives. In total, we coded over 2,100 instances of modal utterances, culled from the more than 10,600 utterances we had collected. All coding of each language was done by native speakers after extensive discussion of the code and practice coding among the collaborators.

TABLE 8.1
Semantic Functions Expressed by Modal Words

Semantic Category	Semantic Function	Example
Permission	Expresses or request consent to do an act.	"You can choose the page we read."
Obligation	Expresses commitment to the performance of an act or behavior.	"You must stay there."
Necessity	Expresses the belief that a state of affairs is unavoidable, inevitable, or undeniable	"You'll have to take one of these three."
Possibility	Expresses the potential for or the probability of an act, event, or state of affairs.	"That can come off."
Conditional	Expresses the necessity of setting up a prerequisite condition so that an action can be done.	"You have to line up the train's wheels with the track."
Enablement	Expresses that an action can be done since the prerequisite conditions have been set up.	"Now you can do it."
Willingness/ Agreement	Expresses willingness or agreement to participate in an act.	"Yes, I'll read you the bunny book."
Intention/ Volition	Expresses determination, desire, or choice to do an act or create a state.	"I'm gonna build a tower."

Our findings were that American mothers used significantly more modals than German mothers, about one in every four sentences they spoke to their children, as compared to one in five for the German mothers. However, the German mothers on average used significantly more of the semantic categories (eight) than did the American mothers (six). For both groups of mothers, the most frequent semantic categories were intention and possibility. Nonetheless, American mothers used these categories significantly more than did the German mothers. German mothers, on the other hand talked relatively more about necessity than did American mothers, and the number of German mothers who talked about necessity at both observation times and obligation, permission, and conditionality at the first observation time differed significantly from the number of American mothers who did so. Mothers also differed significantly in the frequency of modal utterances that were questions or negatives, with American mothers producing more modal questions, and German mothers producing more modal negatives (Shatz, Grimm, Wilcox, & Niemeier–Wind, 1989).

In speech style terms, the German mothers can be characterized as focusing more than the American mothers on necessity and obligation and using more negatives, whereas the American mothers focus more on intention and possibility, and ask more questions. Indeed, when we developed composite measures characterizing these two styles, and rank ordered the groups of mothers, the German mothers ranked significantly higher than the American mothers on the "German" style measure, and the reverse was true for the "American" style measure.

What about the children? Both groups of children were learning their respective modal systems during the period of our observations. The German children were even more advanced than the Americans with regard to measures like frequency of modal use and number of different modal words used. Of interest here is the finding that the correlations between parents and children on the frequency of types of modal words were significant for both language groups, and the correlation on the frequency of semantic categories was significant for the Germans. Thus, the frequencies with which parents used certain words were already reflected in their children's vocabularies, and, for the German children, they showed an equivalent effect on modal meanings as well. For example, a few German children were already making obligation statements, whereas no American children were. Also, with regard to the particular words used, *müssen* was the second most frequent modal for both mothers and children in German, but American mothers rarely used *must* (*have to* was fifth most frequent) and American children never produced it (*have to* was seventh most frequent). It appears, then, that even for children under the age of 3 years, the different parental speech styles were being taken up by the children and were conveying information to them about underlying social values.

In sum, our comparison of German and American mothers has revealed some measurable differences in child–directed speech that seem to reflect cultural values related to parenting reported by others relying on very different methods. Using specific measures of language, we have demonstrated that those sorts of differences are conveyed even to toddlers via maternal speech. Moreover, we have seen that such young children are already starting to reflect those differences in their own speech.

Comparing British and American Mothers

How can we be sure that the differences we observed between German and American maternal speech were indeed differences of parenting style and not ones determined primarily by irrelevant characteristics of the different languages spoken? After all, although German and English have some common ancestry and share many typological characteristics, nonetheless, they are distinctly different languages. Even within the modal verb system, there are some major differences. For example, English modals are generally considered to be auxiliaries rather than main verbs, whereas in German, the reverse is true (although for both languages there is considerable controversy among linguists about how to categorize modals grammatically). Semantically, too, there are differences. Even the number of words we searched for that expressed the range of meanings of interest to us varied from 16 in English to 8 in German. Although there are rough equivalents in one language for many of the modals in the other language, there are some words which are not easily translated on a one–for–one basis. Moreover, some words, like *müssen* and *must* which look equivalent may have very different rates of occurrence in the two languages in part because one can carry a broader range of meanings than the other.

Determining which of these linguistic differences is reflective of some cultural difference and which is irrelevant is a knotty problem. Obviously, only some structural characteristics of languages are reflective of the social values of the cultures in which they are spoken. Japanese morphology for honorifics is one example of such a characteristic. The broad range of meanings that *müssen* can carry may well be another. Even though the strong obligation sense of *müssen* can be qualified by the addition of various particles, nonetheless, the use of the term carries with it some connotation of commitment. Yet, differences in cultural values can be carried not only by differences in the specific forms of two languages, but also by parental lexical choices and by the relative frequency of the forms and meanings expressed. Thus, if the parental hypothesis holds generally, we should be able to find evidence for it even in two societies that speak the same language so long as the societies differ in cultural beliefs about socialization. (Similarly, this argument—and the proposed research framework—could be applied to subgroups within a culture.)

The next study was done with this hypothesis in mind. Sharon Wilcox, Tamara Halle, and I examined data from British families to compare their speech patterns to those in the American sample. Because American parents are often characterized as the most egalitarian and individualistically oriented of any, we expected that British parents would fall somewhat below the Americans in their emphasis on the child's intentions and possibilities for action. We also suspected they might be more negative and ask fewer questions of their children.

Our sample consisted of six British families from a slightly wider class range than the American sample. The parents were observed regularly for an hour at a time at home with their 2–year–olds and an older sibling during the course of a year (see Dunn & Shatz, 1989, for details of the data set and procedures of data collection). For the comparison to the American sample, we selected two observation times 4 months apart, starting when the children were 2 years, 2 months. Thus, the British children were a bit younger than the American sample. Another difference between the samples is that in the British sample, the older child was present during the audiotapings, whereas the American and German data consisted only of dyadic interactions. The presence of the older sibling may have influenced the speech of the mothers, even when they were directly addressing the younger children. Because of these sampling differences, our findings must be taken as only suggestive.

We followed the same procedures for analyzing the British data as had been done for the German and American data. The mothers' toddler–directed speech was searched for uses of modals, and then the utterances containing a modal were coded for type of word and semantic function as in Table 8.1. We then compared the frequency and kinds of modals and their functions found in the British data to those from the American data.

On average, American mothers used significantly more modals than did British mothers. Moreover, a significantly larger proportion of their speech included modals expressing notions of intention and possibility than occurred in the speech of the British mothers. There was no difference in the frequency with which American and British mothers produced questions with modals, but British mothers did produce significantly more negative utterances with modals than did Americans. Thus, our hypotheses about possible differences between the British mothers' speech and the American mothers' speech were largely confirmed. Even in two groups of mothers speaking the same language, we found differences in the way the language was used in social interaction with toddlers. It is unlikely, then, that the differences we observed in the German and American data can all be attributed to differences in language structure alone.

CONCLUSIONS

The research reported here suggests that we can learn much about social development from controlled studies comparing the language behavior of people from different cultures. It appears that the way language is used in different cultures, even with very young children, can have profound effects on their cognitive functioning and their social understandings. Without this kind of research, we have only descriptions of how cultures differ but little understanding of whether and how those differences matter in development.

Moreover, we can gain insights about development not just from the study of cultures very different from one another. Our work shows that cultures (and their languages) which are often assumed to be much alike can be different in important ways, and even societies that share a common language can use it in ways that may result in different outcomes for child development. We have seen that Korean–

speaking children function on certain language processing tasks more like English–speaking children than like Japanese speakers, even though their language shares many general characteristics with Japanese. We have seen that middle–class mothers from two highly industrialized societies (Germany and the United States) can differ significantly in the ways they use modal language when interacting with their children and that those differences are beginning to influence even their 2–year–olds. We have also seen that British mothers differ from American mothers in the way they use modal language, despite the commonality of their language. Thus, measures of language use can demonstrate subtle differences between cultural groups that appear to have much in common. As yet, we know relatively little about which of such subtleties are most important to children's development as functioning members of their societies, but comparative cross–cultural studies of language use provide us a means of directly investigating the question of how, indeed, Japanese or Koreans or Germans or Americans generally come to be different from one another.

It is important to remember that the studies presented are intended as illustrative examples of the kinds of direct, comparative research that can be done on questions of language socialization. In both studies, the arguments for cultural differences existing between the groups had been suggested independently by other researchers using other methods. Thus, the point of the work presented here is not to show that Japanese are more polite to their interlocutors than are Koreans and Americans, or that German parents are more authoritative in style than American parents. Others have made such claims based on other data. Rather, the point is that if characteristics like these are associated with certain groups, then one should be able to find correlates of them in the language spoken to and acquired by the children in those groups.

Obviously, it is not sensible to make broad generalizations from small samples of subjects to whole societies on the basis of a handful of studies. Moreover, there are bound to be individual, intra–cultural differences among members of the same cultural group, or among subcultural groups, and these have not been addressed here. Nonetheless, cultures do differ in significant and documentable ways, and it is important for us to discover the nature and range of those differences, how they are articulated, and how they are perpetuated. Studying the language behavior of samples of subjects drawn from those cultures is one way of doing some of that work.

There are many possibilities for future research in the area of language socialization. It is important to have studies that can draw on larger sample sizes. How language functions in different cultures in a variety of situations would be important to investigate, as would the question of the range of speech, and speech roles, to which a child is exposed. Similarly, it would be useful to have some longitudinal comparisons to assess the different communicative influences on children as they pass through, say, educational systems in different cultures. How uniform is the message of cultural values they receive from socializing agents beyond the immediate family? What influences on reasoning do the early socialization practices have; what influences on motivation? How do children whose parental styles differ from the cultural norms develop? How much intra–cultural variation is there, and how does this affect socialization outcomes? These are some of the questions that such research can begin to address. The cross–cultural study of the role of language use in development promises to help us discover how we humans acquire the social skills and cognitive capacities that are required to be functioning members of a society.

ACKNOWLEDGMENTS

I wish to thank Judy Dunn and Penny Munn for access to their data on British families. A Fulbright research grant helped in the preparation of those data. The Social Sciences Research Council provided partial support for the German–American study, as did the Office of the Vice President for Research at the University of Michigan. The empirical research discussed here could not have been done without the dedicated collaboration of my colleagues: Jeansue Lee Kim and M. Michael Akiyama for the Japanese, Korean, and English study; Hannelore Grimm, Karin Niemeier–Wind, and Sharon A. Wilcox for the German–American study; and Sharon A. Wilcox and Tamara Halle for the American–British comparison. Two of them, M. Michael Akiyama and Sharon A. Wilcox, were kind enough to read and comment on an earlier version of this manuscript. Of course, my arguments regarding the role research like this plays in understanding language and socialization across cultures are my own.

REFERENCES

Akiyama, M. M. Are language–acquisition strategies universal? *Developmental Psychology*, 1984, *20*, 219–228.

Akiyama, M. M. Denials in young children from a cross–linguistic perspective. *Child Development*, 1985, *56*, 95–102.

Akiyama, M. M. Task specificity and language effects in verification: Comments on "Development of the concept of truth functional negation." *Developmental Psychology*, 1986, *22*, 415–418.

Bowerman, M. What shapes children's grammars? In D. I. Slobin (Ed.), *The crosslinguistic study of language acquisition* (Vol. 2, pp. 1257–1319). Hillsdale, NJ: Lawrence Erlbaum Associates, 1985.

Choi, S., & Zubin, D. Acquisition of negation. In S. Kuno, J. Whitman, I. Lee, & Y. Kang (Eds.), *Harvard studies in Korean linguistics* (Vol. 1, pp. 135–144). Cambridge: Harvard University Press, 1985.

Clancy, P. M. The acquisition of communicative style in Japanese. In B.B. Schieffelin & E. Ochs (Eds.), *Language socialization across cultures* (pp. 213–250). Cambridge: Cambridge University Press, 1986.

Dunn, J., & Munn, P. Becoming a family member: Family conflict and the development of social understanding. *Child Development*, 1985, *56*, 480–492.

Dunn, J., & Shatz, M. Becoming a conversationalist despite (or because of) having an older sibling. *Child Development*, 1989, *60*, 399–410.

Givon, T. Function, structure, and language acquisition. In D. I. Slobin (Ed.), *The crosslinguistic study of language acquisition* (Vol. 2, pp. 1005–1027). Hillsdale, NJ: Lawrence Erlbaum Associates, 1985.

Grossman, K, Grossman, K. E., Spangler, G., Suess, G., & Unzner, L. Maternal sensitivity and newborns' orientation responses as related to quality of attachment in Northern Germany. In I. Bretherton & E.

Waters (Eds.), *Growing points of attachment theory and research. Monographs of the Society for Research in Child Development*, 1985, *50*, 233–254.

Kim, J. L., Shatz, M., & Akiyama, M. M. The effects of language and task on children's patterns of sentence verification and denial. *Developmental Psychology*, 1990, *26*, 821-829.

Kim, K. J. Development of the concept of truth–functional negation. *Developmental Psychology*, 1985, *21*, 462–472.

Lewin, K. *Resolving social conflicts. Selected papers on group dynamics*. New York: Harper, 1948.

Makino, S. *Kurikaeshi–no Bumpo*. (The grammar of repetition). Tokyo: Taishukan, 1980.

Ochs, E. Talking to children in Western Samoa. *Language in Society*, 1982, *11*, 77–104.

Ochs, E. Introduction. In B. B. Schieffelin & E. Ochs (Eds.), *Language socialization across cultures* (pp. 1-13). Cambridge: Cambridge University Press, 1986.

Ochs, E., & Schieffelin, B. B. Language acquisition and socialization: Three developmental stories. In R. Shweder & R. LeVine (Eds.), *Culture theory: Essays on mind, self, and emotion* (pp. 276–320). Cambridge: Cambridge University Press, 1984.

Schieffelin, B. B. Getting it togther: an ethnographic approach to the study of the development of communicative competence. In E. Ochs & B. B. Schieffelin (Eds.), *Developmental pragmatics* (pp. 73–108). New York: Academic Press, 1979.

Schieffelin, B. B., & Ochs, E. Language socialization. *Annual Review of Anthropology*, 1986, *15*, 163–191.

Shatz, M., Grimm, H., Wilcox, S. A., & Niemeier–Wind, K. *The uses of modal expressions in conversations between German and American mothers and their 2–year–olds*. Paper presented at the Biennial Meeting of the Society for Research in Child Development. Kansas City, 1989.

Shweder, R. A. *The problem of rationality*. Colloquium delivered at the Institute for Social Research. Ann Arbor: 1989.

Slobin, D. I. Cognitive prerequisites for the development of grammar. In C. A. Ferguson & D. I. Slobin (Eds.), *Studies of child language development* (pp. 175–208). New York: Holt, Rinehart, & Winston, 1973.

Slobin, D. I. Crosslinguistic evidence for the language–making capacity. In D. I. Slobin (Ed.), *The crosslinguistic study of language acquisition* (Vol. 2, pp. 1157–256). Hillsdale, NJ: Lawrence Erlbaum Associates, 1985.

Triandis, H. C. The self and social behavior in differing cultural contexts. *Psychological Review*, 1989, *96*, 506–520.

Whitehurst, G. J., Falco, F. L., Lonigan, C. J., Fischel, J. E., DeBaryshe, B. D., Valdez–Menchaca, M. C., & Caulfield, M. Accelerating language development through picture book reading. *Developmental Psychology*, 1988, *24*, 552–559.

Becoming American or English? Talking about the Social World in England and the United States

9

Judy Dunn and Jane Brown
Pennsylvania State University

INTRODUCTION

The nature and extent of the differences between the cultures of the United States and of England have puzzled and intrigued writers from both worlds for at least a century and a half. Even without the sensibility of Henry James, most transatlantic travellers respond to such differences—with reactions that can range from a sense of amusement at relatively trivial matters of difference in greetings or public manner, to an unease at hints of chasms between two sets of beliefs about deeper social issues. If we reflect for a moment on the experiences of small children and their parents in those two cultures two sets of questions—each with profoundly important developmental implications—arise. The first set concerns the nature of children as cultural selves. In what sense is a preschool child growing up in the States today an *American* child? How are preschool–aged *English* children different from their peers in the US? If sense–of–self is a product of a particular culture, then are 2– and 3–year–olds, whose sense of self is in the making, already influenced by whether they are growing up in Cambridge, Massachusetts as opposed to Cambridge, England, or Lancaster, Pennsylvania as opposed to Lancaster, Lancashire?

To focus on the issue is to raise a series of notoriously intractable questions. What is the nature of children's sense of self in the early years? If acquiring language is acquiring culture, as argued by anthropologists—in what dimensions then is the language of the Pennsylvanian child different from that of the Lancastrian? Most importantly, do differences *within* each group outweigh differences between them? Are educational or social class differences between the parents within each cultural group, or the contrast between rural and urban families, for instance, in fact more salient in accounting for the development of individual differences than the cross–national differences? Both within the United States and within Britain there are notably wide differences in cultural experience, as the illuminating work of Brice–Heath (1983), Miller, (Miller & Sperry, 1987), and the Newsons (Newson & Newson, 1968) have each illustrated.

The second set of developmental questions concerns the nature of the processes by which differences between or within the groups are formed; here the role of parent–child relationships obviously is a potentially key one. But what aspects of the parent–child relationship are important here? Where should we begin to explore the possible differences in what happens between parents and children in the two worlds? Parents are such crucial architects of the lives of their babies and young children: What aspects of that architecture should we examine? We could focus on the broad structure of the children's lives: How much time do they spend with their parents, how much time do they watch television or read books? Such a focus on the "ecological context" of children's lives in different cultures has been employed for instance by the Whitings and their colleagues (Whiting & Edwards, 1988) and by Super and Harkness (1986). In contrast, we could choose to examine more fine grained details of children's social relationships in their different worlds, features of parent–child interaction that current developmental theories propose are important. For example, how responsive are the parents to their children's needs and demands? What is the nature of the cognitive demands that they place on their children? How do the "narratives"that parents and children construct together about the child as a social self differ?

Where we chose to look for differences in parenting between the two cultures will of course depend on what aspects of children's development we are attempting to understand, as well as our own theoretical predilections. If we are trying to explain broad differences in nutritional status or health, we would obviously look at rather different parental processes from those that we would guess to be implicated in differences in, say, politeness or intellectual style. But even with a relatively circumscribed developmental outcome in mind, such as differences in cognitive style, the range of parental practices that might be important in contributing to differences in outcome is very great. If our concern is with the nature of differences in children's social understanding and sense–of–self—aspects of that vague notion "cultural self"—then the question of where it would be appropriate to look for relevant differences in parenting practice is one for which we have rather little guidance in current theory or empirical work. But themes in recent anthropological and developmental writings stand out as signposts for us.

Most significantly, there has been what Bruner (1986, p. 90) terms a revolution in the definition of human culture:

> It takes the form of a move away from the strict structuralism that held that culture was a set of interconnected rules from which people derive particular behaviors to fit particular situations, to the idea of culture as implicit and only semiconnected knowledge of the world from which, through negotiation, people arrive at satisfactory ways of acting in given contexts. The anthropologist Clifford Geertz likens the process of acting in a culture to that of interpreting an ambiguous text.

As part of this shift towards a view of culture as implicit, negotiated knowledge, there is a focus on the implicit and explicit messages in daily practices and interaction of members of a culture. The arguments of Rosaldo (1984, p. 140) are frequently quoted as expositions of this view:

> What is important here is the claim that meaning is a fact of public life, and secondly that cultural patterns—social facts—provide the template for all human action, growth and understanding. Culture so construed is ... a matter less of artifacts and propositions, rules, schematic programs, or beliefs, than of associative chains and images that tell what can be reasonably linked up with what; we come to know it through collective stories that suggest the nature of coherence, probability and sense within the actor's world. Culture is, then, always richer than the traits recorded in the ethnographer's accounts because its truth resides not in explicit formulations of the rituals of daily life but in the daily practices of persons who in acting take for granted an account of who they are and how to understand their fellows' moves.

The argument that we should examine the implicit and explicit cultural messages in daily interactions is convincing—but very general in its formulation. Where within that rich and complex tapestry of interactions should we look for distinctive differences in the messages children receive about their cultural world, and about themselves as members of that world?

There are a number of good candidates that have been suggested in recent work, and in this chapter we will consider four such aspects of discourse about the social world in which implicit and explicit messages are conveyed to the child. First, interactions over transgressions of social rules, and discussion of prescriptions more generally, are likely to reveal differences in the nature of prescriptions between cultural groups. Further, they are likely to be the context in which children learn what's expected, allowed, negotiable—and forbidden in their world. Haste (1987, p. 163), commenting on common aphorisms in North America and Britain such as "You shouldn't hit people; it hurts" or "Real men don't eat quiche" notes that:

> Such rules are the grammar of social relations. They are a model for ordering and organizing one's experience; they reflect, and prescribe, a range of explanations of the social and physical world. In acquiring these rules, the child learns the basis for interaction with others, and the shared cultural framework for making sense of the world.

A second arena in which distinctive cultural messages may well be conveyed concerns discourse about feelings. Marked cultural differences in such discourse about affect have been described between different American cultures (Miller & Sperry, 1987). These differences take on especial significance in light of recent evidence that differences in talk about feelings during early childhood have been shown to be associated with later differences in children's judgments about the feelings of others (Dunn, Brown, & Beardsall, in press). Thirdly, the fantasies in which children and their parents become engaged in the different cultures could provide another window on children's and parents' views of their world. And a fourth domain of interaction between parents and children that is currently receiving attention for its cross–cultural significance is the joint construction of *narratives about the self* (Miller, Potts, Fung, Hoogstra, & Mintz, in press).

Our plan in this chapter is to discuss each of these contexts that involve discourse about the social world, and to explore their potential for generating similarities and differences in children's development across the two cultures. But first, one significant theme in recent developmental work that underlines the potential importance of these aspects of discourse should be noted. We now know that children from very early in life are both interested in and participate in discourse about such matters. Their moral and social understanding is well underway by their second and third years (Dunn, 1988). Notions of harm, responsibility, culpability, principles of positive justice, and excuses of intent are all in place, and this understanding forms a central core in children's armory of justification and reasoning within the power politics of the family; it is an understanding that is evident not only in their disputes but in their jokes and their pretend play. The significance of this evidence for our present purposes is, of course, that these are principles of the wider world outside the family that are already understood and used by children. That children are already participant in discourse about the social rules and roles of their world—including principles beyond the idiosyncratic practices of particular families—suggests that such discourse may be a promising place to look for the development of cultural differences. And, perhaps more important, examining such discourse in families from different cultures may highlight developmental processes of more *general* significance.

In this chapter we explore these four aspects of discourse between parents and young children about the social world: prescriptions, feeling state talk, joint fantasies, and joint narratives about the self. For the first three we draw on data from two longitudinal studies of young children at home with their mothers and siblings: 50 families in Centre County Pennsylvania and 43 families in Cambridge, in England. The discussion on narratives will chiefly refer to the work of Miller and her associates. What follows is essentially an exploration of possible domains for further work, rather than a presentation of finished research.

DISCOURSE ABOUT THE SOCIAL WORLD

The 50 Pennsylvanian families we studied were recruited from consecutive birth announcements in the local paper of a county that includes a large State University, small industries, and a rural farming population. In terms of occupational status and education, the sample is diverse, representative of the County, and includes families within the town community and relatively isolated rural families, some of whom were relatively disadvantaged. The fathers' occupational status assessed with the National Opinion Research Corporation prestige rating ranged from 15 to 88 (mean 51.5, SD 16.3); for the U.S. white labor force the NORC rating is 41.7 (SD 13.9), thus although the Pennsylvania sample has a higher occupational rating than the working US population, the variance is similar. The English families studied lived in Cambridge and surrounding villages, and also included a range of occupational and educational backgrounds—though the diversity was less extreme. The fathers' occupation classified according to the Registrar General (1973) was Professional/managerial for 27 families, White collar for four families, Skilled manual for nine families, and Unskilled manual for three.

Each family had at least two children, and the focus of each study was upon the second–born child: we were interested in the contribution of older siblings, as well as parents, to the development of social understanding in early childhood. The methods of data collection were similar in the two studies. Two one–hour naturalistic observations were made in the home at each time point studied; audiotape recordings of family conversation were made, while a single observer who was familiar with the family kept paper–and–pencil record of certain aspects of the interactions and context (see Dunn, 1988 for details). Observations were made on the U.S. sample when the secondborn children were 33 and 39 months old, in the English sample when the children were 18, 24, and 36 months old. The focus of this paper will be on comparisons between the Pennsylvanian and Cambridge samples when the children were 33—39 months, and 36 months old, respectively.

A brief note should be taken of the contexts in which these family conversations took place, and of the frequency of parent–child talk in the two samples. The observations were completely unstructured; we explained to the mothers that we wished to observe the children in their daily routines, and to disrupt family life as little as possible. Thus, during the observations mothers were usually busy preparing meals or clearing up, doing housework, cleaning; they often stopped for a cup of coffee or tea, and some watched TV; many talked on the phone. The children played, quarrelled, talked, and got in and out of trouble, in a way that their mothers commented was pretty representative of their usual daily pattern. Test–retest correlations for measures of maternal talk were significantly positive (e.g., for the frequency of maternal speaker turns to child per hour of observation, $r = .74, p <$ .05), indicating that the 2 hours of time sampled gave reasonably reliable data on these variables.

The houses in both samples ranged widely in size and comfort, however there was a tendency for the American houses to be larger, and for the children in the American sample to spend more time away from their mothers, and alone with their siblings. (Mother and child were together on average 70% of observation time in the U.S. sample, 78% in the U.K. sample, $X^2 (1) = 5.2, p < .05$). The MLU of the children in the two samples was not significantly different (3.77 in the U.K., 3.67 in the U.S.), nor was the amount the mothers talked to the children (the mean number of mother to child turns of talk per hour of home observation was 134 in the U.K. sample and 139 in the U.S. sample).

Discussion of Social Rules, Transgressions, and Prescriptions

In the world of 2– and 3–year–old children—whether American or English—messages about what is allowed and what is not, about what is acceptable, preferable, or absolutely forbidden are a common feature of daily life. We have explored a number of features of such prescriptive messages (e.g., Dunn & Munn, 1987); in this first, exploratory comparison of discourse concerning social rules in the two samples, three general aspects of mothers' talk about prescriptions in the two cultures were considered. The first was the *topics* on which mothers' prescriptions were focused in the two cultures. Was prominence given to a different set of issues in Cambridge from those emphasized in Centre County? In drawing attention to what is normative and desirable behavior, do mothers in the two samples emphasize different aspects of the social world?

The second general aspect of the mothers' prescriptions we explored was the question of *how* these messages were sent to the children? Here our interest was in the distinction among (1) explicit prescriptions articulated in a normative formulation (e.g., "Dirty shoes don't go on the table" or "Kids aren't supposed to do that."), (2) more indirect formulations of a prescription (e.g., "Where do those shoes go?" or "Was that Daddy's, that you used?"), and (3) direct prohibitions of individual actions (e.g., "Take your shoes off the table.") in which disapproval or control was articulated in terms of the child's particular actions rather than in terms of a general rule.

The third general feature considered was whether the prescriptive message was accompanied by an evaluative comment or label. Here we were interested in whether moral evaluative messages (e.g., good, naughty, not nice) concerning the transgression or behavior were included in the prescription.

For this exploratory examination, data were compared from 20 families from the two cultural groups, in which pairs of children from each group were matched in terms of child gender and occupational and educational background of the families. With such a very small sample, results of comparisons must be treated simply as pilot data that can identify suitable targets for more systematic study with larger samples. Although that caveat must be borne in mind, the results of the comparisons do highlight some points of general interest concerning the children's experiences in the two cultural groups.

The initial general point is that there were very large within–group differences. The issue of effect size is one that must be taken seriously, in any work comparing sub–cultures in the U.S. or Britain. Even where we find mean differences between groups, we have to bear in mind that there may be significant—developmentally significant—within–group variation. There were, nevertheless, interesting cross–cultural differences in each of the aspects of social rule discussion that we considered, and these will be briefly summarized.

Topic of social rules discussed. The issues discussed during the observations were categorized according to a system that distinguished the topics of *Rights* (possession), *Positive justice* (sharing, taking turns), *Harm* to others (kindness, aggression), *Destruction*, and *Rules of the house* (issues of daily routine, politeness, tidiness, appropriate clothes). Comparison of the proportions of maternal speaker turns that focused on prescriptions in these different categories showed that a higher proportion of such maternal turns focused on the issue of Rights in the Centre County families than in those in Cambridge, and the issue of Harm was more

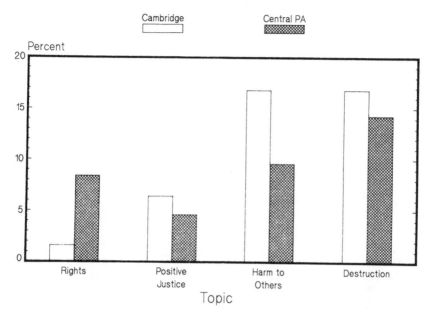

Figure 9.1. Topic of rules: Percentage of prescriptions referring to different topics. (*Note that prescriptions referring to "rules-of-the-house" are not included in the table.*)

prominent in Cambridge (see Figure 9.1). The differences in the proportion of prescriptions focused on these topics in the two groups were significant, $z = 2.67$ for Rights, $z = 18.9$ for Harm to others, $ps < .05$. Issues of Destruction and Positive justice were discussed with similar frequency in the two groups.

Rules–of–the–house (not shown in Figure 9.1) was much the most prominent issue discussed in both cultures, accounting for 63.2% and 58.4% of prescriptions in Centre County and Cambridge, respectively. We took a closer look at the prescriptions within this general category, distinguishing rules concerned with politeness/appropriate mealtime behavior, noisiness, tidiness/things in their proper place; again, differences within each cultural group were marked, but there were also some differences between the groups. For example, appropriate meal time behavior and politeness stood out in the Cambridge sample as relatively common topics, and were less prominent in the American sample, while noisiness and wild behavior were more commonly a matter of social–rule–talk by the American than the English mothers (see Figure 9.2). The differences between the two groups were significant, for appropriate meal time behavior, $z = 3.52$, and for noisiness/wild behavior, $z = 2.40, p < .05$. These pilot data, then, indicate that as early as 33–36 months, different aspects of the social world are being emphasized for these children in Cambridge and in Pennsylvania—but that there is striking within–group variation in each cultural group.

Explicitness and directness in prescriptions. The second aspect of mothers' prescriptions that we examined concerned the form of the message sent in the two

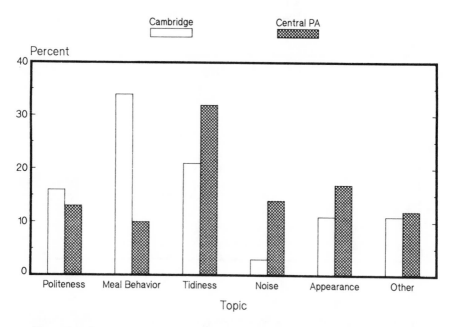

Figure 9.2. Prescriptions referring to "rules-of-the-house": Percentage focused on different topics.

samples. Here the data show considerable mean differences. The American mothers more often directed messages to their children about what is acceptable or unacceptable behavior in terms of the children's individual actions (the direct prohibitions shown in Figure 9.3) than the English mothers, $z = 3.40$, $p < .05$, while prescriptions in the form of explicit rules about behavior couched in general normative language were more commonly given by the English than the American mothers, $z = 2.22$, $p < .05$. In Cambridge, that is, mothers were more likely to discuss matters of behavior in terms of the norms of a wider social world than they were in Centre County; the following examples that come from Cambridge mothers illustrate such comments:

E.g. 1
CHILD TO MOTHER: I want to kick you! I want to kick you!
MOTHER TO CHILD: You mustn't kick people.

E.g. 2
[Following dispute about whether child can have the umbrella]
CHILD TO MOTHER: Where's the umbrella?
MOTHER TO CHILD: The umbrella's out hanging on the pegs because that's where umbrellas live, isn't it?

E.g. 3
CHILD TO SIBLING: I hate you!
MOTHER TO CHILD: You don't really do you? He's your brother!

E.g. 4
[Child and sibling are on table]
MOTHER TO CHILD: Tables aren't for walking on!

In Centre County maternal control attempts came in the form of directives or comments about the children's individual actions more often than they did in Cambridge [see Figure 9.3].

E.g. 5
MOTHER TO CHILD: Don't do that in here!

E.g. 6
Child is fussing because she knocked herself while rushing around:
MOTHER TO CHILD: That's because you weren't watching what you were doing!

Evaluative prescriptions. The third aspect of the prescriptions on which we focused was the issue of whether evaluative comments or labels accompanied the mothers' prescriptions. Here again, both within– and between–group differences were marked. In Cambridge, children were much more likely to receive evaluative, moral messages along with the prescription—both in positive and in negative terms—than the children in Centre County. In the Cambridge families, 19% of maternal prescriptions were accompanied by an evaluative label; in Centre County, only 5%. The difference is highly significant, $X^2 (1) = 17.43, p < .01$, and it raises questions about whether such evaluative discourse affects children's attitudes and responses to issues of social transgression—and indeed to their sense of self worth.

In summary, while differences within each cultural group were notable, there were also differences between the cultural groups that are worth attention. In Centre

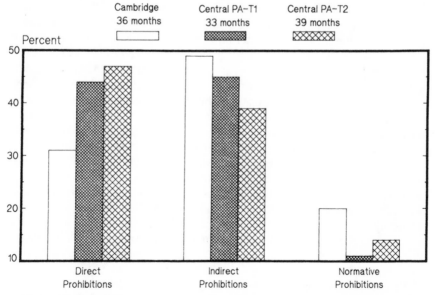

Figure 9.3. Prescriptions: Percentage of direct prohibitions, indirect prohibitions, and normative prescriptions.

County, the rights of the individual were frequently stressed, in Cambridge, harm to others; in Cambridge, politeness and appropriate behavior were commented on with some frequency, in Centre County, noisiness and wild behavior. The prescriptive messages were sent to the English children in terms of general normative rules, as if the mothers presumed that 36–month–olds can understand normative expectations of how people in general behave. The appeal to the child was in terms of shared beliefs about how it is desirable for people in general to behave, an appeal to what the child "knows" people do. In Centre County, the prescriptions were addressed to a child in terms of his or her own personal actions—and they were much less likely to carry an evaluative message. The moral tone of the mothers' comments was less explicit. It is tempting to extrapolate from such findings to national characteristics; however for the moment we should of course treat these pilot data with much caution, their usefulness lying in the illumination they provide for planning future research.

Discussion of Feeling States within the Family

The second domain on which we focused was the discussion of feeling states in the two groups. Previous work had shown that differences in the frequency of such discourse about feelings in the preschool period were correlated with children's ability to judge others' emotions, as assessed in the Rothenberg Test of Social Sensitivity (Dunn et al., in press; Rothenberg, 1970). Were there differences in the frequency or nature of such discourse in the two samples? We examined data from the full sample of families in each group (50 U.S. and 43 English families), and considered the thematic content and social context in which family discussions about feelings took place, in addition to the frequency with which they occurred.

As with discussions of social rules, differences in mothers' talk about feelings within each cultural group stand out as well as the contrasts between mothers' talk between the two. Mothers in Cambridge made reference to feelings on average eight times an hour, and mothers in central Pennsylvania averaged 11 feeling state turns per hour. The difference in these two means was not statistically significant, in large part because of the great variability within each sample. During the observations some English mothers made no references, others as many as 21 references per hour; the American mothers' references showed a similar range.

Twenty different emotion-descriptive themes were identified in the mothers' feeling state talk in both countries. When we looked for differences in the number of mothers who referred to particular themes in the two groups we found that significantly more of the mothers in Pennsylvania talked about dislike of actions and things, pain, disgust, remorse and affection, and by contrast concern and sympathy were referred to by a larger proportion of the English mothers. On average, the American mothers also referred to a wider range of emotion themes than the English mothers, U.S. mean was 5.9 and U.K. mean was 4.2, $t = 3.61, p < .05$.

Further examination of the themes and context in which mothers talked about feelings revealed an interesting pattern of differences. Emotion themes were divided into three groups: those with explicitly negative hedonic tone (e.g., pain, distress, dislike, anger), those with explicitly positive hedonic tone (e.g., pleasure, amusement, sympathy, affection), and those which were neither explicitly positive or negative, or were blends (e.g., surprise, concern, fatigue). In the Pennsylvanian homes negative emotion themes were more likely to be referred to than in the English homes, both in terms of the proportion of feeling state references (64% versus 38%) and the actual number of times per hour than mothers made such references (7.52 versus 3.37), $t = 2.69$, $p < .05$. In fact it is likely that references to negative emotions in the American sample account for the greater "diversity" of themes noted in these mothers' talk. Positive themes were referred to about equally in the two groups, and mothers talked about positive feelings less often than negative feelings in both cultural groups.

Not only did the mothers in Pennsylvania refer to negative emotions more often, the context in which they talked about feelings was more likely to be conflictual than the feeling state discussions in the English homes. Again, both the proportion and frequency measures showed feeling state talk was more often in the context of disputes: proportion means were 33% in the U.S. and 24% in the U.K., X^2 (1) = 9.9, $p < .05$; frequency means were 3.54 versus 1.91 turns per hour, $t = 2.5$, $p < .05$.

In summary, in both countries, mothers made frequent references to feelings in conversation with their young children. In the course of daily interactions the American mothers referred more often to negative feelings, to a wider range of feelings, and made their references more often in the context of disputes than the English mothers.

It may be helpful to interpret this pattern of feeling state talk in light of our finding that mothers' talk about social rules may have been precipitated more often by battling siblings in the U.S. than in the English homes. It seems plausible that in the relatively large U.S. homes mothers may have been drawn to where the children were playing by sounds of rough–housing or distress, resulting in a greater frequency of references to negative feelings and a higher proportion of such talk occurring in the context of disputes.

But what of the implications of these differences for the children growing up in the two cultures? In particular, can we suggest that the observed differences in family talk will be associated with differences in children's ability to understand emotions in the two countries? Interestingly, two of the differences noted between the two cultures—the diversity of themes discussed, and the frequency of feeling state discussion occurring in disputes—have been previously found to correlate positively with the English children's social understanding at age 6 (Dunn et al., in press). Whether these same variables are implicated in the development of in-dividual differences in children's understanding of emotions in the Pennsylvanian families is currently being investigated.

Pretend Play within the Family

The selection of pretend as a domain for examining potential cross–cultural differences and similarities is made on several grounds. First, pretend play is notable as a context in which children begin to explore the social rules and roles of their world (Garvey, 1977); it provides a window on the nature of their understanding of that world (Bretherton, 1984); and—it is widely argued—pretend may well be a context in which such understanding is fostered. Second, marked differences in parental interest and involvement in such pretend have been described in different sub–cultural groups in Britain (Dunn, 1980; Dunn & Wooding, 1977; Newson & Newson, 1968) and in the U.S. (Miller et al., in press). How far such differences in parental involvement contribute to differences in outcome remains a matter of controversy, but a plausible a priori case can be made for their significance (see, for example, Tough, 1977).

For the exploration of differences between the Centre County families and those in Cambridge, we examined the data from the observation of the 20 pilot families, and focused specifically upon two questions: Are there differences in the themes of the children's fantasy play in the two cultural groups, and are there differences in the involvement and participation of the mothers in the groups—specifically in the frequency of their verbal turns concerned with pretend?

The overall rate of social pretend play was similar in the two groups: For the Pennsylvanian families, on average 53.0 speaker turns per hour were made in pretend play, for the Cambridge families, 51.6 on average. There were, however, differences in the themes of the play in the two groups, shown in Figure 9.4 as the proportion of pretend turns focused on particular themes. The most noticeable

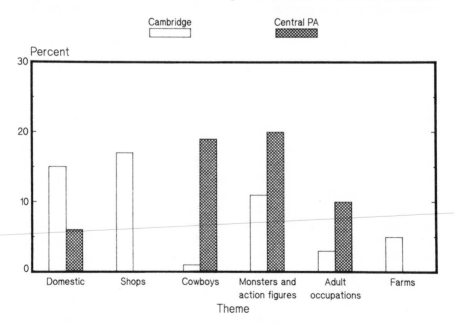

Figure 9.4. Themes of pretend play: Percentage of pretend turns focused on particular themes.

differences are that the American children engaged in more play about cowboys and horses, action figures, fantasy figures such as monsters, and "adult" dolls, whereas the English children engaged in more play related to farms, shopping, and domestic activities.

Mothers in the English sample engaged in almost twice as many pretend turns as the Pennsylvanian mothers (17.13 versus 9.50 per hour of observation time). We distinguished between turns that involved *participating, supervising*, or *soliciting* pretend play, and found that the proportion of the mothers' pretend turns in each of these categories was similar in the two samples. In summary, the experience of joint play in a shared fantasy world with the mother was more common for the Cambridge children, and already there were differences in the fantasy roles that they enacted. The Wild West was already salient for the Pennsylvanian children, whereas the English children played at more domestic roles. Napoleon's description of the English as a nation of shopkeepers appears still to be apt—a national characteristic that is evident astonishingly early!

Narratives and the Development of Cultural Selves

The final domain to be considered, in this search for fruitful arenas for cross–cultural comparisons, concerns personal story–telling—narratives about the self—and mothers' roles in co–constructing such accounts with young children. The significance of narrative in the development of sense of self has been cogently argued for by writers from anthropology, psychology, and sociology (e.g., Bruner, 1986; Gergen, 1989; Goffman 1959, 1974). Children are passionately interested in narrative, and their interest shows us how powerful narrative images are in generating a particular self in a particular culture. As Bruner (1986, p. 66) put it, stories "provide ... a map of possible worlds in which action, thought, and self–definition are permissible (and desirable)."

The proposition that personal story–telling plays an important role in the social construction of self is a plausible one; for very young children such talk is chiefly structured by adults (Eisenberg, 1985; Sachs, 1983), but by the third year children become more active participants in such joint stories about the child's past (Fivush, Gray, & Fromhoff, 1987). The work of Fivush (in press) and of Miller and her colleagues illustrate how illuminating attention to this domain can be. Miller's research has focused on the beginnings of this process of social construction. She has shown that the everyday practices in which mothers and children talk about their personal experiences provide a rich context in which children receive messages about who they are, what's special, exciting, funny, or deplorable about them, about which of their actions or sayings are approvable, or lamentable (Miller & Moore, 1989). She emphasizes "the socializing potential of the informal, mundane, and often pervasive narrative accounts that people give of their personal experiences ... even when such stories are told informally and without didactic intent, even when they are not addressed specifically to the young, they may play a powerful role in childhood socialization" (Miller et al., in press).

Most relevant for our present concerns, mothers differ in the style in which they structure such conversations (Fivush, in press; Fromhoff, 1988), and such differences appear to be linked to later differences in children's style. Miller and her colleagues have shown that the role of parents in the construction of personal stories concerning children varies very much among cultures within the U.S. The construction of stories by parents and their young children is compared in a number of different communities; this data set is used to highlight the dimensions that differentiate the interventions in joint narratives by caregivers in these different cultural groups. The researchers contrast, for example, the didactic nature of Chinese American parental contributions to joint stories, and their explicit moral messages, with those of the low–income African American and working–class white groups. "In these groups moral messages are embodied in caregivers' interventions but they tend to be implicit; the density of explicit references to moral rules and transgressions is lacking" (Miller et al., in press). Here the parallels with our comparison of Cambridge and Centre County mothers discussion of prescriptions is notable.

Another dimension of differences between the cultural groups that Miller and her colleagues emphasize concerns fantasy, or the distinction between literal and fictional. Caregivers from Chinese and low–income African American families, they note, were more tolerant of fictional elaborations of the "story of what happened", while a stricter adherence to the truth was wanted by the low–income working class white mothers. Again the parallels with the differences we have noted between the Cambridge and Centre County families in attitude to fantasy are noteworthy—though, again, we should stress that the within–group differences were marked, as well.

During our observations of the families in Cambridge and Central Pennsylvania stories about the child occurred, though somewhat less frequently than the data reported by Miller and Sperry (1988). They reported an average of 2.2 episodes per hour in the families they observed when the children were 2½ years old. In our samples, the English mothers and children engaged in an average of 1.4 episodes per hour of observation (range 0 – 3.5), but such talk occurred less often in the American families (mean 0.8 per hour, range 0 – 4.2). Given the small sample size and the large within–culture variability, it is not surprising that this difference did not reach statistical significance, $t = .88$. More of the English mothers told stories about their children's past experiences, 8 of the 10 versus 5 of the 10 Pennsylvania mothers, but the average lengths of the story–telling episodes were not significantly different (English mean = 8.1 turns versus U.S. mean = 6.6 turns; $t = .35$).

Following Miller and Sperry (1988), we examined the content of the stories, separating recounted events into *good* events, *bad* events, and *odd* events. Among the good events were: the child's achievements, recalling of pleasant occasions like holidays, positive social interactions, and signs of the child's mature behavior (e.g., not crying at preschool). *Bad* events included: stories about the child being injured and the child's transgressions. The category *odd* was reserved for those stories, some of which included transgressions, in which some novel or peculiar event was recounted. In the following example from the U.S., the "mystery" of the jumping fish is the central feature of the story, no reference to misbehavior is made:

CHILD TO MOTHER: Mom, one of my fish got on my floor.
MOTHER TO CHILD: Yup.
MOTHER TO OBSERVER: One of his fish got on his floor. He came outside, I was working in the garden. He said, "It jumped down and it was dead and wait til you see how far it jumped."
MOTHER TO CHILD: Show her. Let's show her.
SIBLING TO OBSERVER: It didn't jump.
MOTHER TO SIBLING: Hmm hmm. [smiling]
SIBLING TO MOTHER: It didn't jump.
CHILD TO MOTHER: I got it out with a net. Mom, I got it out with a net.
MOTHER TO CHILD: You got it out with a net! [smiling] I don't know what net!
MOTHER TO OBSERVER: But it was still alive!
CHILD TO MOTHER: It was right here! [pointing]
MOTHER TO CHILD: It was right there! It jumped the whole way! [laughing] Poor Pebbles (fish), we didn't know if she was going to make it, but she did![laughing]

Good events dominated the English families personal stories (69%); a quarter of their stories concerned *bad* events, and 6% were categorized as *odd*. In the American families *bad* events were most often recounted (43%) with *good* and *odd* events each comprising about one quarter of the total (29% *good*, 28% *odd*).

Unfortunately, there were too few episodes to make comparisons between the English and American mothers' use of explicit moral messages in the stories they told. Given the differences already noted in mothers' discussions of social rules in the two samples, further study of how moral messages are conveyed in personal narratives may be a fruitful avenue to explore; whether the same pattern would be found in personal stories remains an intriguing question. In general, moral messages were implicit in the stories. Occasionally any prescriptive message was made more ambiguous by the obvious delight with which the stories were told. For example, this English mother was clearly amused by an incident in which the child had refused to do as she was told.

SIBLING TO MOTHER: I just don't mind what I get do I?
MOTHER TO SIBLING: You just accept what jumpers go with which. Right. You know which ones match, don't you? But Julie sometimes wants ... What did she want to do this morning?
MOTHER TO CHILD: Which pair of tights did you want?
CHILD TO MOTHER: The ones with the hole in!
MOTHER TO CHILD: You did, didn't you?
CHILD TO MOTHER: Yes.
MOTHER TO CHILD: You had to have them on for about an hour before we managed to change them, didn't we?

One final note. Not only did mothers and children tell stories about the child, older siblings often participated as well, particularly among the English sample where older siblings joined in the telling of 75% of the stories. In the American sample older siblings participated a little less than half of the time (43%). Whether this difference reflects a true cultural difference remains an intriguing question. But, coupled with our finding of more frequent story–telling in the English homes, it raises the interesting possibility that these English children are growing up with greater expectation that their lives and exploits will be the subject of public scrutiny than are the American children we studied.

CONCLUSIONS

The results of this exploratory comparison highlight a number of general issues, to be taken seriously in future work on cross–cultural comparisons of parenting. First, the differences revealed in each of these domains, but especially in discussions of social rules, show how early distinctive cultural messages shape children's lives and their talk. Children are cultural creatures by the time they are 3; their fantasies and the rules that shape their lives and style are not just those of the family but those of the wider culture beyond the family.

However it is important to take seriously the differences within each cultural group. The great variability within the groups reminds us that we cannot presume that what is transmitted to children is a unitary culture, either in Central Pennsylvania or within a particular city in England. Even though these families were not from identified "sub–cultures" within either national group, we still found great differences in each. Parental educational, socioeconomic status, and the rural/urban differences within these particular groups are likely to have contributed to the differences. We must add to Geertz's observation that acting in a culture is like interpreting an ambiguous text the comment that there is not simply one text to disambiguate but several.

Moving from the general to the specific, the particulars of the differences revealed in these pilot analyses are intriguing. It is tempting to link the differences to national stereotypes: In the U.S., the emphasis on individual rights, on prescriptions in terms of a person's actions rather than in terms of general social rules, with more frequent discussion of negative emotions; in the U.K., the emphasis on politeness and appropriate behavior, on avoiding harm to others, on general normative prescriptions and moral evaluation. Some of these differences could be linked to the differences in the "cultural ecology" of the children's lives (Super & Harkness, 1986): In the U.S., larger houses, less time close to the mother may lead to wilder noisier behavior, and thus to a greater emphasis in the mother–child discourse on noisiness and destruction, and more prominence of disputes and discussion of negative emotions in the talk about feelings. But given the small size of the sample, it is obviously imprudent to speculate further on such particulars until analyses are complete for a larger sample—analyses that can take proper account of the possible contribution of variables such as time–close–to–mother, space within the house, and so on *within* each culture as well as *between*.

If we find that individual differences in one culture are associated with particular outcomes, can we assume that such differences are implicated in a similar pattern of development in another culture? For example, we have argued from data on English children that disputes and situations in which a child is faced with another's different point of view may have special developmental significance (see Dunn, 1988); do they have the same significance for the Pennsylvanian children? If so might we expect these children to develop some powers of social understanding earlier than the Cambridge children?

Finally, the differences evident in this small–scale comparison of English–speaking children growing up in different cultures raise a number of issues of some social importance. What are the developmental implications of the experience of growing up in the micro-culture of a family and then becoming a member of another, different—and dominant—culture at the point of school entry? Consider for example, the experiences of Mexican American, Chinese American or African American children in the U.S., or of West Indian, or Bangladeshi children in England. (Pomerleau, Malcuit, and Sabatier begin to address some of these issues in their chapter in this volume.) Further, what is the impact of the cultural images of the media, presented to the child even within that family world, yet contrasting often with the cultural messages that parents may be trying to transmit. The study of the interaction of family culture and the wider cultures that the children may already be exposed to is clearly of such social significance that we should surely place it high on our research agenda.

ACKNOWLEDGMENTS

The study in Cambridge was supported by the Medical Research Council; the study in Pennsylvania was supported by a grant from the National Institute for Child Health and Human Development (HD23158–02). We are very grateful to Lise Youngblade for making available her analysis of pretend play.

REFERENCES

Bretherton, I. *Symbolic development: The development of social understanding*. New York: Academic Press, 1984.

Brice–Heath, S. *Ways with words: Language, life and work in communities and classrooms*. Cambridge: Cambridge University Press, 1983.

Bruner, J. *Actual minds, possible worlds*. Cambridge, MA: Harvard University Press, 1986.

Dunn, J. Playing in speech. In L. Michaels & C. Ricks (Eds.), *The state of the language* (pp. 202–212). Berkeley: University of California Press, 1980.

Dunn, J. *The beginnings of social understanding*. Cambridge, MA: Harvard University Press, 1988.

Dunn, J., Brown, J., & Beardsall, L. Family talk about emotions, and children's later understanding of others' emotions. *Developmental Psychology*, in press.

Dunn, J., & Munn, P. The development of justification in disputes with other and sibling. *Developmental Psychology*, 1987, *23*, 791–798.

Dunn, J., & Wooding, C. Play in the home and its implications for learning. In B. Tizard & D. Harvey (Eds.), *The biology of play* (pp. 45–58). London: Heinemann, 1977.

Eisenberg, A. R. Learning to describe past experience in conversation. *Discourse Processes*, 1985, *8*, 177–204.

Fivush, R. The social construction of personal narratives. *Merrill-Palmer Quarterly*, in press.

Fivush, R., & Fromhoff, F. A. Style and structure in mother-child conversations about the past. *Discourse Processes*, 1988, *11*, 337–355.

Fivush, R., Gray, J. T., Fromhoff, F. A. Two–year–olds talk about the past. *Cognitive Development*, 1988, *2*, 393–409.

Garvey, C. *Play*. Cambridge, MA: Harvard University Press, 1977.

Gergen, K. J. Social understanding and the inscription of self. In J. W. Stigler, R. A. Shweder, & G. Herdt (Eds.), *Cultural psychology: The Chicago symposia on culture and human development* (pp. 569–606). Cambridge: Cambridge University Press, 1989.

Goffman, E. *The presentation of self in everyday life*. New York: Doubleday Anchor Books, 1959.

Goffman, E. *Frame analysis: An essay on the organization of experience*. Cambridge: Cambridge University Press, 1974.

Haste, H. Growing into rules. In J. Bruner & H. Haste (Eds.), *Making sense* (pp. 163–195). London: Methuen, 1987.

Miller, P. J., & Moore, B. B. Narrative conjunctions of caregiver and child: A comparative perspective on socialization through stories. *Ethos*, 1989, *17*, 43–64.

Miller, P. J., & Sperry, L. The socialization of anger and aggression. *Merrill-Palmer Quarterly*, 1987, *33*, 1–31.

Miller, P. J., & Sperry, L. Early talk about the past: The origins of conversational stories of personal experience. *Journal of Child Language*, 1988, *15*, 293–315.

Miller, P. J., Potts, R., Fung, H., Hoogstra, L., & Mintz, J. Narrative practices and the social construction of self in childhood. *American Ethnologist*, in press.

Newson, J., & Newson, J. *Four years old in an urban community*. Harmondsworth: Penguin books, 1968.

Registrar General. *Great Britain Summary Tables, Census 1971*. London: Her Majesty's Stationary Office, 1973.

Rothenberg, B. Children's social sensitivity and the relationship to interpersonal competence, intrapersonal comfort and intellectual level. *Developmental Psychology*, 1970, *2*, 335–350.

Rosaldo, M. Toward an anthropology of self and feeling. In R. Schweder & R. LeVine (Eds.), *Culture theory: Essays on mind, self and emotion* (pp. 137–157). Cambridge: Cambridge University Press, 1984.

Sachs, J. Talking about the there and then: The emergence of displaced reference in parent–child discourse. In K. E. Nelson (Eds.), *Children's language* (Vol. 4, pp. 1–27). New York: Gardner Press, 1983.

Super, C., & Harkness, S. M. The developmental niche: A conceptualization at the interface of child and culture. *International Journal of Behavioral Development*, 1986, *9*, 545–569.

Tough, J. *Talking and learning*. London: Ward Lock Educational, 1977.

Whiting, B. B., & Edwards, C. P. *Children of different worlds*. Cambridge, MA: Harvard University Press, 1988.

Cultural Variation in the Role Relations of Toddlers and Their Families

10

Barbara Rogoff
University of Utah
Jayanthi Mistry
Tufts University
Artin Göncü
University of Illinois—Chicago
Christine Mosier
University of Utah

INTRODUCTION

Most research on the social context of young children's development focuses on their relationships with one other person. Frequently, this is the child's mother and occasionally it is instead the father or a peer. Only rarely do observations and discussions consider the child's multiple and embedded relationships within larger groups (but see Lewis, 1984, and Wilson, 1989).

Although the dyadic focus of research is partially due to the complications that ensue in analyzing observations with more than two people, it may also result from assumptions that the dyadic (especially the mother–child) relationship is the unique or ideal prototype of children's social relationships.

In this paper, we examine that assumption, arguing that in many cultural communities, children's development occurs in the context of structured and diverse relationships with a variety of other people (including the mother) in groups larger than dyads. The mother–child dyad, though universally important to children's survival and development, may not be such an exclusive and all–encompassing relationship in communities where families contain a number of children, living near other kin, and entwined in long–term support and obligation with other community members. Children may have varied relationships with different people playing specialized roles with them.

We begin by providing a brief conceptual background to our view of development as a process of *apprenticeship*, which necessarily involves structured relationships with a variety of partners, and our interpretation of cultural variations and similarities in general. Then we examine cultural variation in parental roles and children's opportunities to take part in adult activities, the orientation of children to community groups, and dyadic parent–child interaction versus group interaction as prototypes for social engagement. We base our discussion of children's role relations on our observations of 14 toddlers (12 to 24 months) from each of four cultural communities, as they interacted with their families in a home childrearing interview and observation of interaction around everyday problem solving. This age group was chosen because the children are old enough to have some communicative skill and young enough to still require supervision by mothers and their delegates.

The four communities, a peasant town in Guatemala, a middle–class urban community in the United States, a poor tribal community in India, and an urban middle–class community in Turkey, were chosen to represent a variety of arrangements for childrearing and took advantage of the existing familiarity of the researchers with each setting. In all four communities, the researcher responsible spoke at least one of the local languages and had lived or worked previously in that community or another in that nation. With many of the families, the researchers were personally familiar in long–term relationships.

DEVELOPMENT AS APPRENTICESHIP WITHIN RICHLY ORGANIZED RELATIONSHIPS

We consider children's development to occur as they participate in organized sociocultural activities with their close relations, in a process resembling apprenticeship (Adams & Bullock, 1986; Bruner, 1983; John–Steiner, 1985; Lave, 1988; Rogoff, 1990). Using apprenticeship as a conceptual model for development focuses attention on the active role of children in organizing development, the active support and use of other people in social interaction and arrangements of tasks and activities, and the socioculturally ordered nature of institutional contexts, technologies, and goals of activities.

In addition to emphasizing shared problem solving in which active learners participate in culturally organized activities with others varying in skill, apprenticeship involves other central features of guided participation (Rogoff, 1990): a focus on routine activities, tacit as well as explicit communication, supportive structuring of novices' efforts, and transfer of responsibility for handling situations as novices progress in understanding. Lave (1988, p. 2) suggests that "apprentices learn to think, argue, act, and interact in increasingly knowledgeable ways with people who do something well, by doing it with them as legitimate, peripheral participants."

Most important for the purposes of the present paper, the apprenticeship model and concept of guided participation include more people than a single expert and a single novice. The apprenticeship system often involves groups of novices and masters. The novices (peers) serve as resources for each other, aiding and challenging exploration in the new domain, and differ among themselves in expertise and perspective in useful ways. Several experts, relatively more skilled than the novices and with greater responsibility for the overall process, may collaborate in the activity and in the supervision of novices, sometimes with specialization of roles. Apprenticeship provides a model involving active learners in a *community* of people who support, challenge, and guide them as they increasingly participate in common purposes within valued sociocultural activities.

CULTURAL VARIATION AND SIMILARITIES

Across differing cultural communities, there are essential similarities as well as differences in childrearing and development. Although many scholars assume that variations in a phenomenon across different cultural communities indicate cultural processes and that similarities across communities demonstrate biological processes, we argue that both variation and similarities across groups involve cultural as well as biological processes (see Rogoff, 1990). For example, different groups *differ* in eye color, a characteristic that has clear genetic contributions, and are *similar* in arranging for the shelter and protection of young infants, practices with clear cultural contributions. Rather than assuming that culture and biology are opposing or even separable factors, we assume that as a species, humans are biologically social creatures. Part of our species heritage is the wide flexibility as well as the human similarities in cultural arrangements that characterize varying communities.

In this chapter, we do not regard the cultural variation that we explore in children's relations with parents, other family members, and neighbors as categorical differences (where one community has only one kind of relationship, and another has another) but as variations on a theme. Greater emphasis on multi-way relationships in some communities can bring to our attention their importance, even if less frequent, in communities that may often focus their relationships more dyadically. Our aim is to call attention to children's embeddedness in communities—in all cultural settings—by examining variations across communities in the prevalence of multi-way relationships involving a variety of other people in children's lives.

We refer to communities or cultural communities, rather than cultures, to avoid the danger of generalizing to national groups from observations of a few people in a single community from each nation. Our observations in each of the four cultural communities are not necessarily applicable beyond the communities that we have observed to other communities in the same country. By community we mean groups of people having some common local organization and similarities in values and practices.

CULTURAL VARIATION IN ROLES OF PARENTS AND OTHER FAMILY MEMBERS

Parent and Child Roles in Teaching and Learning

Although processes of guided participation are widespread around the world, important variation appears in the teaching/learning roles of children and parents (Dixon, LeVine, Richman, & Brazelton, 1984; Heath, 1983; Ochs & Schieffelin, 1984; Rogoff, 1981, 1990; Ward, 1971; Watson–Gegeo & Gegeo, 1986). In some settings, parents see their role as instructing children, playing with them, and entering into conversations as peers with children in contexts adapted to children's interests and understanding. In other settings, children are expected to learn through participation and active observation in adult settings.

Whiting and Edwards (1988) note that of the 12 cultural groups they studied, the U.S. middle–class mothers ranked highest in sociability with children—interacting in a friendly, playful, or conversational way, treating children at times as status equals—whereas in the other communities, mothers stressed training or nurturant involvement with children —maintaining authority and dominance with respect to children.

Extended Family Roles

Accompanying the differences in roles of parents in varying cultures are differences in the roles of siblings and other children, grandparents, and the broader community. In settings where mothers and fathers do not see themselves as conversational partners with children, there are other people who converse with children. The nuclear family situation, with one or two parents living in a separate dwelling far from kin, is a quite different childrearing environment from that experienced by children surrounded by siblings, cousins, grandparents, and other related and nonrelated familiar people (Watson–Gegeo & Gegeo, 1989; Whiting & Edwards, 1988; Whiting & Whiting, 1975).

In the middle–class communities we observed in the United States and Turkey, toddlers generally lived with only parents and siblings and often slept in rooms of their own. In the Mayan and Indian settings, in contrast, toddlers were in the company of many people who were engaged in the business of life. They generally lived in compounds near other related families who often shared a courtyard and water and washing facilities, and they always slept in the same room and usually in the same bed as other family members.

In all four communities, the availability of other family members related to the caregiving environment for the child. In the Turkish, Guatemalan, and Indian communities, most of the families had relatives living in the same neighborhood or town, and for half or more of the families in each community, these other relatives helped in caregiving by tending the children at times (Mistry, Rogoff, & Göncü, in preparation). The U.S. families were less likely to have relatives living nearby, but those relatives who were nearby usually participated in the toddlers' care.

Distinctions in the Roles of Mothers and Others

Whereas the U.S. and Turkish middle–class mothers whom we visited considered it part of their role to play with their children, in other cultures that role belongs to other people, not mothers. Some of the Guatemalan Mayan mothers in our sample laughed with embarrassment at the idea of playing with their children, as this is the role of other children and occasionally grandparents (Rogoff, Mosier, Mistry, & Göncü, in press).

A similar separation in roles was noted by Ward (1971) in her description of the social partners of Black children in Louisiana. The children watch and listen to adults; they play and talk and tumble with other children. Older children are involved in taking care of younger children, and teach social and intellectual skills: "Alphabets, colors, numbers, rhymes, word games, pen and pencil games are learned, if at all, from older children. No child, even the firstborn, is without such tutelage, since cousins, aunts, and uncles of their own age and older are always on hand" (Ward, 1971, p. 25). Similar observations have been made by Farran, Mistry, Ai–Chang, and Herman (in press) indicating that native Hawaiian preschoolers are involved with an average of 17 people who are active in the children's caregiving and entertainment, and by Leiderman and Leiderman (1973) who noted that in monomatric family systems the mother is the main purveyor of physical and social stimuli for the infant, whereas in polymatric systems the mother may remain the primary agent for meeting physical needs while others meet social needs.

The Importance of Child Caregivers and Peer Relations

In many communities, child care is largely carried out by children between ages 5 and 10, who tend children past the earliest months of infancy (Weisner & Gallimore, 1977; Wenger, 1983; Whiting & Edwards, 1988; Whiting & Whiting, 1975). Children may carry a younger sibling or cousin around on their back or hip to be entertained with the sights and sounds of the community and the play of the other children. If the young one becomes hungry, the child caregiver may return to the mother to allow the child to nurse. Adults are available to supervise the child caregivers, but the entertainment of young children falls to other children. Whiting (1979) notes that Kenyan graduate students at Harvard are surprised to see U.S. children seeking interaction with their parents in preference to siblings.

Care by siblings may provide infants with special intellectual opportunities, particularly in communities in which such caregiving arrangements are commonplace. Watson–Gegeo and Gegeo (1989) state that Kwara'ae (Solomon Island) sibling caregiving provides infants with a great diversity of cognitive and social stimulation, both from their mobility and from their skill, which is moderate at age 3 and requires no supervision after age 6 to 7. Heath (1983) notes that the playsongs invented by working–class black girls are tailored to language teaching for young children, with nonsense wordplay, counting, and naming body parts—topics handled in middle–class adult–child interaction through nursery rhymes and routines but not included in adult–child interaction in the Carolina working–class black community that Heath studied.

Compared with young child partners, however, even middle–class adult caregivers may be less likely to seek playful interaction with a child or to enter into collaboration in pretense or in playful exploration in the way that child companions frequently do. Dunn and Dale (1984) noted that 2–year–olds playing with siblings engaged in collaborative pretend games involving transformations of role identity, location, or psychological state, whereas their play with mothers was more likely to involve labeling or acting on a replica object, supporting but not entering play in pretend roles or actions.

Children's Opportunities to Take Part in Adult Activities

Variations in parent–child roles and responsibility for teaching and learning may relate to the opportunity that children have to take part in the varied and valued cultural activities of adults versus being segregated into specialized child settings (Rogoff, 1990). Historical analyses of Western societies link the lack of separation of workplace from home (typical in the colonial period) with a pattern of child–rearing that involved many people (siblings, other relatives, and nonrelatives) and learning by participation in daily activities and tasks (Harevan, 1989).

We noted great variation in toddlers' opportunities to observe adult economic activity and to engage with a variety of people in daily life (Mistry, Rogoff, & Göncü, in preparation). Guatemalan Mayan toddlers could routinely observe the home–based economic activities (sewing and weaving) of their mothers; Indian Tribal toddlers could observe their mothers work in the fields or in daily–paid labor outside the home because they accompanied their mothers. In contrast, almost all of the middle–class Turkish toddlers stayed home with mothers whose work did not include economic activity beyond homemaking, and middle–class U.S. toddlers either stayed home with homemaking mothers or stayed in other settings in which the adults' economic activity was to tend them!

Such varying opportunities to observe adult economic activities and adult social relationships may limit the chances that young children have to begin to make sense of the more mature roles towards which they are directed. Without the opportunity to observe and participate in mature activities of their communities, young children may need to have adult guides (e.g., teachers, child–focused parents) who special-ize in introducing them to mature skills in specialized settings, out of the context of adult work and everyday life.

The further segregation of children according to age into peer groups is an unusual circumstance, speaking globally, that requires sufficient numbers of children in a small territory in order to provide enough children of the same age (Konner, 1975). Age segregation, even with many children available and even in an urban setting in the U.S., is uncommon outside of bureaucratic institutions such as schooling or camp, where age groups are formed for adult convenience (Ellis, Rogoff, & Cromer, 1981; Rogoff, 1981). Nonetheless, a large proportion of U.S. children's time is spent in such age–graded bureaucratic institutions.

Such age segregation limits children's opportunities to learn by being embedded in the activities of somewhat more mature members of their cultural community. In communities in which children are not segregated from observation of and participation in the activities of their elders (adults or older children), the responsibility for child development may fall more on those who 'raise' the children instead of on the children themselves 'coming up' (the metaphor for child development used in Heath's, 1983, working–class Black community) as they are embedded in the everyday lives and work of extended family and neighbors.

ORIENTATION OF CHILDREN TO COMMUNITY GROUPS

Beyond children's engagement with extended family, it is important to recognize that in some communities, children are members of an even larger social unit, including nonkin in the neighborhood or larger community. In some communities, supervision of children may be the responsibility of the whole community, without the need for any particular adult to devote attention to the pack of children. Ward (1971) states that in the Louisiana black community she studied, caregiving and disciplinary duties belong to anyone who is near the child. Tronick, Morelli, and Winn (1987; Morelli & Tronick, in this volume) observe that the care and nursing of infants among the Efe of Zaire is shared among the women of the community, with efforts made to extend infants' maternal relationships beyond those with the biological mother. Our observations of Indian and Guatemalan children indicate that toddlers are often involved in multi-age packs of children that serve caregiving functions as they roam around together, with intervention as necessary from whatever adult is nearby (Mistry et al., in preparation).

Indian toddlers have been noted to experience a fluid socialization environment, with responsibility for caregiving diffused through a neighborhood group. Neighbors are often related, and if not, they have been living next to each other for generations and behave like relatives through their sense of community and belongingness. Indian babies are usually surrounded by relatives and nonkin neighbors of many ages, who take responsibility for them when the mother is away or busy (Rohner & Chaki–Sirkar, 1988; Saraswathi & Dutta, 1988); similar caregiving occurs for native Hawaiian families (Gallimore, Boggs, & Jordan, 1974) and among the Lijembe of Africa (Munroe & Munroe, 1975).

In our observations of Indian toddlers, neighbors related to the family not by kinship but by long association made their opinions known regarding anyone's treatment of a child and took over with rights usually reserved for parents in the U.S. middle class (Mistry, Rogoff, & Göncü, in preparation). Nonrelatives were almost always present in our home visits with the Indian toddlers (in 92% of the sessions), but they were not commonly present in the visits with toddlers from the U.S. (7%), from Turkey (29%), or from Guatemala (36%). This easy availability of nonkin who take a responsible role with toddlers means that the circle of a child's reciprocal relationships may be much more varied than those of children who have little contact with nonkin neighbors and other community members. When nonrelatives were present in the U.S., Turkey, or Guatemala, they primarily took a spectator or uninvolved role, whereas in the Indian sample, nonrelatives participated at least as extensively as did relatives. They commented, made suggestions (e.g., how to get the child to hold still or how to distract the child), and directed the mother and the toddler in caregiving and play. They regulated the behavior of the toddlers' siblings and engaged the toddlers in playful teasing interactions, demonstrating direct relationships with toddlers that may be reserved for kin or childcare professionals in other communities.

Although responsibility for caregiving is assumed by an extended group in many communities, mothers around the world usually have primary responsibility for caregiving with infants and toddlers. In describing the expanded caregiving system of Hawaiian families, Gallimore, Boggs, and Jordan (1974) point out that even when mothers report active contributions by others they describe themselves as centrally concerned and responsible. Mothers have a central role with infants and toddlers, whether they are involved directly with the children, delegate responsibility to other caregivers, or supervise the shared care and responsibility for their children.

DYADIC PARENT–CHILD INTERACTION VERSUS GROUP INTERACTION AS PROTOTYPES FOR SOCIAL ENGAGEMENT

In communities varying in caregiving arrangements and in involvement of the larger community, one would expect differences in the orientation of children toward their parents as primary social partners (as in the U.S. middle class) or toward the larger group. In our observations of the direction of U.S. and Guatemalan Mayan toddlers' attention, we noted that whereas the U.S. toddlers and their mothers tended to focus exclusively on their own activities or on their dyadic interactions, or to alternate their attention with other social events, the Mayan toddlers as well as their mothers often attended simultaneously to other ongoing social activities while they engaged with each other or with their own activities (Rogoff, Mosier, Mistry, & Göncü, in press). For example, they might closely monitor a conversation involving other people while they work together to figure out how a novel object functions.

The sort of intimate face–to–face mother–infant interaction that is the subject of U.S. research on infant social interaction may be very unusual in cultural settings where infants are not being brought up as conversational partners with their mothers but as less individually–focused and more group–focused members of the community. There appears to be great cultural variation in the extent to which mothers rely on the face–to–face position for communication. Mothers in many cultures commonly hold infants facing away from them (Martini & Kirkpatrick, 1981; Sostek, Vietze, Zaslow, Kreiss, van der Waals, & Rubinstein, 1981). This is sometimes interpreted as a position revealing a lack of social interaction between mother and infant. However, variation in infant positioning from facing the mother to facing the same way as the mother reflects cultural values regarding the social world in which the child is becoming embedded, as well as the means of communication.

Martini and Kirkpatrick (1981) note that Marquesan mothers (in the South Pacific) appear strained and awkward when asked to interact with their babies in a face–to–face orientation. In everyday activities, babies are usually held facing outward and encouraged to interact with and attend to others (especially slightly older siblings) instead of interacting face–to–face with the mother. The authors report that this is consistent with a general cultural value of embeddedness in a complex social world. Marquesan infants learn a different lesson in their interactions than do U.S. infants engaged in face–to–face interaction, but mothers in both societies provide guidance in developing culturally appropriate skills and values. Marquesan mothers actively arrange infants' social interactions with others; if babies appear to get self–absorbed, mothers interrupt and urge attention to the broader social environment:

> [Mothers] consistently provided the infant with an interactively stimulating world, first by interacting, next by encouraging and making effective his attempts to make contact, and finally by directing others to interact with the infant. Caregivers . . . shaped the infants' attention towards others and objects, and shaped their movements towards effective contact and locomotion. By the end of the first year, infants were becoming interactants able to accompany and learn from older children in an environment supervised by adults (Martini & Kirkpatrick, 1981, p. 209).

Face–to–face interaction may also be a prototype in most research on mother–child communication because of the dyadic didactic role assumed by middle–class U.S. mothers, who often rely on their own efforts to motivate children to learn. This contrasts with the group–focused interactions of mothers and children in cultural communities in which children have the responsibility to learn and have many other social partners in the process.

CONCLUSIONS

Middle–class children from small families, isolated from kin and separated from neighbors by distance as well as by lack of shared networks and obligations, spending most of their time in age–segregated institutions from early years, have limited opportunities for engagement in age–diverse children's groups that interface with their parents' social worlds. Their relationships with related and unrelated adults are similarly limited by the institutional arrangements of their care and by their parents' distant and invisible (to the children) work environments.

For young children around the world, mothers typically have a uniquely important role. In many communities, however, the relationship between mother and infant is not exclusive—it is neither the infants' sole important relationship, nor is the relation with the mother necessarily one that focuses on her to the exclusion of other family and community members present. We suggest that the understanding of young children's social worlds may be enhanced by taking a broader view of children's social relationships as mutually constituted with others who share relations with each other and who may specialize in their roles with children.

For young middle-class children, a primacy of dyadic interactions especially with mothers may predominate in ways not shared in many other communities. However, even with middle-class children, a focus on their dyadic relations with one other person is likely to overlook their important and mutually embedded relations with other family members and with important nonfamily companions and caregivers. The observations of cultural variation in toddlers' roles with their family and nonkin relations may open our eyes to the richly organized social relations in which toddlers here and elsewhere participate.

ACKNOWLEDGMENTS

The authors are grateful for the collaboration of the children and their families and communities in the four research sites. The research reported here has been supported by the University Research Committee (University of Utah) and by the National Institute of Mental Health (#41060).

REFERENCES

Adams, A. K., & Bullock, D. Apprenticeship in word use: Social convergence processes in learning categorically related nouns. In S. A. Kuczaj & M. D. Barrett (Eds.), *The development of word meaning: Progress in cognitive development research* (pp. 155–197). NY: Springer–Verlag, 1986.

Bruner, J. S. *Child's talk: Learning to use language.* NY: Norton, 1983.

Dixon, S. D., LeVine, R. A., Richman, A., & Brazelton, T. B. Mother–child interaction around a teaching task: An African–American comparison. *Child Development*, 1984, *55*, 1252–1264.

Dunn, J., & Dale, N. I a daddy: 2–year–olds' collaboration in joint pretend with sibling and with mother. In I. Bretherton (Ed.), *Symbolic play: The development of social understanding* (pp. 131–158). Orlando, FL: Academic, 1984.

Ellis, S., Rogoff, B., & Cromer, C. C. Age segregation in children's social interactions. *Developmental Psychology*, 1981, *17*, 399–407.

Farran, D., Mistry, J., Ai–Chang, M., & Herman, H. Kin and calabash: The social networks of preschool part–Hawaiian children. In R. Roberts (Ed.), *The learning environments of young children at risk.* NY: Ablex, in press.

Gallimore, R., Boggs, S., & Jordan, C. *Culture, behavior, and education: A study of Hawaiian-Americans.* Beverly Hills, CA: Sage, 1974.

Harevan, T. K. Historical changes in children's networks in the family and community. In D. Belle (Ed.), *Children's social networks and social supports* (pp. 15–36). NY: Wiley, 1989.

Heath, S. B. *Ways with words: Language, life, and work in communities and classrooms.* Cambridge, England: Cambridge University Press, 1983.

John–Steiner, V. *Notebooks of the mind: Explorations of thinking.* Albuquerque: University of New Mexico Press, 1985.

Konner, M. Relations among infants and juveniles in comparative perspective. In M. Lewis & L. A. Rosenblum (Eds.), *Friendship and peer relations.* NY: Wiley, 1975.

Lave, J. The culture of acquisition and the practice of understanding. (Report no. IRL 88–0007). Palo Alto, CA: Institute for Research on Learning, 1975.

Leiderman, H. P., & Leiderman, G. F. *Polymatric infant care in the East African highlands: Some affective and cognitive consequences.* Paper presented at the Minnesota Symposium on Child Development, Minneapolis, MN, 1973.

Lewis, M. (Ed.). *Beyond the dyad.* NY: Plenum, 1984.

Martini, M., & Kirkpatrick, J. Early interactions in the Marquesas Islands. In T. M. Field, A. M. Sostek, P. Vietze, & P. H. Leiderman (Eds.), *Culture and early interactions* (pp. 189–213). Hillsdale, NJ: Lawrence Erlbaum Associates, 1981.

Mistry, J., Rogoff, B., & Göncü, A. *Variations in role relations of toddlers and their families in four cultural communities,* in preparation.

Munroe, R. H., & Munroe, R. L. *Infant care and childhood performance in East Africa.* Paper presented at the meetings of the Society for Research in Child Development, Denver, 1975.

Ochs, E., & Schieffelin, B. B. Language acquisition and socialization: Three developmental stories and their implications. In R. Schweder & R. LeVine (Eds.), *Culture and its acquisition.* Chicago: University of Chicago Press, 1984.

Rohner, R., & Chaki–Sirkar, M. *Women and children in a Bengali village.* Hanover, NH: University Press of New England, 1988.

Rogoff, B. Adults and peers as agents of socialization: A Highland Guatemalan profile. *Ethos,* 1981, *9,* 18–36.

Rogoff, B. *Apprenticeship in thinking: Cognitive development in social context.* New York: Oxford University Press, 1990.

Rogoff, B., Mosier, C., Mistry, J., & Göncü, A. Sixteen toddlers' guided participation in cultural activity. In E. Forman, N. Minick, & A. Stone (Eds.), *The institutional and social context of mind.* New York: Oxford University Press, in press.

Saraswathi, T. S., & Dutta, R. *Invisible boundaries: Grooming for adult roles.* New Delhi: Northern Book Center, 1988.

Sostek, A. M., Vietze, P., Zaslow, M., Kreiss, L., van der Waals, F., & Rubinstein, D. Social context in caregiver–infant interaction: A film study of Fais and the United States. In T. M. Field, A. M. Sostek, P. Vietze, & P. H. Leiderman (Eds.), *Culture and early interactions.* Hillsdale, New Jersey: Lawrence Erlbaum Associates, 1981.

Tronick, E., Morelli, G. A., & Winn, S. Multiple caretaking of Efe (Pygmy) infants. *American Anthropologist,* 1987, *89,* 96–106.

Ward, M. C. *Them children: A study in language learning.* NY: Holt, Rinehart and Winston, 1971.

Watson–Gegeo, K. A., & Gegeo, D. W. The social world of Kwara'ae children: Acquisition of language and values. In J. Cook–Gumperz, W. Corsaro, & J. Streeck (Eds.), *Children's language and children's worlds.* The Hague: Mouton, 1986.

Watson–Gegeo, K. A., & Gegeo, D. W. The role of sibling interaction in child socialization. In P. Zukow (Ed.) *Sibling interaction across cultures: Theoretical and methodological issues.* New York: Springer–Verlag, 1989.

Weisner, T. S., & Gallimore, R. My brother's keeper: Child and sibling caretaking. *Current Anthropology,* 1977, *18,* 169–190.

Wenger, M. *Gender role socialization in an East African community: Social interaction between 2– to 3–year–olds and older children in social ecological perspective.* Unpublished doctoral dissertation, Harvard University, 1983.

Whiting, B. B. *Maternal behavior in cross-cultural perspective.* Paper presented at the meeting of the Society for Cross–Cultural Research, Charlottesville, VA, 1979.

Whiting, B. B., & Edwards, C. P. *Children of different worlds: The formation of social behavior.* Cambridge, MA: Harvard University Press, 1988.

Whiting, B. B., & Whiting, J. W. M. *Children of six cultures: A psycho–cultural analysis.* Cambridge, MA: Harvard University Press, 1975.

Wilson, M. Child development in the context of the black extended family. *American Psychologist,* 1989, *44,* 380–385.

11 Commentary: Dynamics of Enculturation

William Kessen

Yale University

INTRODUCTION

Sir Francis Galton went into Southern Africa in 1850 "to fill up that blank in our maps which [lies] between the Cape Colony and the western Portuguese settlements ..." (Galton, 1853, p. iii). He carried with him, not only servants, five oxen, a cart drawn by eight mules, and half a ton of supplies, but also a set of beliefs and convictions that guided his tour. It may help us to understand the advances and the losses in the discipline of the present book over the past century and a half if we loosely compare Galton's trek to the adventures we have described. Uneven historical recollection does not make new method; it may make new mind.

When Galton went into Africa, as the first European explorer, he carried with him a curious baggage of well–formed but not always explicit principles; he cared little about children, to be sure, but he was governed by the overarching Western conviction—that it was important *to find out*, that to know was all. I shall return to the persistent and times–linking vision of Knowledge as Power.

And Galton wore principles more secular than Christian charity and less universal than the omnipotence of information. He was certain that the people he discovered (as though they began to exist with his observation) would be primitive (his cousin Darwin was convincing), that he possessed new scientific attitudes and procedures that would make his research permanent, and that, in time, the natives might be brought to the high levels of English civilization.

Galton's principle of primitivity was questioned first—by thoughtful anthropologists, by philosophers, and, most recently, by generous–minded thinkers such as Geertz. Nonetheless, as we shall see, the evolutionary attitude is not gone from developmental thinking. The principle of method—the glories of Western science—has stumbled a bit but remains strong; it runs like a ground bass through our book. The principle of development remains almost in full force—witness the derogatory "developing or underdeveloped nation"—save that the ideal civilization has become American and that Galton's undiscovered cultures are becoming largely persuaded of our superiority.

Let me begin my commentary with a story that contains, all wrapped together, the messages of science, guesthood, and superiority.

A TALE OF THE PAST

About sixty years ago, as Arnold Gesell was completing the construction of his Clinic of Child Development, he designed an apartment on one of the upper floors. The space had all the usual apparatus of an ordinary apartment—living room, bedroom, kitchen, bath—*and* a wall of one–way–vision screen that would permit Gesell and his colleagues to observe scientifically the lives of a real family. It may not surprise the reader to learn that Gesell never found anyone to live in his invention and that the area became a place for the testing of children[1]; nonetheless, Gesell's arrogance and his cool distancing will stand as models for students of cross–cultural parenting to beware. The arrogance was his own, much like Galton's, and, happily, not duplicated in the pages of this book; the distancing will become a recurrent theme in my discussion.

FROM THE LABORATORY TO THE BUSH

In the transition from vague unease to Bronfenbrenner's systematic attack (Bronfenbrenner, 1979), the laboratory as a setting for the study of development has become suspect. In the long catenary that stretches from the Papoušeks to Rogoff and her colleagues, we can appreciate the restraint and skill of the Papoušeks' use of a fixed environment. Within a standardized procedure (that "... certainly emphasizes cross–cultural similarities ..."), they present evidence that the mothers of three cultures show notably similar "... species–specific behavioral patterns ..." in the way they address 2–month–old babies. Two ideas thread through the Papoušeks' paper—the conviction that evolutionary processes have guided the preparation of human beings for parenting and their desire to end the long era of mother–blaming, an era that runs earlier than Galton and flourishes today[2]. Their defense of intuitive patterns of mothering, together with suggestive similar findings by Sigman and Wachs, make engaging psychology.

The Papoušeks' fine paper also introduces a question that can be addressed several times over the foregoing chapters. How shall cross–cultural observation deal with the *absence* of demonstrated differences, especially when the difficulties of the investigatory task make large samples cumbersome or impossible? The most obvious answers are, first, to wait until someone demonstrates differences by conventional procedures and, second, to adopt a hypothesis–fitting statistical procedure that will heavily demand precision of theory and stability of outcome.

---

[1] I may write with excessive confidence; the "family observation unit" has been tried several times in the last decades and recently.

[2] John Watson's dedication of this baby–care book to "the first mother who brings up a happy child" (Watson, 1928, dedication page) can stand at the top of the mother–blaming era. See Ben Bradley's "Infancy as Paradise" (*Human Development*, in press) for a prologue to his historical critique of the record.

Surely, in the meantime, the observations of intuitive parenting in the conversations of mothers and young infants will give pause to the folks who want to dismiss characteristics independent of cultural differences.

But we cannot forget the artificiality of the laboratory, particularly in the study of early social exchange. What young mother in a formal study asks where the television set is or wanders off to telephone a friend? How much discussion is there about Ghostbusters or Teenage Mutant Ninja Turtles or Super Mario III? The questions are important because in the laboratory the mother and her child are special *guests*, and in the bush the researcher is a special *guest*; in every culture there are subtle and widely varying rules for the proper behavior of hosts and guests. In a serious and often restrictive way, *our observations are wrapped in the rules of guesthood*. Galton was not insensitive to the requirements of guesthood[3], but he would not have seen his entire enterprise (surely fabulous to the Africans) as tied tightly to the perception and social cognitions of his hosts, or, for that matter, that they were in any sense his hosts. One of the most winning changes in attitude that the present book affords is the representation of politeness and good sense that is reflected in Pomerleau et al.'s use of co–linguistic interviewers and in Bornstein et al.'s invariable use of culture natives to make observations. Perhaps the first move in every cross–cultural study (and the first passage in our reports) should be an

---

[3] Galton, like all other Europeans, was impressed by the standard of South African beauty, especially by the pendulous buttocks admired by the Hottentots. He will tell his tale of the conflict between the gentlemanly code and the pressure for knowledge.

> ...a charming person, not only a Hottentot in figure, but in that respect a Venus among Hottentots. I was perfectly aghast at her development, and made inquiries upon that delicate point as far as I dared among my missionary friends. The result is, that I believe Mrs. Petrus to be the lady who ranks second among all the Hottentots for the beautiful outline that her back affords, Jonker's wife ranking as the first; the latter, however, was slightly *passée*, while Mrs. Petrus was in full *embonpoint*. I profess to being a scientific man, and was exceedingly anxious to obtain accurate measurements of her shape; but there was a difficulty in doing this. I did not know a word of Hottentot, and could never therefore have explained to the lady what the object of my footrule could be; and I really dared not ask my worthy missionary host to interpret for me. I therefore felt in a dilemma as I gazed at her form, that gift of bounteous nature to this favoured race, which no mantua–maker, with all her crinoline and stuffing, can do otherwise than humbly imitate. The object of my admiration stood under a tree, and was turning herself about to all points of the compass, as ladies who wish to be admired usually do. Of a sudden my eye fell upon my sextant; the bright thought struck me, and I took a series of observations upon her figure in every direction, up and down, crossways, diagonally, and so forth, and I registered them carefully upon an outline drawing for fear of any mistake; this being done, I boldly pulled out my measuring–tape, and measured the distance from where I was to the place she stood, and having this obtained both base and angles, I worked out the results by trigonometry and logarithms (Galton, 1853, p. 87f).

account of the constraints and expectations of being a host or being a guest in the visited culture. We cannot drown our lodgement in our own culture, but we seem to be learning how to make guesthood a part of our study and our concern.

Scientism blunts our everyday sensitivity to the problems of being a guest. Enamored of our apparatus and our measures, as recently as thirty years ago we believed that good method made people of all ages, from newborn to aged, into subjects. How strange, how inhuman! I will not rehearse the often amusing, often ludicrous contretemps we managed—although it is tempting to chart the potential errors that ran from the newborn infant dolled up in wires to the 6–year–old asked about grammaticality to the college sophomore on the five–thousandth trial of a tachistoscope study to the pregnant woman completing a questionnaire about life expectations. I have, on purpose, chosen my cases from middle–class American culture—the culture many of us grew up in; when we move the questions of guesthood to Bed–Stuy or Haiti or Japan, the complications become prodigious.

Let me be clear. I am not scoring either our predecessors (after all, there was a context in 1850 and 1900 and 1950) nor our contemporary attempts to find out; rather, I am reminding all of us that our present search for truth is as context–bound as it ever was. The everlasting task, and I believe it to be everlasting, is to seek out the humane and decent and wise ways to stand back from our moment. We need distance from our cogitations, not from our observed colleagues. Of course, I do not raise an unrecognized problem; the papers that illuminate this book are the best of a noble stock. They speak to the complexities of observing in cultures where the rules of social exchange differ so markedly from the ones familiar to us. They demonstrate that, for all our zeal, if we do not fully understand the context into which observers are placed by the people being observed, we cannot comprehend what we think we see.

UNIFORMITY AND DIVERSITY

No psychologist can ignore the eternal tension between the Search for Uniform Being, on one hand, and the Celebration of Diversity, on the other. But the psychologist who works in different cultures bears an awesome responsibility. In the foregoing papers, we have seen the clear reach for Uniform Being, in Papoušeks' paper and in Morelli and Tronick, markedly—the finding, despite differences in climate and in history, that all babies are essentially the same, that we can eliminate the distractions of accident to find the core truth. But, sitting side by side with the search for uniformity, is the equally enticing lure of variation—the ethnographic impulse to see different ways of dealing with human dilemmas and human ambiguities, the perception of diversity that Pomerleau and her colleagues state most boldly—"... a competent mother will be competent only within her own culture." The disjunction is an antique one, clearly shown in the work of early Greek philosophers and threading its way through all Western history to appear in research, novels, wars, and pogroms. The only sure lesson that I can draw from the jumble of shifting values is: *We almost always see too little diversity.* Michael

Zuckerman speaks of our myths and our methods when he indicts historical writing for its compression of variety into the forms of high cultural value. Hear him.

> Once we begin to unravel the social fabric, there is no end to the process. A generation ago, historians who took ethnicity seriously took their investigations of, say, the Irish or Italians of Boston as surrogates for studies of the Irish or Italians of America. . . . Today, such assumptive allowances are untenable. . . . Irish immigrants and their offspring met far different fates in Boston, where they were effectively ghettoized, in Philadelphia, where they were less excluded from the larger life of the city, and in the smaller urban centers of the middle and far west, where they were scarcely isolated at all (Zuckerman, 1984, p. 229).

Zuckerman's indictment of historical writing is relevant for the cross–cultural study of parenting; whatever is the case for the students of the hyperstudied Irish–Americans is true in spades for students of small samples in cultures that differ critically from academic America in conceptions of gender, hierarchy, power, and mind. In our first observing move in another setting, American or not, we take several steps that simplify our task and complicate our interpretation. I will discuss the defining steps shortly but it is worth noting that very nearly all of them serve a common purpose—to reduce the range and the variability of *what is there*. Again, we walk in a minefield. In order to bring order to the flood of impressions that might be recorded as observation in someone else's place, we must simplify, we must organize, and we must cut away some of the entangling complexity, a fact that is becoming painfully clear to all serious students of cultural variation. But how? Let me say a word about procedures in use in cross–cultural studies and, then, turn back to my prickly question.

WAYS OF DISTANCING

Not only should we attend to the rules of guesthood, not only should we be alert to lurking diversity, but we Westerners must try to recognize that one of the best practiced and most accepted procedures of academic researchers is to put the objects of study *at a distance*.

There are a number of ways to separate ourselves from our *subjects*; perhaps the most pervasive is exactly to consider the people we are observing as *subjects*. But, beyond such a move—made easier in the past by such protections as "aboriginal" and "primitive"—there are intertwined and reinforcing methods of making sure (for scientific and extrascientific reasons) that we do not confuse who is the *looker* and who is the *looked–at*.

A Surefire Method

The sturdiest weapon of Western science against ignorance has been Galton's (and *all* his successors') commitment to a cool and *objective* method—the conviction that the diversity and complexity of the world would submit to distancing maneuvers that preserved the sureness and the separation of the observer. I elide many commentaries of the last decades to say that no such surefire method exists, certainly not for cross–cultural study, and we all start with the recognition that any method, however carefully wrought, imposes chastening limitations on our work.

Perhaps the best summary of the method of distancing by method is: We will continue to need all the methods used by the contributors to this book—from experiment to poetry—in order to comprehend the diversity we meet. And, we had better maintain our sensitivity to the boundary conditions of method, those limitations of our procedures that keep us astigmatic.

A subdivision of sure method—sure data handling, sure statistics—requires a word. Here, the papers have been less sure–footed in their strategies; with numbers of the observed that run from 8 to 150, with statistical techniques that run from narrative to factor analysis, no coherent analytic theory has emerged. What is wonderfully clear is, first, the absence of a singular canonical procedure of analysis—the magic bullet of procedural certainty—and second, the presence of a devoted attention to analytic detail. Bornstein and his colleagues use the armory of statistical manipulation with talent and restraint; they catch the abiding numerical spirit of Francis Galton—the patriarch of statistics as well as the patriarch of exploration—without falling into his conviction about hereditary genius. Rather, there is a shared search for *finding*, for *fact*, that seems to use any data–reduction method that will yield what we accept as findings and facts. It is to such a grand theme that I will return at the end.

The Making of Categories

Next to method in the Western scientific quiver is category–making, a mental and technological procedure that can range from observation scale (mother–child interaction schedules, patterns of fantasy play) to the organization of a journal article. We are constantly breaking up our experience in smaller pieces, giving the pieces names, and seeing the world again in the pieces of our invention. It is a subtle and corrosive practice that may run too deep in Western culture to be rethought. Geertz (1983, p. 74) puts the case with striking clarity.

> Yet we are reluctant ... to draw ... the conclusion that science, ideology, art, religion, or philosophy, or at least the impulses they serve, are not the common property of all mankind.

But, for Geertz and for many other observers of cultural variation, the conclusion is inescapable—if we approach another people with the categories of academic Americans filtering our vision, we will not see the people as they live. What a pickle! If we study only our own culture (the culture of universities, I am afraid, or the culture of educated Western adults), our categories will be both familiar and useful *but* we will find it difficult to escape the boundaries of the categories to penetrate to the footings of culture. If we study other cultures, we carry with us a powerful set of defining categories and, although we may find the other culture strangely or (in Galton's word, aghastingly) *different*, we may not be able to shed our biases fully enough to see the wellsprings of the differences.

In a commentary as elementary as mine, it is easy to mislead or to misstate. I do *not* believe that there is some *Ur*–being, some universally true expression of humanity waiting abroad to be discovered. Nor do I believe that there is some Cultural Truth about the Japanese or the Kenyans or the Turks that dutiful ethnographers will eventually reveal. What I want to assert is that every social grouping—as small as a couple, as large as a nation—lives within a set of specifying rules (categories, if you wish) that guide the vision and the passion and the thought of the grouping.

More, there exists in some cultures a specialized grouping—the Researchers, the Knowers—whose assigned task it is to understand the world. Whether guru or theoretical physicist, the Knowers manage their charge by *bounding* it and *organizing* it; the resulting bounded organization becomes an active process that screens the world and defines the world. The work of the steady researchers who have written their accounts here (how fractional a representation of their splendid careers the present book offers!) is a step in the long struggle to bound and to organize the world of parenting in ways that will be revealing in different cultural arrangements *without solving the problems by the way they are stated*. In skeptical moments, it is hard for me to anticipate a rigorous and self–correcting scheme for understanding human parenting without the lifelong commitment of the knower, the researcher, to each particular culture of interest. Shatz states the promise and the problem well when she points out that "... even societies that share a common language can use it in ways that may result in different outcomes for child development," a conclusion that her work and that of Dunn and Brown demonstrate beyond our doubting. Again, the notable gain of the present endeavor lies in its toughminded unwillingness to claim simple answers and the shared ability to concentrate the researcher's attention on the subtle variations of a visited culture.

The Others as Objects

Just a word on the old saw about distancing by objectifying. When the social sciences were invented in the last century, the central claim of psychology and sociology and anthropology *as science* was that we would not fall into the trap of poets, historians, and philosophers; we would not confuse the knower and the known, the looker and the looked–at. Such confusion lies at the heart of the present day spirited debate about the nature of social science. How do we maintain the analytic and critical attitudes that have been built over the last semimillenium to solve the problems of nuclear fracturing and space astronomy and overpopulation and poverty and prejudice? How can we, particularly the students of culture, be scientists in the tradition of the Royal Society and the Academy while we try to understand cultures that do not play by the rules of Societies and Academies?

I have no answer to propose. The current Americanization of the world may remove the problem from our agenda without our ever having faced it down, but such a solution is hardly appealing. My optimistic guess is that the distancing of objectification can only be tackled by groups like the people who have reported here, people steeped in the analytic and critical tradition who frankly stare at the apparent insufficiency of the analytic and critical tradition.

The Move to Narrative

Lurking for years at the edges and now moving to the center of our search is the promise of narrative. Led by the literary critics and the anthropologists, a number of students of cultural variation have toyed with *narrative* accounts of their observations, giving up the scientistic patterns in order to express, in a story, the richness of human diversity. Rogoff, in her recent book (1990), has shown the enriching competence of such a move, just as she has in her chapter here. The move seems, on the face of it, to be the best way to escape the crippling dilemmas of the field. But I would not be true to my role as Lachesis if I did not warn the new narrativists, who try to imitate Rogoff, that on either side of their shiny yellow road are the swamps of sloppiness and sludgy thinking. The proper use of ethnographic narrative requires the same self–critical spirit and the same analytic temper that we have traditionally demanded of our more usual procedures.

CONCLUSION

At last, I return to the question I raised a while back; how shall we simplify, how shall we organize, how shall we comprehend the entangling complexity of cultural variation?

Aside from the racism of his time, Galton possessed two simplifying convictions—the sure march of evolution and the certainty of scientific method. We have seen the current expression of the evolutionary dogma in Morelli and Tronick's description of child behavior as "... proximal ... enactments of more distal evolutionary processes." There may still be explanatory life in the Darwinian vision and the question is worthy of an examination as open and as responsive as the present book.

Yet the chief link between Galton's time and ours is the uniform commitment to knowing; looping through the foregoing pages, with the unexamined uniformity of a cultural principle, is the implicit statement that our heart task is to plumb, to dig, to root up, to discover, to dissect, to find out. No matter the form—from laboratory experiment to social rules, from ANOVA to metaphor, from 2–month–olds to school–age children—the *investigator* commands. The shared article of faith would have delighted all your predecessors of the last century and a half; it expresses convincingly the confidence and the optimism of the West.

However, there is a movement of the intellectual community in the chapters of this book that would not have pleased Galton, a continental shift of cognitive value. Final truth, the uniformity of simple and sufficient knowledge, applicable across the entire range of our interests, seems to be absent; no one has maintained a singular all–encompassing Answer. Geertz has again caught the core of the shift in his promulgation of local knowledge—"... the shapes of knowledge are always ineluctably local, indivisible from their instruments and their encasements" (Geertz, 1983, p. 4).

The gathering of cross–cultural workers represented here is, of itself, the best news of the day. Only by sharing our discomforts and our triumphs, only by asking the other scholar the questions we fear to ask ourselves, only by abandoning dreams of final truth, only then will we have the confidence, the stamina, and the humility to withstand the necessary tension of our task and to carry on the search for trustable knowledge.

REFERENCES

Bradley, B. S. Infancy as paradise. *Human Development*, in press.

Bronfenbrenner, U. *The ecology of human development: Experiments by nature and design*. Cambridge, MA: Harvard University Press, 1979.

Galton, F. *The narrative of an explorer in tropical South Africa*. London: John Murray, 1853.

Geertz, C. *Local knowledge: Further essays in interpretive anthropology*. New York: Basic Books, 1983.

Rogoff, B. *Apprenticeship in thinking: Cognitive development in social context*. New York: Oxford University Press, 1990.

Watson, J. B. *Psychological care of infant and child*. New York: Norton, 1928.

Zuckerman, M. Myth and method: The current crisis in American historical writing. *The History Teacher*, 1984, *17*, 219–245.

About the Authors

MARC H. BORNSTEIN is Senior Research Scientist and Head, Section on Child and Family Research, at the National Institute of Child Health and Human Development. He holds a B.A. from Columbia College and M.S. and Ph.D. degrees from Yale University. Bornstein has received the C. S. Ford Cross-Cultural Research Award from the Human Relations Area Files and the B. R. McCandless Young Scientist Award from the American Psychological Association. He was a J. S. Guggenheim Foundation Fellow, and he received a Research Career Development Award from the National Institute of Child Health and Human Development. Bornstein has held academic appointments in Princeton, Munich, London, Paris, New York, and Tokyo. He is coauthor of *Development in Infancy* and *Perceiving Similarity and Comprehending Metaphor*. He is general editor of seven volumes in *The Crosscurrents in Contemporary Psychology Series*, and he has also edited *Maternal Responsiveness: Characteristics and Consequences* and coedited *Developmental Psychology: An Advanced Textbook, Stability and Continuity in Mental Development*, and *Contemporary Constructions of the Child*. He is author of the children's books *Wide World* and *Wide World in Action*. Bornstein's research covers human experimental, methodological, comparative, developmental, cross-cultural, and aesthetic psychology.

T. BERRY BRAZELTON is Clinical Professor Emeritus of Pediatrics at Harvard Medical School, founder of the Child Development Unit at the Children's Hospital in Boston, and Professor of Psychiatry and Human Development at Brown University, Providence, Rhode Island. Brazelton graduated from Columbia University College of Physicians and Surgeons. He has published 20 books and numerous articles on child development, including *Infants and Mothers, Working and Caring*, and *Families: Crisis and Caring*. Brazelton was president of the Society for Research in Child Development and is president of the National Center for Clinical Infant Programs. His research has centered around the behavior of the neonate and the parent–infant dyad, the development of attachment in the first months of life, cross–cultural studies of infant behavior and parenting practices, the importance of early intervention with at–risk infants and parents, and the opportunities presented in infancy for strengthening families.

JANE BROWN is a doctoral student in the Department of Human Development and Family Studies at the Pennsylvania State University. She received her B.A.

from the University of California at Santa Cruz and her M.S. at the Pennsylvania State University.

JUDY DUNN is Professor of Human Development at the Pennsylvania State University. Her B.A., M.A., and Ph.D. degrees are all from Cambridge University. Before coming to the Pennsylvania State, she carried out research at the Medical Research Council Unit on the Development and Integration of Behaviour, University of Cambridge. She has been a Fellow at the Center for Advanced Study in Behavioral Sciences at Stanford and at the Van Leer Foundation in Jerusalem. Her interests center on children's relationships and the development of social understanding. Dunn is author of *The Beginnings of Social Understanding*.

ARTİN GÖNCÜ is Assistant Professor of Educational Psychology and Coordinator of Early Childhood Education at the University of Illinois at Chicago. He received his B.A. from Hacettepe University in Ankara, Turkey, and his Ph.D. from the University of Houston. Göncü was a postdoctoral fellow in developmental psychology at the University of Utah. He is coeditor of *Analyzing Children's Play Dialogues* and conducts research on young children's play and teaching interactions with peers and adults.

WILLIAM KESSEN is Eugene Higgens Professor of Psychology and Professor of Pediatrics in Yale University. He is author of *The Child*. Kessen was raised and taught in Florida, he has spent the bulk of his work time studying newborn infants, and he has recently turned to the history of the social sciences.

GÉRARD MALCUIT is Professor of Psychology at Université du Québec à Montréal, Québec, Canada. He received his Ph.D. from Université de Montréal, Québec, and spent a postdoctoral year at the University of Massachusetts. Malcuit is interested in infant development, attention and learning in infants, language acquisition, and early environment. He is coauthor of *L'Enfant et Son Environment: Une Étude Fonctionnelle de la Première Enfance*.

JAYANTHI MISTRY is Assistant Professor in the Eliot-Pearson Department of Child Study at Tufts University. She received her M.S. degree from M. S. University of Baroda, India, and her Ph.D. from Purdue University. Mistry had a postdoctoral fellowship at the University of Utah, and has worked for the Pre-kindergarten Education Programs of Kamehameha Schools, Hawaii, conducting research on the sociocultural learning environments of Hawaiian preschoolers. Her publications deal with cross-cultural perspectives on development, and focus on cognitive and language development in infancy and early childhood.

GILDA ANN MORELLI is Assistant Professor of Psychology at Boston College. She received her Ph.D. from the University of Massachusetts–Amherst and was an NIMH postdoctoral fellow at the University of Utah. Morelli is co–principal investigator and project director of research on the development of forager infants' relationships with caregivers. This research continues her earlier work conducted in Zaïre on forager and farmer 1 to 3 year olds. Morelli is also co-principal investigator on research comparing young children's engagement in cultural activity in communities varying in technological complexity and formal schooling. Her interest is in studying the social development of young children from a cultural perspective, and her present work focuses on gender–role development, the role of males in parenting, and the development of early relationships.

CHRISTINE MOSIER is a graduate student in Developmental Psychology at the University of Utah. She received her B.A. from Pomona College. Her research focuses on infants' cognitive and communicative development in social context and the cultural context of young children's relationships with siblings and other family members.

HANUŠ PAPOUŠEK received his doctorate in medicine from the Purkinje University, Brno, and a doctorate in science from the Charles University, Prague, Czechoslovakia. He recently retired from the position as Head of Projects in Developmental Psychobiology in the Max-Planck Institute for Research in Psychiatry in Munich, German Federal Republic, and became a Special Professor in Developmental Psychology at the Free University of Amsterdam, The Netherlands, Departments of Developmental Psychology and Human Movement Sciences. His basic research programs in pediatrics and psychobiology have focused on the early development of learning, cognition, and social communication.

MECHTHILD PAPOUŠEK is Senior Scientist and Head of Programs on Preverbal Parent-Infant Relationships at the Institute for Social Pediatrics, University of Munich. She received her M.D. from the University of Tuebingen, Federal Republic of Germany, and her specialization in clinical neurology and psychiatry in Munich. She served in the Developmental Psychobiology Research Group at the Max-Planck-Institute for Psychiatry. Her scientific publications have centered on preverbal parent-infant communication, infant vocal development, precursors to speech acquisition, babytalk, and intuitive parental caregiving.

ANDRÉE POMERLEAU is a Professor of Psychology at Université du Québec à Montréal, Québec, Canada. She received her doctorate from Université Laval, Québec, after the completion of her Ph.D. research at the University of Massachusetts, Amherst. Pomerleau is interested in infant development, especially attention and learning in infants, mother–infant interaction, and early rearing conditions. She is coauthor of L'Enfant et Son Environment: Une Étude Fonctionnelle de la Première Enfance.

BARBARA ROGOFF is Professor of Psychology at the University of Utah. She received her B.A. from Pomona College and her Ph.D. from Harvard University. Rogoff is Editor of the Newsletter of the Society for Research in Child Development and was a fellow at the Stanford University Center for Advanced Study in the

Behavioral Sciences. Her research interests focus on the sociocultural context of development, as children collaborate with others in solving problems involved in cultural activity. She is the author of *Apprenticeship in Thinking: Cognitive Development in Social Context*.

COLETTE SABATIER is a postdoctoral fellow at Queen's University in Kingston, Ontario, Canada. She received her Ph.D. from the Université du Québec à Montréal, Québec, Canada. She has a long experience as therapist in child psychiatric outpatient clinics and as consultant in daycare centers. Sabatier has been interested in socioemotional development especially with babies. Currently, her main interests are centered on socio–adaptation of minority children and on their specific contexts of development.

MARILYN SHATZ is Professor of Psychology at the University of Michigan. She received her Ph.D. from the University of Pennsylvania. She has been a visiting scholar at the University of California – Berkeley, Harvard University, New York University, the University of Wisconsin, Cambridge University, and the Max–Planck Institute of Psycholinguistics. A recipient of NIE, Guggenheim, and Fulbright research fellowships, she has published extensively on the topics of language acquisition and the development of communication skills.

MARIAN SIGMAN is Professor of Psychiatry and Psychology at the University of California, Los Angeles. She received her B.A. from Oberlin College and her Ph.D. from Boston University. She is currently an Associate Editor of *Child Development*. Sigman is co–editor of two volumes, *Preterm Birth and Psychological Development* and *Children with Emotional Disorders and Developmental Disabilities*.

JOSEPH TAL is a Statistician in the Child and Family Research Section at the National Institute of Child Health and Human Development. He received his doctorate from Northwestern University. His interests include psychometrics and experimental design.

CATHERINE S. TAMIS–LEMONDA is Assistant Research Professor of Psychology at New York University. She received her B.A. and Ph.D from New York University. Her research focuses on early cognitive development and its environmental correlates. Her specific interests are in the areas of perception, memory, language, play, and mother–infant interaction.

EDWARD Z. TRONICK is Associate Professor of Pediatrics at the Harvard Medical School, Associate Professor of Human Development at the Harvard School of Education, and Chief of the Child Development Unit, Children's Hospital, Boston. He received a Master's degree in Comparative Psychology from Cornell University and the Ph.D. in Developmental Psychology from the University of Wisconsin, Madison. His research has focused on social and emotional development, infant behavioral assessment, and mother–child interaction in normal and high–risk children in the U.S.A. and several other countries, including Zambia, Kenya, and Peru.

THEODORE D. WACHS is Professor of Psychology at Purdue University. He received his B.A. from Muhlenberg College and his Ph.D. from George Peabody College. He has been a visiting faculty member at the Institute of Child Development, University of Minnesota, and the Departments of Psychology at York University and Indiana University. He has also been an NIH postdoctoral fellow at the Child and Family Research Branch, National Institute of Child Health and Human Development. He is currently on the editorial board of *Child Development*. His interests include the study of environmental influences on early development and the study of individual differences in reaction to the environment. He is coauthor of *Early Experience and Human Development* and *Assessment of Young Developmentally Disabled Children*.

AUTHOR INDEX

A

Adams, A. K., 174, *182*
Ai-Chang, M., 177, *182*
Akiyama, M. M., 143, 144, 145, *152, 153*
Alleton, V., 38, 39, *41*
Altmann, J., 98, *112*
Ary, D., 75, *89*
Azuma, H., 70, 71, 74, 76, *85, 86, 88,* 124, *136*

B

Bailey, R. C., 96, *112*
Balderston, J., 127, *136*
Ban, P., 74, *88*
Barnard, K. E., 61, 67, 70, *86*
Barnett, R. K., 26, 35, *44*
Bastide, E., 48, *67*
Bates, J. E., 70, *88*
Bayles, K., 70, *88*
Beardsall, L., 157, 164, *171*
Beaton, G., 127, *136*
Beckwith, L., 70, *86*
Bee, H. L., 70, *86*
Befu, H., 71, *86*
Bell, R. Q., 70, *86*
Belsky, J., 70, 75, *86*
Benedict, R., 6, 17, *18*
Benjamin, J. D., 120, *120*
Berry, J. W., 5, *18,* 73, *86,* 123, 124, *137*

Bertrand, M., 74, *86*
Black, J., 134, *137*
Blackburn, T. C., 71, *89*
Boggs, S., 179, 180, *182*
Bornstein, M. H., 23, 24, 26, 36, 38, *41, 42, 43,* 46, 47, *67,* 70, 71, 72, 73, 74, 75, 76, *86, 88, 89,* 123, 124, 133, *136*
Bowerman, M., 140, *152*
Bowlby, J., 71, *86*
Boysson-Bardies, B., 34, 35, 37, *42*
Bradley, B. S., 186*n, 193*
Bradley, R. H., 47, 61, *67,* 70, *86*
Brazelton, T. B., 47, 51, *67,* 73, *88,* 116, 117, 120, *120,* 124, *137,* 176, *182*
Breckenridge, J. N., 47, *68*
Bretherton, I., 166, *171*
Brice-Heath, S., 156, *171*
Bril, B., 46, *67*
Brim, D., 123, *136*
Brislin, R. W., 73, *86*
Brody, S., 72, *86*
Bronfenbrenner, U., 4, 17, *18,* 186, *193*
Brown, J., 157, 164, *171*
Bruner, J. S., 24, 26, *42,* 73, *87,* 156, 167, *171,* 174, *182*
Bullock, D., 174, *182*
Bwibo, N., 70, 74, *89*

C

Caldwell, B. M., 47, 61, *67,* 70, *86*

201

SUBJECT INDEX

A

Active Learning, 174–175
Adaptation, 24–25, 117
Age Segregation, 178–179
American Parenting, 28–32, 34–35, 37–38, 69, 71–72, 75–84, 146, 148, 158–171, 174, 176–180
Apprenticeship Model, 174–175

B

Behavioral Phenotype, 118

C

Caregiver Behaviors, Continuity of, 128, 130–132, 134
Caregiver-Child Interactions, 127–135
See also Verbal Interactions
Caregiving Behaviors, 98–104, 108
See also Parental Investment Strategies
Caregiving Contexts, 32, 34–35
Caregiving Environment, 176, 179
Caregiving Melodies, 29–30, 36, 38
Caregiving v. Entertainment, 177
Caretaker Teaching Behaviors, 25–26
Caretaking Forms, 24
Child Caregivers, 100–102, 104, 108–109, 134, 177–179

Continuous Care and Contact Models (CCC), 91

Cross-Cultural Developmental Research, 3–8, 18, 23–25, 28, 73–74, 115–116, 140–141, 192–193
methods, 83, 120, 190–192
problems, 14–17, 49–50, 64, 81–82, 117, 124–125, 186–192
Cultural Community, 175
See also Culture
Cultural Ecology, 170
Cultural Norms, Parental Beliefs and Child-Rearing Practices, 46–47, 60–66, 71–72, 78–80, 83–85
Cultural Processes v. Biological Processes, 24, 29–30, 41, 116–118, 175
Culture, 16–17, 73, 156–157

D

Direction of Infant Attention, 180–181
Distancing, 186, 189–192
Diversity, 13, 188–192
Dyadic Parenting Relationships, 23–24, 173, 180–182
See also Mother-Infant Interaction

E

Efe (Zaïre) Parenting, 92–111
Egyptian Parenting, 125–126, 128–131, 133–135